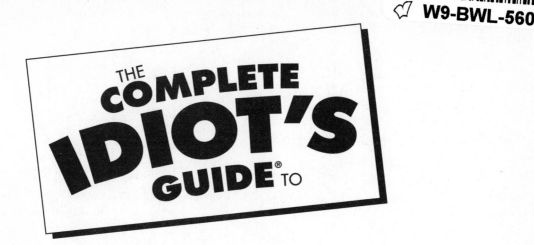

THE
# COMPLETE
# IDIOT'S
GUIDE® TO

# Writing
# Christian Fiction

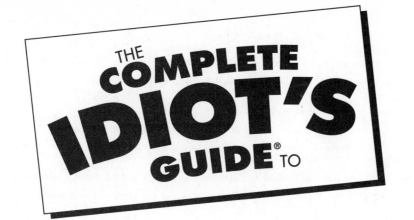

THE COMPLETE **IDIOT'S** GUIDE® TO

# Writing
# Christian Fiction

*by Ron Benrey*

**ALPHA**

A member of Penguin Group (USA) Inc.

## ALPHA BOOKS

Published by the Penguin Group

Penguin Group (USA) Inc., 375 Hudson Street, New York, New York 10014, USA

Penguin Group (Canada), 90 Eglinton Avenue East, Suite 700, Toronto, Ontario M4P 2Y3, Canada (a division of Pearson Penguin Canada Inc.)

Penguin Books Ltd., 80 Strand, London WC2R 0RL, England

Penguin Ireland, 25 St. Stephen's Green, Dublin 2, Ireland (a division of Penguin Books Ltd.)

Penguin Group (Australia), 250 Camberwell Road, Camberwell, Victoria 3124, Australia (a division of Pearson Australia Group Pty. Ltd.)

Penguin Books India Pvt. Ltd., 11 Community Centre, Panchsheel Park, New Delhi—110 017, India

Penguin Group (NZ), 67 Apollo Drive, Rosedale, North Shore, Auckland 1311, New Zealand (a division of Pearson New Zealand Ltd.)

Penguin Books (South Africa) (Pty.) Ltd., 24 Sturdee Avenue, Rosebank, Johannesburg 2196, South Africa

Penguin Books Ltd., Registered Offices: 80 Strand, London WC2R 0RL, England

International Standard Book Number: 978-1-59257-681-4
Library of Congress Catalog Card Number: 2007930855

09   08   07        8   7   6   5   4   3   2   1

Interpretation of the printing code: The rightmost number of the first series of numbers is the year of the book's printing; the rightmost number of the second series of numbers is the number of the book's printing. For example, a printing code of 07-1 shows that the first printing occurred in 2007.

*Printed in the United States of America*

**Note:** This publication contains the opinions and ideas of its author. It is intended to provide helpful and informative material on the subject matter covered. It is sold with the understanding that the author and publisher are not engaged in rendering professional services in the book. If the reader requires personal assistance or advice, a competent professional should be consulted.

The author and publisher specifically disclaim any responsibility for any liability, loss, or risk, personal or otherwise, which is incurred as a consequence, directly or indirectly, of the use and application of any of the contents of this book.

Most Alpha books are available at special quantity discounts for bulk purchases for sales promotions, premiums, fund-raising, or educational use. Special books, or book excerpts, can also be created to fit specific needs.

For details, write: Special Markets, Alpha Books, 375 Hudson Street, New York, NY 10014.

**Publisher:** *Marie Butler-Knight*
**Editorial Director:** *Mike Sanders*
**Managing Editor:** *Billy Fields*
**Executive Editor:** *Randy Ladenheim-Gil*
**Development Editor:** *Lynn Northrup*
**Senior Production Editor:** *Janette Lynn*
**Copy Editor:** *Jeff Rose*

**Cartoonist:** *Steve Barr*
**Cover Designer:** *Kurt Owens*
**Book Designer:** *Trina Wurst*
**Indexer:** *Brad Herriman*
**Layout:** *Brian Massey*
**Proofreader:** *John Etchison*

# Contents at a Glance

# Contents

## Part 2: Writing Publishable Christian Fiction 55

### 5 Publishability and the Fictional Dream 57

### 6 The Most Popular Christian Fiction Genres 69

# Introduction

These are exciting times for Christian publishers—and happy days for Christian novelists. Why?

- Christian fiction is the fastest-growing segment in the fiction marketplace.

- Leading bookstore chains have expanded their "Inspirational Fiction" shelves.

- Carloads of Christian novels are sold in Wal-Mart and supermarkets.

- Mainstream publishers have launched Christian imprints and acquired leading Christian publishers.

- *Publishers Weekly, Booklist, Library Journal,* and other leading industry publications review the latest Christian novels.

- Libraries across the United States have "Inspirational Fiction" or "Christian Fiction" sections.

- Readers can buy large-print versions and audio books of bestselling Christian novels.

- There are increasing international sales and reprints overseas of Christian novels by North American authors.

- An increasing number of Christian novelists have built solid, full-time careers writing Christian fiction.

- There are literary agents that specialize in representing Christian books.

- Several fast-growing national organizations provide support for Christian novelists.

- Christian novelists can network and fine-tune their craft at dozens of Christian-focused writers' conferences.

Curiously, if you look a mere two decades into the past, you'll see a decidedly different picture. Back then, Christian fiction was widely viewed as the impoverished relation of "real fiction"—little more than a slipshod genre of sweet stories populated with cardboard characters and filled with heavy-duty Christian preaching that seemed better suited for religious tracts.

One of my friends put it this way: "Old Christian novels would move along at a good pace, but suddenly the action would stop, a curtain would open, a pulpit would appear, and a key character would deliver a sermonlike lecture that seemed totally unnatural. When he or she finished, the curtain would close, allowing the action to start again. This was ... *dumb writing.*"

It's no wonder that mainstream bookstores snubbed early Christian fiction. The few critics who would review Christian novels usually dismissed them out of hand as formulaic, parochial, and boring. Worst of all, most readers—including many Christians—assumed that Christian fiction was corny, preachy, simple-minded, and dull. Few writers wanted to author a Christian novel. Or were willing to read a book like this one.

But no longer.

The days are past when anyone—writer, editor, or publisher—need apologize for producing a Christian novel. In fact, Christian fiction is widely recognized as the Cinderella of publishing. It has outgrown its former status as a mere publishing genre or subcategory to become a full-fledged market segment with dozens of its own genres, including women's fiction, romance, biblical, "chick lit," historical, suspense, mystery, cozy mystery, private-eye, adventure, fantasy/science fiction, Southern fiction, western, allegorical, literary, African-American, young adult … the list goes on and on.

The credit for these changes goes not to a fairy godmother, but to the first-rate writers, expert editors, and determined publishers who worked together to produce excellent Christian novels.

Quality has proved to be the secret of Christian fiction's success. The Christianity is still there, but the best of today's Christian novels can stand toe to toe with their mainstream counterparts and meet virtually any quality yardstick a persnickety literary critic might care to apply.

A handful of Christian novelists typically get the credit for blazing the trail that led to the broad acceptance of Christian fiction:

◆ Janet Oke—began writing her collection of more than 75 Christian historical "prairie romances" in 1979. Her novels established a reader base for Christian fiction and proved, to both bookstores and publishers, that there was a market for good Christian fiction.

◆ Frank Peretti—*This Present Darkness*, his novel of spiritual warfare, was published in 1989. Many industry observers consider this the breakthrough novel that established Christian fiction as "real fiction."

◆ Jerry Jenkins and Tim LaHaye—Their *Left Behind* series (*Left Behind*, the first novel, was published in 1995) has sold more 65 million books, proving that Christian fiction can achieve blockbuster sales.

Many industry observers include Jan Karon on this short list. Her bestselling *Mitford* series is currently published by a mainstream publisher and has significant "crossover" readership among readers who wouldn't dream of visiting a Christian bookstore but love Karon's charming, thoroughly Christian, stories.

The rapidly increasing readership for Christian fiction means new opportunities for unpublished authors to join the burgeoning list of successful Christian novelists.

The bottom line: you've chosen the perfect time to learn how to write a Christian novel. So sit back and join me on a fascinating journey as we explore the ins and outs of writing Christian fiction.

## What You'll Learn in This Book

This guide focuses on the specifics of writing Christian fiction. That means I intentionally didn't try to duplicate the many good books out there about writing fiction, including *The Complete Idiot's Guide to Writing a Novel*. There's not much difference, for example, in the basic skills you need to tell an exciting mainstream story or a compelling Christian story. But to write a successful Christian novel you'll need to know more. The pages that follow are about the more.

I've organized the book into four parts that cover the distinctively Christian aspects of writing successful fiction:

**Part 1, "Understanding Christian Fiction,"** helps you appreciate—and master— the characteristics of novels we label *Christian fiction*. The most significant of these is the explicit Christian content. I also examine the forces that are shaping Christian fiction today, the notion that Christian fiction can be a ministry for both writers and publishers, and the important differences between Christian and mainstream publishers. These are details you need to know when you plan a Christian novel.

**Part 2, "Writing a Publishable Christian Novel,"** gives you the foundational information you need to write a Christian novel that will stand tall enough among the competition to attract the interest of a literary agent and editor. I take an especially close look at the practical boundaries of topics, genres, and language in Christian novels. In today's competitive marketplace, submitting a manuscript that an editor deems publishable is the key to your success as a Christian novelist.

**Part 3, "Sitting Down to Write Christian Fiction,"** explains the nitty-gritty aspects of writing Christian fiction and looks at the unique challenges that every Christian writer must cope with when writing a novel.

**Part 4, "Get Your Christian Novel Published,"** is your introduction to the realities of Christian publishing, including the inevitable business aspects of publishing and the gauntlet of agents, editors, and publishing executives your novel must satisfy on its journey to publication.

I won't kid you; there are many first-time Christian novelists trying to get published, so it's tough to find an agent and a publisher. Knowing the information in this section will make it more likely that you attract the attention of an agent or editor.

## Extras

I've included a number of different sidebars throughout the chapters that supplement the chief explanations and teaching. They are identified by the following labels:

**Literary Sins**

The way to publishing success is narrow. Lots of writers get lost—and lose valuable time—by making the easy-to-avoid missteps I'll describe in these sidebars.

**Chapter and Verse**

These are the words and terms you should have at your fingertips when you plan your Christian novel—and at the tip of your tongue when you talk about Christian fiction.

**A Lamp Unto Your Feet**

Here you'll find useful hints and tips to teach you practical "best practices" and "lessons learned" about writing Christian fiction.

**It Is Written ...**

Check out these boxes for intriguing—and pertinent—quotations from well-known Christian and secular novelists.

**Wisdom and Knowledge**

These tidbits of insider information will help you accelerate your pace as a writer of Christian fiction.

## Acknowledgments

I offer a special thank you to Brandilyn Collins for her help in launching this project. Once underway, she and many other Christian novelists, agents, and editors responded to my pleas for assistance. They include Hannah Alexander (Cheryl and Mel Hodde), Lynn Austin, Karen Ball, James Scott Bell, Janet Benrey, Kristen Billerbeck, Austin Boyd, Sue Brower, Terry Burns, Colleen Coble, Athena Dean, Joy DeKok, Rosey Dow, Alton Gansky, Jeff Gerke, Becky Germany, Joan Marlow Golan, Len Goss,

Linda Hall, Nick Harrison, Robin Lee Hatcher, B. J. Hoff, Dave Horton, Angie Hunt, Jim Jordan, Karen Kingsbury, Dave Lambert, Yvonne Lehman, Chip Macgregor, Gail Martin, Andy McGuire, Rod Morris, Tom Morrisey, Nancy Moser, Deb Raney, Lisa Samson, Jan Stob, Krista Strover, Camy Tang, Ann Tatlock, and Stephanie Grace Whitson.

Randy Ladenheim-Gil, Executive Director at Alpha Books; Lynn Northrup, my Development Editor; and Janette Lynn, Senior Production Editor, made the editorial process painless for me. For that, I am truly grateful.

Finally, a hearty cheer and wave to Marilyn Allen, my literary agent, for her confidence in me.

## Trademarks

All terms mentioned in this book that are known to be or are suspected of being trademarks or service marks have been appropriately capitalized. Alpha Books and Penguin Group (USA) Inc. cannot attest to the accuracy of this information. Use of a term in this book should not be regarded as affecting the validity of any trademark or service mark.

# Part 1

# Understanding Christian Fiction

If you want to write Christian fiction, you should know what makes it Christian—and what makes it tick. Surprisingly, there are more details to understand than many new writers assume. I say that with complete conviction because I charged ahead and began writing my idea of a Christian novel before I had a solid grasp on the distinctive features and requirements of Christian fiction.

That unsold manuscript still sits on a shelf in my office. It's not publishable because it violates too many conventions and guidelines of Christian publishing. One of these days I'll get around to a complete rewrite.

This part of the book is aimed at helping you appreciate—and master—the characteristics of novels the world labels *Christian fiction* so that you'll be able to write a publishable manuscript from the get-go. Even more important, the information presented here will help you develop a more effective Christian novel—a book that truly helps to advance the Kingdom of God.

# What Is Christian Fiction?

## In This Chapter

- How Christian fiction differs from secular fiction
- Crafting Christian messages
- A spectrum of spiritual possibilities
- "Conversion scenes" are optional
- Incorporating Christian worldview
- Christian content must be nondenominational

What makes a Christian novel *Christian?* More to the point, what ingredients must you add to the novel you plan to write to make an editor say, "There's a fine example of Christian fiction that we should publish"?

That's the vital question I'll answer in this chapter. You'll discover that the primary distinction of Christian fiction is its explicitly Christian content. You'll also learn about the range and variety of Christian messages that readers and editors expect to find in a Christian novel.

## Christian Fiction Is ...

Think of two successful novels you've read—one Christian and one *secular*—and imagine that you've placed them side-by-side. Now tell me why the two books are different.

**Chapter and Verse**

Throughout this book I'll often use the word **secular** to contrast Christian, when I write about fiction, publishers, agents, writers, and readers. "Secular" means worldly, rather than sacred or religious. I need to use a label other than "non-Christian" or "non-believer," because many secular readers, agents, and editors are believing Christians. When appropriate, I'll also use the word "mainstream" to indicate other-than-Christian publishing activities.

I predict that you'll identify an astonishingly short list of distinguishing factors, because the two novels actually have much in common. Both authors …

- Told exciting stories set in interesting places.

- Created fascinating characters.

- Wrote entertaining dialogue.

- Generated compelling fictional dreams (I'll discuss fictional dreams in Chapters 3 and 5).

- Kept readers engrossed—and turning pages quickly.

- Honored the rules of grammar, usage, and point of view.

- Researched the facts they presented.

- Met the distinct requirements of their specific genres.

- Followed similar formatting guidelines for their manuscripts.

But there is one overarching difference.

Let's begin by looking at three definitions of Christian fiction:

1. Novels in popular genres that are written by Christians mostly for Christians. They contain clear Christian themes—often depicting the journey of the hero or heroine's soul—and are designed to be sold in Christian bookstores.

2. Novels and novellas that tell stories from the perspective of a Christian worldview. The author seeks to persuade the reader to make the Christian worldview his or her own.

3. Stories that encompass religious themes found in the Old and New Testaments, including God as creator, the sinful nature of humankind, the need for a savior, the role of Jesus Christ in bringing salvation, and the role of the Holy Spirit. A key element of each story is the protagonist's relationship with God, which typically grows and solidifies as the action moves forward.

Did you spot the common denominator in these three seemingly different definitions? The chief difference exhibited by a Christian novel is its explicit Christianity. At least part of the novel will reflect the Gospel of Jesus Christ.

# Secular "Christian Novels"

Before you say *Duh!* at my "obvious" statement, consider that countless secular novels have religious and moral themes. Their heroes and heroines believe in God and often honor Christian values.

These books about Christians contain central stories about clergymen, Christian history, saints, Christians who sin, Christians who triumph over sin, nonbelievers who accept Christ, and occasionally even Jesus Christ, Himself. *The Robe*, by Lloyd C. Douglas, is a good example. So is *The Testament*, by John Grisham, and the series of Church of England novels written by Susan Howatch, a popular British author.

These Christian-themed books are wonderful reads that tell gripping stories of characters on Christian journeys, yet they are not classified as Christian fiction or sold in most Christian bookstores.

## Why Aren't They Christian Novels?

You may be tempted to answer that some of these titles don't meet the general standards of Christian fiction—that list of defining factors that seems to characterize most Christian novels:

- Conservative Christian values
- Christian characters who don't drink alcoholic beverages, play cards, dance, or gamble
- No profanity
- No strong violence
- No overt sexuality
- Chaste relationships that downplay the physical component of love while emphasizing the emotional side

In fact, these decades-old prohibitions are beginning to soften as a few leading Christian publishers move toward "edgier" Christian fiction. The traditional features have stopped being reliable indicators you can use to separate Christian from secular fiction.

What hasn't changed—and what is unlikely to change—is the reader expectation that Christian fiction contain explicit Christian content.

## Nonbelievers Also Read Christian Fiction

Another flagging distinction of Christian fiction is the notion that Christian novels are read only by Christians. These days, we see many examples of so-called *crossover novels* that have become bestsellers among secular readers (including many nonbelievers).

**Chapter and Verse** _____

**Crossover novels** are Christian novels that have won a following among readers who'll probably never shop at a Christian bookstore. The *Mitford* series and the *Left Behind* series are the leading examples of explicitly Christian novels that became wildly successful crossover novels. As you would expect, most Christian crossovers have subdued Christian content. Many Christian novels are also purchased by people who don't seek a Christian message but prefer "gentle reads" (books without profanity, overt sexuality, or in-your-face violence).

Secular novels about Christianity usually fall short of true Christian fiction for a variety of reasons. They may not be explicitly Christian, despite their religious themes. Or they may not have a distinctively Christian viewpoint—the concept of a Creator God who chose to enter His creation, a God who loves and forgives, a God who seeks our prayers and answers them. Or they may not sufficiently emphasize redemption and salvation from a grace-based Christian perspective.

Labeling a novel as Christian or secular may demand that we walk a tricky line—and use vague language. Is *The Pilgrim's Progress*, by John Bunyan, an early Christian novel? Some people say yes, others no. What about *Crime and Punishment*, by Fyodor Dostoyevsky, and *The Lord of the Rings*, by J.R.R. Tolkien? Both authors were steadfast Christians and both novels incorporate powerful Christian themes. Again, some readers say these books are Christian, others insist they're not.

# Evangelical Fiction

A number of Christian writers prefer the term "evangelical fiction" because their Christian novels strongly proclaim the Christian message and depict leading characters journeying from nonbelievers to born-again Christians. The trouble with this label is that many contemporary Christian novels have significantly less Christian content than a truly evangelical book, yet still pass muster as Christian fiction.

We'll revisit this important topic later in this chapter when I discuss required Christian content. For now, we'll agree that no one has invented a hard-and-fast formula we can use to make our novels explicitly Christian. However, we do have a useful rule of thumb: a novel that delivers a clear, unambiguous Christian message is probably Christian fiction. A novel that doesn't deliver a Christian message is probably secular—even though the story may be full of Christian themes and characters.

It's worth noting the difference between "Christian fiction" and "inspirational fiction." These terms are interchangeable in many contexts—for example, Christian novelists will often describe their work as inspirational fiction when they speak at secular writers' conferences. But there can be an important difference between Christian and inspirational fiction in some settings. For example, the "inspirational fiction" aisle at a mainstream bookstore or your local public library is likely to include novels of other faiths—Jewish, Buddhist, Hindu, Muslim, and Wiccan—alongside the Christian fiction.

At the end of the day, what Potter Stewart, Associate Justice of the U.S. Supreme Court, famously said about pornography also applies to Christian fiction: "I know it when I see it." Readers seem to have no trouble recognizing a novel that seeks to witness to the nature and work of Jesus Christ. And therein lies the essence of Christian fiction.

# Christian Content Is a Spectrum of Spirituality

I have some good news to share with you. Despite what you may have heard about Christian fiction, you actually have great flexibility when you develop the Christian content for your novel.

Many of the new writers I meet at writers' conferences assume that Christian publishers promulgate hard-and-fast rules that define the required Christian content in the novels they publish. A widespread misconception is that every Christian novel must show at least one character accepting Christ as his or her Lord and Savior.

Although this may have been true during the early days of Christian fiction, publishers and readers have become used to a range of explicit Christianity—a spectrum of spirituality, if you like. You can almost always incorporate the right amount of Christian content to fit your genre, your story, and your personal vision of Christian fiction.

> **Wisdom and Knowledge** _____
>
> Experienced Christian writers often use two acronyms as labels for the parallel
> worlds of Christian and secular publishing. *ABA* (American Booksellers Association),
> an organization of independent bookstores founded in 1900, is a fast way of saying
> "secular publishing." *CBA* (Christian Booksellers Association), a comparable organiza-
> tion founded in 1950, has become shorthand for "Christian publishing." Attend any
> Christian writers' conference and you'll hear talk about "ABA publishers," "CBA imprints,"
> "ABA book distributors," and "CBA agents." At one time, "ABA" and "CBA" stood for
> distinctly separate secular and Christian markets. Although the labels are still used today,
> a handful of large publishing conglomerates now own most of the publishers and book
> distributors on both sides of the fence.

## At the High End: The Conversion Scene

Let's label one end of the explicit Christianity spectrum "high Christian content."
Here, you will tell a complete story that shows God's grace in action.

Specifically, your main plot will involve a hero who starts out as a determined nonbeliever—possibly an atheist. He will suffer the consequences of a life separated from
God, hit rock bottom, cry out to Jesus for help, and receive salvation. Along the
way, other characters will explain Christianity to your hero and otherwise assist his
journey to redemption. A high point of this kind of story is the so-called conversion
scene, where the hero will speak some form of the "Sinner's Prayer" and become a
born-again Christian.

A popular alternative version of the story begins by introducing Heroine (a faithful
Christian) and Villain (a determined nonbeliever). Villain commits an evil act that
impacts Heroine. She has every right to condemn Villain, but she appreciates that he is both a horrific sinner and a human being created in the image of God.

To everyone's amazement, Heroine forgives Villain, triggering his own realization that he is a sinner in need of salvation, and beginning the process that leads to his eventual redemption and personal conversion. The story ends with Former Villain—now a born-again Christian— "doing the right thing." This can include making restitution for the wrongs he's done, or even turning himself in to the authorities to receive appropriate punishment.

> **A Lamp Unto Your Feet** _____
>
> Christian publishers usually
> produce submission guide-
> lines that spell out their require-
> ments for Christian content. These
> are available on their websites.
> Comparing the guidelines from
> several publishers will give you
> a snapshot view of current expec-
> tations for the Christian fiction
> marketplace.

If you are a fan of Christian fiction—and you should certainly read Christian novels if you intend to write them—you've probably come across many similar stories in your favorite reads. Redemption plotlines are staples of Christian fiction and have been told thousands of different ways, starring all manner of heroes, heroines, and villains. There's really no surprise here; most secular stories echo a small set of recurring themes. Redemption is one of the most popular in all branches of fiction.

## The Middle Ground: Jesus at Work

If you choose to write in the middle of the Christian content spectrum, your stories will likely illustrate the impact of Jesus Christ on the lives of one, or possibly two, leading characters. They may or may not be Christians when the action begins, but the faith they develop during the course of the story will help them to solve their problems—and change the way they view the world around them.

Here's an example of what I mean: Heroine, already a Christian, always seems to have relationship problems. No matter how carefully she chooses the men in her life, things invariably go wrong, leaving her with yet another broken heart.

Heroine decides that she doesn't want to be hurt again; from this day forward she won't enter into any more relationships with men. She works hard to keep the men in her life at arm's length.

But then Heroine meets Hero, a determined Christian. She rejects him at first—and at second, and third. Hero doesn't stop trying to create a relationship with Heroine and eventually reminds her of the fact that she has obviously forgotten: her future is in God's hands, not her own. As Heroine's faith grows, she comes to realize that God wants her to build a relationship with Hero.

Here's another story from this range on the spectrum: Hero, a relatively new Christian, meets and falls in love with Heroine. When she returns his affections, Hero decides to propose marriage—but a problem intervenes. Hero is haunted by the many infidelities he committed before he accepted Christ. How can he ask Heroine to trust him when he doesn't trust himself? As the story moves to its climax, Hero eventually recognizes that becoming a Christian made him a new creation, and that he now has the power *not* to succumb to temptation and fall into sin. He feels free to marry the woman he loves.

A middle-ground story can readily become the stuff of a Christian subplot in your novel. This leaves you free to devote your central story to a complex plotline appropriate for romance, mystery, suspense, woman's fiction, or another genre.

**Literary Sins**

Regardless of the amount of Christian content in your stories, excessive preachiness will scuttle your Christian novel. Avoid excess sermonizing or out-of-place teaching in your stories. When readers complain that a book is "preachy," they usually mean the explicit Christianity was not smoothly integrated into the story. These days, editors expect a writer to apply both skill and planning to "submerge" the Christian message inside the plotline, rather than letting it float on the surface of the story. I'll describe various techniques to accomplish this trick later on in this book.

## At the Very Least ...

At the other end of the spectrum, the Christian message is fairly mild. It can be as simple as showing significant progress in a lead character's Christian walk. The character starts the story as a Christian and struggles to become a stronger Christian during the course of the novel. By the end of the book, the character must have become a solid believer in Christianity and a member of a church community. This seems to be widely accepted by many as the absolute minimum explicit Christianity in true Christian fiction.

One of the most familiar stories of this kind has Hero starting out mad at God—or abandoned by God—perhaps because of a tragedy in his past. As Hero interacts with other characters, he comes to realize that God has never left his side. Hero's personal relationship with God is restored.

Another popular story pattern begins with Heroine refusing to be part of a church community, possibly because she's been hurt or disappointed by the non-Christian behavior of church leaders sometime in the past. As Heroine moves forward through the story—and onward in her faith journey—she recognizes that everyone is a sinner. She learns to forgive the earlier trespasses committed against her. By the end of the story, she has joined a new church and has come to think of herself as a Christian once again. Stories this simple may not even warrant a complete subplot. Instead, you can incorporate details into the central story.

Does mild Christian content share the message of Christ? One can argue that it does, on the theory that non-Christians are more likely to read these kinds of stories to the end—and to not consider them "Christian propaganda."

Equally important, the Christians who read them (and most readers of Christian fiction are believers) may be comforted by stories that reaffirm their faith. Countless Christians experience doubts about the faith and doubts about their church. As a result, "fairly mild" stories can have a powerful impact on readers, despite their limited religiosity.

> **Wisdom and Knowledge** _____
>
> Many Christian writers use a recurring Christian theme in their novels. Several of the cozy mysteries I co-wrote with my wife, Janet, for example, had Christian subplots about characters who stopped being churchgoing Christians. Something—or someone— drove them away from formal religion. At the start of each novel, Hero or Heroine doesn't attend church, although he or she hasn't stopped believing in God. As the story progresses, circumstances re-energize the character's Christianity. By the end, Hero or Heroine are back in the fold—and in church. This pattern (at the "fairly mild" end of the Christian content spectrum, a level appropriate for cozy mysteries) emerged in our writing without any preplanning—at least on our part. We do not retell over and over. Rather, we write variations on a common theme, which lets us probe more deeply into a problem that plagues the contemporary Christian community. We all know people who can tell similar stories for real.

# Not Everyone Agrees

Given the origins of Christian fiction—and the almost universal use of conversion stories in early novels—it's not surprising to find that some Christian novelists reject the idea of a spectrum of spirituality.

## The Arguments for a Conversion Scene

Several successful authors I know insist that every Christian novel must show grace in action—a character who needs grace both receiving and accepting it via an industrial-strength conversion scene. These novelists go beyond theology to make their case. They also point out that many long-time readers of Christian fiction expect to read a full-fledged conversion scene in every Christian novel they buy. This is the climactic moment of high drama, a grand finale equivalent to the underdog vanquishing the villain in an adventure story; a Christian story doesn't seem complete without one.

Finally, writers who routinely include conversion scenes can show you impressive stacks of letters from readers who say the novels changed their lives by helping to bring them to Christ.

## The Arguments Against a Conversion Scene

These are powerful arguments, difficult to refute, yet other writers claim with equal conviction that we shouldn't set *any* minimums for explicit Christian content in Christian fiction. Press them for an explanation and you'll hear something like this: "I'm a Christian who happens to write novels. That means I have a Christian worldview—a set of beliefs and assumptions that are in my mind whenever I sit down to write. Therefore, my novels will automatically …

- Convey Christian values via actions rather than words.
- Communicate key elements of my Christian worldview to readers.
- Deliver an indirect Christian message, again through the actions and behaviors of the leading characters."

The worldview-only advocates also have thank-you letters from readers whose lives changed for the better after reading their books. These writers note that because their novels are less propagandistic, they are much more likely to be read by non-Christians, whereas high-Christian-content fiction aimed at Christian readers mostly ends up preaching to the choir.

## When Nonbelievers Read Christian Fiction

Lastly, worldview-only advocates point to an obvious problem with fiction that contains an explicit Christian message designed to evangelize: the book's purpose—and the author's agenda—are completely apparent to a nonbelieving reader. Rather than being caught up in a compelling story, a non-Christian reader feels manipulated by a transparent attempt to change his or her core beliefs.

The heart of the worldview argument—really a spin on "loving actions speak louder than clever words"—goes back a long time. Saint Francis reputedly urged Christians to "Preach the gospel at all times. Use words if necessary." (If his quotation isn't true, it should be.)

And more than 50 years ago, C. S. Lewis wrote in *God in the Dock* that "We must attack the enemy's line of communication. What we want is not more little books about Christianity, but more little books by Christians on other subjects—with their Christianity latent."

## The Bottom Line

Frankly, neither of these views—must have a conversion scene; don't need any explicit Christian content—reflects the state of Christian publishing today. I say this not to criticize either viewpoint, but to focus on the expectations of most gatekeepers and publishers.

The consensus among literary agents and acquisitions editors seems to be that a Christian novel needs more than mere "niceness" and a few head-nods to faith and prayer; it should contain demonstrably Christian content. On the other hand, most publishers realize that our storytelling would suffer a serious cramp if every Christian novel was required to incorporate a nonbeliever accepting Christ.

### Literary Sins

Never use Christian polemic to deliver an explicit Christian message in your novel. The dictionary defines polemic as "argumentative or disputatious"—in other words, writing that drives home your viewpoint with a sledgehammer. Keep in mind that Christians are called to "Always be prepared to give an answer to everyone who asks you to give the reason for the hope that you have. But do this with gentleness and respect …" (1 Peter 3:15 NIV) This is equally good advice for Christian novelists.

# The Power of Christian Worldview

We talked about worldview briefly in the last section—too briefly to indicate its great potential in Christian fiction. Worldview is an extremely powerful concept that every Christian novelist can use intentionally, along with explicit Christian content. Let's return for a closer look.

## Worldview Is …

Simply defined, worldview is the framework we use to interpret, and interact with, the world around us. Our worldview is made up of the various beliefs and assumptions we apply when we think about things.

A Christian worldview, for example, begins with the belief that we were put here for a purpose by a Creator God, and that his love for us gives us an innate value. Consequently, Christians stress love for neighbors and enemies, because all people were created by God and are loved by him. By contrast, a worldview based on the assumption that people were created more or less by accident through a series of random processes may lead to indifference for people outside one's immediate family or clan.

The point to remember is that behavior based on a Christian worldview is likely to be significantly different than behavior based on a secular worldview.

## Using Christian Worldview in Fiction

You can make good use of this fact when you plot your Christian novel. The heroes, heroines, and villains I sketched earlier in the chapter all had one thing in common: their worldviews became increasingly Christian as their stories progressed. As their worldviews became more Christian, so did their behavior.

In real life, a person's worldview changes slowly; in fiction, readers will accept fairly rapid changes. Thus, as characters make progress in their Christian walk, they will …

   ◆ Start loving the unlovable, including their enemies.

   ◆ Forgive people who trespass against them.

   ◆ Abandon revenge for the wrongs done them.

   ◆ Increasingly lean on God.

   ◆ Avoid lies, or deceit, or the use of foul language.

   ◆ Join a church community.

   ◆ Discover that the "foolishness" of the Gospel (to use Paul's word) makes sense.

I'm sure you recognize these improving behaviors as aspects of the plots I described earlier in this chapter. Changing worldview is a convenient way to link a character's actions to the explicit Christian content in your novel.

# Christian Fiction: A Denomination-Free Zone

When you study submission guidelines from different Christian publishers, you'll probably see some variation of the following instruction again and again:

> Please do not name specific Christian denominations in your novel. We prefer New Song Community Church to New Song Methodist (or Presbyterian, or Baptist, etc.) Church.

You'll also be asked to avoid denominational distinctives, such as the mode and age of baptism, speaking in tongues, election, and the role of women in leadership positions.

There's an obvious reason to keep Christian fiction as free of potential hot buttons as possible: we want our Christian novels to teach, convict, and encourage, not to drive wedges between readers who've chosen different interpretations of Scripture.

There are notable exceptions, of course. The hero of Jan Karon's *Mitford* series is an Episcopal clergyman; her millions of readers don't seem to mind. However, it's best to remain denomination-neutral unless your story absolutely, positively requires a specific denominational preference.

The same principle applies if you introduce Christian doctrine in your story. Don't champion specific denominational beliefs that are likely to put chips on shoulders of readers who approach Christianity from another angle. For example, a hero who insists that everyone must believe in predestination is likely not to wind up on a printed page.

# Think "Mere Christianity"

When C. S. Lewis wrote his famous book about the basics of Christian doctrine, he borrowed the well-known title—*Mere Christianity*—from the writings of Richard Baxter, an English clergyman who lived in the fifteenth century. Baxter used the phrase to describe the essential core beliefs held through the ages by all Christians, of all denominations and churches. The doctrines you present in your novels should reflect "mere Christianity."

When I began writing Christian fiction, I visited the website maintained by the Evangelical Christian Publishers Association (ECPA; see Appendix A) and downloaded its statement of faith. Most of the publishers you're likely to write for are members of ECPA and subscribe to its faith statement. Because many of these companies are linked to specific denominations, their endorsement of the statement indicates its broad-based acceptability. I use it to guide the content and language of Christian doctrine I build into my stories.

## The Least You Need to Know

- Don't assume that all fiction about Christianity—or populated with Christian characters—is Christian fiction.
- Your Christian fiction should have explicitly Christian content.

◆ You have significant flexibility when you plan the explicit Christian message for your novel.

◆ Think of Christian content as a spectrum of possibilities.

◆ You can choose to—or choose *not* to—include a conversion scene in your novel.

◆ Avoid denominational distinctives, and keep your Christian fiction free of potential hot buttons.

# Chapter 2

# The Forces That Shape Christian Fiction

## In This Chapter

- ◆ The publication path from writer to reader
- ◆ The forces driving change
- ◆ A look at the different genres
- ◆ Understanding "no-no" lists
- ◆ Pushing the envelope of Christian fiction
- ◆ Proven sales: a troublesome trend for some authors

No Christian novelist writes in a vacuum. To create a successful Christian novel—a novel that stands a chance of being published in today's highly competitive marketplace—you must respond to the major forces that are shaping Christian fiction today.

That's why it's so important that you understand—and anticipate—the shifting environment. I've designed this chapter to give you the essential information you need to think and plan ahead.

# A Dynamic Process

Notice I said "are shaping"—not "have shaped"—the writing of Christian novels. The maturing of Christian fiction is an ongoing dynamic process. The field has changed significantly during the past two decades and will continue to change in the years ahead. Writers must design their novels *years* before readers can purchase them, so planning a Christian novel that meets market requirements is a bit like shooting at a moving target.

I'll use a two-step approach to talk about the changes. First, I'll describe the leading "influencers" that generate the major forces that shape Christian fiction. These are readers, booksellers, publishers, distribution channels, literary agents, and book critics and reviewers.

**It Is Written ...**

The Christian fiction market is changing so rapidly, you can't even judge it by books published a year or two ago. You must judge it by what's being published now.

—Brandilyn Collins, Christian novelist

Next, I'll examine the six most significant forces that are doing the shaping, along with their impact on a Christian novelist like you:

◆ Emphasis on increasing quality

◆ Ebb and flow of new genres

◆ Demand to maintain the old, traditional values of Christian fiction

◆ Call to push the "envelope" of Christian fiction

◆ Consolidation of Christian publishers

◆ Pressure to increase sales of Christian novels

Keeping pace with the changes in Christian fiction is an especially thorny challenge for an unpublished novelist. Both agents and editors are likely to require a finished manuscript, which may take you a year or more to write. (An experienced novelist can often sell a book on the basis of two or three chapters. A bestselling novelist may need nothing more than a title and a few paragraphs that describe the new concept.)

# The Path from Writer to Reader

Not surprisingly, many novelists consider readers to be their primary customers. After all, writers write books and readers read them. In fact, reality is not that simple. While it's possible for an author to sell books directly to readers—Janet and I do at church-sponsored book signings, for example—the vast majority of novels are sold by booksellers who are several links in the sales chain away from the authors.

For most novelists, the connection between reader and author is indirect and fairly complex, as shown in the following figure. More to the point, the many layers of important activities between reader and writer strongly influence Christian fiction.

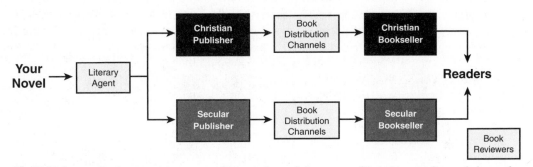

*You'll find several other participants standing on the path between a Christian novelist and the readers of his or her books.*

There are actually two parallel paths that link reader and writer—one Christian, the other secular. Because both involve essentially identical activities, you can think of them as one combined path. Let's begin our travels on the *right* side of the path— with the reader—and move *backward* toward the writer.

## Readers of Christian Fiction

The readers of Christian fiction will be the ultimate consumers of the Christian novels you write. Surveys show that the single largest group of Christian fiction readers in America are Caucasian women, of childbearing through "empty nester" age, who identify themselves as evangelical Christians.

Clearly there are readers of Christian fiction from every demographic category—male, African American, Asian, teenagers, senior citizens, and members of mainstream denominations. Further, the popularity of the *Left Behind* and *Mitford* series among secular readers—plus the steadily increasing demand for gentle reads—proves there are readers for compelling Christian fiction even among nonbelievers.

### Wisdom and Knowledge

The widespread availability of Christian fiction has helped to increase sales. A recent study of readers found that half of all Americans read Christian books and one-third buy them.

Nonetheless, Christian women with the characteristics I mentioned are widely considered to be the target market for Christian fiction.

## Critics and Book Reviewers

Here, I'm specifically talking about critics and book reviewers at major book-industry publications (for example, *Publishers Weekly* and *Library Journal*). While not directly on the writer-to-reader path—few readers of Christian fiction read publishing industry magazines—these reviewers have been influential shapers of Christian fiction because so many editors, agents, and writers pay close attention to their observations, and also to the long-range publishing advice they provide in articles and at industry conferences.

**A Lamp Unto Your Feet**

*Publishers Weekly* magazine is the "bible" of the publishing industry. Subscriptions are fairly expensive, but it's available in most libraries. *PW*, as its friends call it, publishes regular reviews of the best Christian novels and periodically surveys the Christian fiction industry.

What about the book reviewers who evaluate books for newspapers, consumer publications, and websites? Well, while their reviews may influence an individual reader's decision to purchase a Christian novel—and could impact an editor's decision to publish an author's next book—they rarely generate forces strong enough to shape the future of Christian fiction.

## Booksellers

Most of your readers will buy your published novels from booksellers: brick-and-mortar bookstores (both Christian and secular), online booksellers, "big-box stores" (such as Wal-Mart and Target), other retail shops, and, increasingly, supermarkets. The nature of bookselling has changed dramatically in recent years, with large bookstore chains replacing smaller independent bookstores and major book-sale growth in big-box stores and supermarkets.

Industry experts point out that there is too little shelf space at brick-and-mortar booksellers to accommodate the growing variety of Christian novels. This is true both at Christian and secular bookstores. The best selection of Christian fiction can be found at online booksellers.

Christian bookstores—long the champions of Christian fiction—have also changed. The number of independent stores has declined and the makeup of their inventory has changed. At many bookstores, sales of Christian-focused gifts and music generates significantly larger revenue than sales of Christian books. The Christian

Booksellers Association (CBA) has recognized this trend by renaming their annual conference The International Christian Retail Show.

Moreover, even at Christian bookstores that maintain large stocks of novels, sales of Bibles, Christian curricula, and nonfiction works will likely outpace sales of fiction by a considerable margin. Nevertheless, because they supported Christian fiction when few other booksellers did, the members of CBA still retain considerable influence in shaping the content of Christian fiction.

## Book Distribution Channels

I've used "book distribution channels" as a convenient label for the various "middle-men" between publisher and bookseller. These distribution channels include a variety of important functions, such as wholesaling books, warehousing books, shipping books, and visiting bookstores to sell books.

The largest booksellers prefer to buy books directly from publishers. These book-sellers typically have their own warehousing capabilities. Similarly, large publishers are likely to have their own sales staff. Even so, independent book distribution and wholesaling companies remain important links in the author-to-reader chain.

There are specialized distributors and wholesalers who focus on Christian books, but they're likely to be owned by secular firms. For example, Spring Arbor (a firm that distributes more than 110,000 Christian book, video, and music titles) is part of Ingram Book Group, a major secular book distributor/wholesaler.

From the perspective of a novelist writing for a recognized Christian or secular publisher, the single most important distribution-channel function is selling to booksellers. Besides their obvious role of filling shelves at bookstores, the sales force provides essential feedback to publishers. Salespeople know what booksellers are willing to buy today—and what they want to buy in the future.

### It Is Written ...

I am concerned that, as Christian fiction becomes more popular, we may be poisoning the garden that grew it: the little Christian bookstores that were started and nurtured by people who saw such work as a God-given mission. Sometimes today, the mega-chains and online bookstores can sell a title at retail for less than what the little Mom-and-Pop Christian bookstore can buy it at wholesale. That's why so many Christian stores now devote more than 75% of their floor space to what is known in the trade as "Jesus junk"—the hats, T-shirts, action Bible figures, scripture candy, bad art prints and all the rest of it.

—Tom Morrisey, Christian novelist

# Publishers

Publishers buy—more properly, *license*—manuscripts from writers and then transform them into published novels. Publishers do this by editing the manuscripts, coming up with book and cover designs, hiring a specialized book printer to print and bind finished novels, and arranging for distribution to booksellers.

Publishers also do the required marketing and promoting to accomplish two things: first, encourage booksellers to stock the novels on their shelves; and second, encourage readers to purchase the novels from booksellers.

Writers ultimately work for publishers. *They are your prospective customers.* That's a straightforward concept you should write on the wall above your desk. If you want to become a successful Christian novelist, you need to understand how publishers think.

Christian fiction was first published by companies who publish Bibles. Because these companies typically present themselves as more than mere businesses—most produce mission statements that emphasize the ministry aspects of their work—some writers mistakenly assume that Christian publishing is somehow more easygoing and gracious than secular publishing. Well, while the Christian editors I know are some of the most delightful folks I've worked with, the publishers they represent are every bit as demanding as secular publishing houses.

> **Wisdom and Knowledge**
>
> One way that publishers have held the line on front-end investments is to cut back spending on marketing—especially for new and non-bestselling authors. This seems counterproductive, but many published authors have experienced marketing cutbacks. The practice has prompted novelists to step up their own marketing efforts, including websites, blogs, direct mail, newsletters, speaking engagements, and others.

Publishing agreements offered by Christian publishers can be as (or more) complex as contracts written by secular houses—contracts exceeding 18 pages are no longer unusual. Negotiations with Christian publishing houses can be as difficult and as tough as working through the details with a mainstream publisher. As one publishing company vice president told me, "being Christian doesn't mean being a bad businessperson."

Christian publishers want to change lives, but most also expect to make money. No surprise there; they must pay the same kinds of bills and survive the same financial pressures as secular publishing firms. Even more important, they face the same publishing risks.

There's a quip I use when I lecture at writers' conferences: If you want to make a little money publishing novels, start with a lot. The simple fact is that book publishing is a risky business. On average, only about 500 of the 200,000 new books published each year in the United States—fiction, nonfiction, Christian, secular, text books, cookbooks, children's books, Bibles, the lot—become authentic bestsellers, and sell more than 100,000 copies. The great majority of those 200,000 titles (about 80 percent) sell fewer than 100 copies.

The bottom line is that Christian publishers—like all other sensible publishers—are forever trying to minimize risk. They continuously shape, and reshape, the Christian fiction they publish in response to fast-changing business considerations.

## Literary Agents

Literary agents *represent* manuscripts and proposals to publishers. They also perform an initial filtering role by validating whether manuscripts and proposals created by authors are of publishable quality. Finally, agents provide a useful buffer between authors and editors, taking on the knotty chores of contract negotiation and problem resolution.

Some writers mistakenly believe that agents are literary salespeople who merely offer manuscripts to editors. These writers are surprised when an agent sends a rejection letter that says, "I don't love your work enough to represent it." The truth of the matter is that an effective agent must be an enthusiastic supporter of a writer's work—an advocate who believes in a manuscript's potential almost as much as the writer does.

# A Tale of Many Forces

The following graphic shows you which influencers are most responsible for the various forces that continue to shape Christian fiction today. Two check marks represent an especially strong influence.

As a Christian novelist—someone called to write Christian fiction—you must honor these forces, too. Developing a full-length novel represents a mammoth investment in time and effort. It makes little sense to produce a manuscript that has no chance of acceptance in the marketplace.

| | Readers | Reviewers | Booksellers | Distribution Channels | Publishers | Agents |
|---|---|---|---|---|---|---|
| **Improving Quality** | | ✓✓ | | | ✓✓ | |
| **More Genres** | ✓✓ | | | ✓ | | |
| **Traditional Values** | ✓ | | ✓✓ | | ✓ | |
| **"Push the Envelope"** | | ✓✓ | | | ✓✓ | ✓ |
| **Publisher Consolidation** | | | | | ✓✓ | |
| **Increased Sales** | | | ✓✓ | ✓✓ | ✓✓ | ✓ |

*The different links on the chain from writer to reader shape different aspects of Christian fiction.*

# Continuously Improving Quality

Perhaps the single most significant aspect of Christian fiction in recent years has been its continuously improving quality. The complaints of critics and book reviewers that Christian fiction was boring, preachy, formulaic, heavy handed, and clumsily written—coupled with limited readership, even among evangelical Christians—drove Christian publishers to hire editors who truly understood the craft of fiction. In turn, these editors found writers who could write compelling novels that simultaneously delivered explicit Christian content.

Higher-quality Christian fiction enabled many of the other changes I've talked about. Once quality improved, bestselling titles became possible. So did crossover novels that appeal to secular readers, and also increased sales at secular bookstores. The result has been the widespread perception that Christian fiction has "come of age."

## Increasing Quality in Action

Quality begets quality. Editors at Christian publishing companies have set high standards and expect authors to deliver high-quality manuscripts and proposals. Looked at from the other side of the desk, editors (and agents) will quickly reject manuscripts that have weak stories, sloppy prose, poor characterization, tacked-on Christian messages, untied loose ends, and careless points of view.

## How to Respond to the Demand for Higher-Quality Fiction

You have only one option here: write the highest-quality novel you can. To sell manuscripts, all Christian novelists must work harder to come up with compelling stories and characters. Forget formulaic fiction; shun tired storylines; eschew cardboard characterizations.

And get used to copy-editing your work to eliminate typos, loose ends, point-of-view mistakes, and continuity problems. Writers who have editing skills can do it themselves. Others often rely on friends and critique groups. Growing numbers of published and unpublished novelists routinely hire freelance editors to fine-tune their manuscripts and proposals before submission.

I advise every new writer to go the extra mile to produce a publishable manuscript the first time around. Publishers no longer give partial credit for "almost there" manuscripts. Editors (and agents) will read your novel with an eye toward discovering whether it's publishable or not. A publishable novel *may* be accepted; an unpublishable novel *will* be rejected out of hand.

 **It Is Written ...**

> I'm in touch with lots of published Christian novelists, and I don't know a single one who'd say he/she doesn't have room for improvement. We all want to learn more. We strive daily to improve in our craft. And new, aspiring writers are striving to improve as well.
>
> —Brandilyn Collins, Christian novelist

# The Confusing March of the Genres

As the market for Christian fiction grew, readers demanded Christian novels in as many different flavors as secular novels. Publishers responded with a long list of different genres. Alas, some of them had short, not very successful lives. Simply put, they represent failed experiments. Other genres live on, but with only a handful of new examples published each year.

## Let's Hear It for the Ladies

Yes, there's a pattern here. If you browse through a catalog of upcoming books from any Christian publisher, most of the new titles will be women's fiction, romance, female-oriented biblical novels, female-oriented historicals, female-oriented Southern fiction, female-oriented mysteries and thrillers, and what's commonly called "chick-lit."

Many observers say Christian fiction *is* fiction for women. While that's an exaggeration—there are titles aimed at men on bookshelves—it is true that Christian publishers wisely concentrate on the kind of novels that their target markets will buy.

> ### Wisdom and Knowledge
>
> Interestingly, if you review the membership lists of leading organizations for Christian novelists—one of the largest is American Christian Fiction Writers—you'll find that the majority of writers, both published and unpublished, are women. Who better to write the female-oriented fiction genre novels demanded by the target market? Of course, there are many men writing Christian fiction. *Ahem.* I offer myself as an example.

In theory, virtually any genre is appropriate for Christian fiction if the author incorporates traditional values, a Christian worldview, and an explicit Christian message. In practice, publishers have become less willing to experiment with genres that don't have proven sales potential. These include:

- Male-oriented genres—adventure fiction, military fiction, sports fiction, and nautical fiction, for example

- Speculative fiction—science fiction, fantasy, time travel, and supernatural thrillers, for example

- Horror

- Allegory

- Spiritual warfare

While you certainly can find Christian examples of these genres on bookstore shelves, relatively few are published each year—most of them from a handful of proven authors. Consequently, unusual genres represent a hard sell for authors and agents.

## Your Response to New Genres

Go carefully when you plan your Christian novel. Your best course of action is to choose a standard, tried-and-true genre that readers will embrace. Popular genres stay popular for decades—and represent ongoing markets for novelists.

If you're an unpublished author, keep in mind that publishers are likely to seek proven writers when they experiment with new genres. They'll also terminate experiments quickly if they don't prove successful, typically with little notice.

My point is that writing a novel in an unusual genre can be risky—it's all too easy to produce an orphan manuscript that will never find a home. I have one sitting in my closet.

# Gimme That Old-Time Christian Fiction

Christian fiction has, from its beginnings, been a bastion of conservative Christian values, populated with characters who don't drink alcoholic beverages, don't play cards, don't dance, don't gamble, don't use profanity, don't engage in strong violence, don't display overt sexuality, and don't enter unchaste relationships.

Despite a softening of language and content guidelines at some publishers, these values still define the *expectations* of the majority of Christian readers of Christian fiction.

Christian booksellers have long been the strongest advocates of conservative values—probably because they immediately hear the complaints of conservative readers who are offended by the novels they buy.

## The No-No Lists

You've probably heard of them. No-no lists of words you can't use, lists of topics you can't write about, lists of activities that are off-limits. I wish I could tell you they don't exist, but most Christian publishers have them—some on paper, some in the minds of editors.

Most critics—and many writers—insist that the rules are too rigid, that they're meant to prevent "vicarious sinning" by readers. Others point to the fact that specific prohibitions against characters drinking or dancing are cultural or denominational, rather than truly Christian. Still others rail against the apparent parochialism of rules that try to carve out a carefully defined area of "safety" for Evangelical readers of Christian fiction.

**A Lamp Unto Your Feet**

If you want to write a cross-over novel, keep this in mind: when novels are written from the start as crossovers, this is usually done by toning down the Christian message, not violating the no-no list rules.

I've heard many writers grumble that the no-no lists are inconsistent, and even downright silly. Mild obscenities—the kind many Christians use every day—are not allowed, but gory violence can be acceptable. Which means, for example, that an author can spell out the gruesome details of a shooting, but the victim can't say anything stronger than "oh my!" after being shot.

These debates are interesting, but of little value to a writer of Christian fiction. Whether you're for or against them, the limits on language and content reflect the state of the market today, and the current expectations of the majority of Christian readers.

## Don't Fight the System

It may be fun to complain about the conservative values of Christian fiction, but I urge you to honor the limitations on topics and language when you develop your Christian novel.

A good way to think about Christian fiction is to consider it a "super genre" by itself—a branch of fiction that has its own rules and conventions to satisfy readers.

My wife and I write cozy mysteries—a well-established subgenre of the mystery and suspense genre that has well-defined reader expectations. Cozies are kindler, gentler mysteries that don't repel or truly frighten readers. We create worlds for our stories that *could never* exist for real. Cozy mysteries are populated with charming murderers, simpleminded (often inept) policemen, outlandish methods of murder (all of which cause quick, bloodless, and painless deaths), and amateur detectives who always succeed in capturing the murderer and restoring the balance of the Universe a page or two before the novel ends.

Our readers know that it's all make-believe; that's one of the reasons they enjoy reading cozy mysteries. A well-written cozy mystery lets readers escape the unpleasant real world for a few hours of rest and relaxation in a safe imaginary place.

To a great extent, classic Christian fiction also creates nonexistent worlds that traditional readers of Christian novels like to visit. They're safe, predictable environments with little of the nastiness of the real world. No foul language. No abusive drunks. No perverse sexuality. No moral relativism. No ambiguity between right and wrong. No sleazy love affairs. Only the "good" (emotional) side of love.

It's no surprise that Christian bookstores enforce the no-no rules so fiercely. Readers want them to.

As a writer of Christian fiction, you're free to kick against the goads of the no-no lists. But if you do, you'll significantly reduce the number of Christian publishers (and agents) willing to consider your work.

The no-no lists may change, or even disappear, in the future. But it makes no sense today for a novelist to swim upstream against the requirements—not if you want to write a widely publishable manuscript. I'll talk about specific strategies for coping with limitations on language and content in Chapter 11.

# Pushing the Envelope

The word you often hear at writers' conferences is "edgy." Christian fiction is considered edgy when it focuses on difficult topics, or uses foul language, or includes behavior on some publishers' no-no lists.

Urged on by critics and book reviewers, an increasing number of Christian publishers are willing to confront thorny contemporary issues and show characters dealing with "real world" issues. Recent Christian novels have addressed spousal abuse, child abuse, abuse by clergy members, rape, incest, abortion, AIDS, alcoholism, aging, pornography, drug addiction, sex addiction, serial murder, suicide, homosexuality, racism, and strained relations among different religions. Many of these novels wouldn't have passed muster on bookseller shelves five or ten years ago.

The advocates of edgier Christian fiction point out that the Bible is chock-full of nasty behavior—from child slavery to sexual perversions. Writers (and editors) know that because these activities are likely to test a hero or heroine's Christian faith, they can be the stuff of highly dramatic stories.

## How Far Will the Envelope Be Pushed?

The proverbial jury is still out. The final dimensions of the Christian-fiction envelope will ultimately depend on two things:

1. Where the traditional readers of Christian fiction draw the lines that define the acceptable limits of content and topic

2. Whether the expanded envelope generates sufficient new sales among nontraditional readers of Christian novels to compensate for the loss of some traditional sales

Keep in mind that pushing the envelope doesn't mean short-changing the explicit Christian content. Rather, edgy fiction shows Christians and soon-to-be Christians struggling against the challenges of unpleasant realities.

## Should You Write Edgier Fiction?

Your answer will largely depend on your own personal preferences. I know some Christian novelists who are determined envelope-pushers. I know others who don't like to read, or write, edgy Christian fiction; they are content to tell traditional kinds of stories.

A further important consideration is where you are in your career. Christian publishers seem to give less latitude to new or recently published authors and more to their bestselling authors—proven writers who have already established trust with a large audience of readers.

# Another Publisher Bites the Dust

These are exciting times for Christian publishers. Scarcely a month goes by without an announcement that a venerable Christian publisher has been bought by a secular publishing conglomerate—or even by a larger Christian publishing house. The net result has been to dramatically reduce the total number of Christian publishers—and also the number of companies producing specialized genres, such as Christian children books and Christian young adult fiction.

## The Impact of Fewer Publishers

Bigger publishers swallowing up smaller publishers may be good news for shareholders of the companies, but from a Christian novelist's perspective, fewer publishers means fewer places to sell his or her manuscript. It's become increasingly difficult for new Christian novelists to find homes for their work, because large publishing companies often prefer to contract with proven authors.

A published writer—let's call him Bob—can face an equally painful problem. The large house taking over Bob's current publisher may have a different publishing philosophy. The surviving company may not want to publish any more novels in Bob's chosen genre.

Another possibility is that a publishing merger makes some staff members of the combined company redundant. You frequently see an editor or two leave after the dust settles. If Bob's editor departs, Bob's published novels become "orphans," because there may be no one inside the house to advocate them. Bob may not be offered a contract for follow-up books.

Finally, the large publishing company may currently offer novels that compete directly with Bob's books. After the merger, the surviving company is likely to stick with its own authors—and cut Bob adrift.

 **Literary Sins**

Can an orphaned novel find a new home? It can happen, but don't count on it. When a publisher decides to terminate a series of books, the publishing rights usually revert back to the author. Another publisher who sees a strong sales potential may bring the series back to life by "repackaging" the previously published novels.

## How Should You Respond?

In a time of turmoil, write novels that *any* Christian publishing company is willing to publish. Seek out the genres and markets that offer the most reliable opportunities. Women's fiction, romance, suspense, and mystery seem to always be in demand by publishing houses.

# Big, Big Sales in the Past

These days, a rejection note from a large Christian publisher is likely to read: "We loved your story and your writing, but we've decided to pass on your manuscript because you don't have a successful track record of high book sales."

The magic number seems to be 25,000 to 35,000 copies of a previous book sold. This can be a daunting requirement, considering that very few published Christian novels sell more than 15,000 copies.

Demanding significant past sales is a way for a publishing company to reduce its risk. But the secular booksellers who handle Christian fiction—and the salespeople in the distribution channel—also prefer authors who have name recognition among potential customers. And agents find it much easier to represent a new manuscript from a previously successful author.

## The Impact of the Drive for Greater Sales

Ironically, the practice can impact multi-published authors even more than unpublished authors who haven't built a history of previous sales. A publisher may be willing to take a chance on a new voice, but not go with an established novelist who hasn't achieved impressive sales in the past.

## How Should You Respond?

There's really only one response, and it's appropriate both for unpublished writers and for published authors who lack impressive track records: target publishers who don't insist on previous successes. A good way to find them is by going to conferences and speaking to editors and agents.

## The Least You Need to Know

◆ The target market for Christian fiction is Caucasian women, of childbearing through "empty nester" age, who identify themselves as evangelical Christians.

◆ Make sure you deliver a high-quality manuscript when you submit your novel to an agent or editor.

◆ Choose a genre that will always stay popular.

◆ Don't rock the traditional-values boat.

◆ Recognize that "pushing the envelope" may reduce the number of publishers willing to buy your book.

◆ If you haven't built a history of previous sales, target publishers who don't insist on previous successes.

# Chapter 3

# Christian Fiction as Ministry

## In This Chapter

- ◆ Christian fiction has the power to inspire
- ◆ Is writing fiction a valid endeavor for Christians?
- ◆ How evangelizing fits in
- ◆ Christian fiction isn't an alternate route to publication
- ◆ The question of money
- ◆ The importance of writing with a servant's heart

Can reading a Christian novel bring someone to Christ? Or rejuvenate their faith? Or change their life for the better? Many Christian novelists have letters from readers attesting that these very things happened when they read a particular Christian novel. Perhaps you, or someone you know, has had such an experience.

This raises an obvious question: Should evangelizing your readers—or otherwise ministering to them—be your leading goal when you write Christian fiction? Some experienced writers say yes while others say no. You should know *your* answer—your purpose for writing Christian fiction— when you start planning your Christian novel, because your decision will strongly impact the way you think and write. This chapter will help you decide by considering both sides of the issue.

# Why Do Readers Read Christian Fiction?

This is not a trick question. Sooner or later, every novelist must come to grips with the nature of the work he or she does. The reader's perspective is the heart of the matter, because novels are written to be read.

The primary reason people read any kind of fiction is to be entertained. But readers and writers know that fiction provides a distinctive kind of entertainment. Reading well-written fiction can sharpen and enlarge our understanding of life.

Fiction is not "real," but it can convey reality to readers more effectively than nonfiction. Fiction is not "factual," but it can shape the way people view and react to the real world around them. Fiction is usually about people who never existed, but readers may come to know them just as well as flesh-and-blood friends and relatives—and fully understand their emotions, their hopes, their needs, their fears, and their yearnings.

### Chapter and Verse

The **fictional dream** is what happens when a novel engages a reader's imagination, and "puts" the reader into a character's head, in another time and place. John Gardner, a novelist and teacher, coined the term. I'll tell you more about the fictional dream in Chapter 5 and show you the easy way to create it in Chapter 10.

A good novel stretches the imagination and invites the reader to participate vicariously in an aspect of life different from his or her own. By entering what has been called a *fictional dream*, the reader of the novel walks in someone else's shoes, travels to faraway lands, explores different facets of the human experience, and comes to think about the world in new ways. And in the process, the reader may be changed forever.

Good Christian fiction shares all of these attributes, but it also celebrates God's presence in our life and invites readers to experience God working in the world. A good Christian novel combines a delightful story with deep theology and bedrock truths about God.

Nonbelievers are likely to come away from a Christian novel with a fresh awareness of the power of God, and expanded visions of what Christianity is all about. The Holy Spirit can use this new understanding to change their lives—perhaps even help them become Christians.

Consider this excerpt from a letter that Nancy Moser, a popular author of contemporary Christian fiction, received from one of her readers:

Because of your book, I now believe.

Here's another testimony, from a letter sent to Deborah Raney, a leading writer of Christian women's fiction:

> The Lord spoke to my heart anew and I believe that I realize more than I ever have how very important it is to listen to that "still small voice" and to put my life in the hands of my Lord and Savior.

Believing Christians will often have their faith strengthened by reading a Christian novel, as they gain new perspectives on the impact of God in people's lives.

Well-known Christian women's fiction author Stephanie Grace Whitson received these words from one of her readers:

> My life has been in absolute shambles for two years. … [Y]our books have helped me to remember the trials we all go through and if you put faith in God, it will somehow work out. They have given me so much hope, I can't even put into words.

And a reader of bestselling Christian author Angela Hunt wrote:

> I had almost given up my faith in God until my grandma gave me these (your) books to read, which helped restore my faith in God and our relationship.

My point is that Christian novels have the ability to inspire, educate, and even evangelize readers—and have often done so. Keep this in mind while I take a brief detour to examine the truthfulness of Christian fiction.

# Is Christian Fiction a Lie?

There are sincere Christians who believe that writing and reading Christian fiction are *un-Christian* activities, despite the explicit Christian content to be found in Christian novels. These people argue that writing fiction is by definition telling lies on paper. They also feel that a Christian should spend his or her limited free time reading "truthful" literature that enlightens and edifies, rather than books full of untruths designed to entertain.

**It Is Written …**

Fiction is a lie covering up a deep truth.

—Mario Vargas Llosa, Latin American novelist

I believe this argument is based on a flawed conception of what fiction is—and isn't. For starters, fiction is not the opposite of truth; rather, fiction is the opposite of *fact*. Because fiction grows out of the possibilities of human experience, it can capture the essence of reality more effectively than history, which must be tied to what actually happened.

Both writer and reader know that the characters in a novel are not living and breathing people, that the settings are imaginary, and that the events portrayed never happened in the "real world." And yet, a good Christian novel will contain page after page of truth that speaks to the hearts of readers—truth that is inspirational and life-affirming, and that conveys new understanding of life, grace, and redemption.

**It Is Written …**

A 2006 study by LifeWay Christian Resources found that 53 percent of Protestant clergy read fiction! That's good news, because it used to be that pastors not only didn't read fiction, they didn't encourage their congregants to read it either.

—Karen Ball, Christian novelist and editor

Paradoxically, a make-believe story populated with make-believe characters is a proven way to deliver truth to readers. Picasso famously said that "art is a lie that makes us realize the truth." Well, telling stories is probably the oldest art, and one of the most effective ways to convey truth to people.

Consider how often Jesus told stories when He wanted to communicate spiritual truths. His many parables demonstrate the ability of Christian fiction to make people think in new and different ways. Two thousand years later, we're still extracting new meaning from His stories.

Finally, when we talk about the ability of fiction to convey truth, we must keep one caveat in mind: Christian fiction is not Scripture and most Christian novelists are not theologians. Novels can convey important truths about God, humanity, and the human experience, but no reader should use a novel as a Christian reference text. Although authors and publishers work hard to get history and Bible references right, errors sometimes make it into print.

# Where Does Evangelizing Fit In?

Remember those ads for kosher hot dogs that ended with "We answer to a higher authority"? Many writers and publishers of Christian fiction feel the same way about their novels.

Because inspiration and evangelization can be exciting side effects for readers who presumably set out to be entertained by reading Christian novels, some authors believe they have a responsibility to develop fiction that goes beyond "mere entertainment." They see themselves as *ministering* to their readers from the get-go, employing

the power of fiction to turn around readers'
lives and hearts, and especially bringing nonbelievers to Christ.

Other Christian novelists acknowledge that
they've been called to write Christian fiction,
but they leave the use of their books to God.
As Christians who write, they recognize

> **Chapter and Verse**
>
> The word **minister** actually means "servant" in Latin. The root idea of ministry is service.

a responsibility to follow Jesus' admonition to be "salt and light" in the world (see
Matthew 5:13-14)—and use their writing to influence others. But they don't claim
that their novels minister to readers and they don't seek to write prose designed to
evangelize nonbelievers. They recognize these things may happen, but they don't
make evangelization a chief purpose of their writing work.

Are you ready to take a stand yet? As you can see, the two positions involve different
approaches to developing Christian fiction. The first approach makes communicating a compelling Christian Gospel message the primary reason for writing a
Christian novel. The second approach is a step closer to secular fiction; it emphasizes
the importance of good storytelling and treats the ability to communicate Christian
truths as a byproduct.

Clearly, a good Christian novel needs both effective storytelling and an explicit
Christian message. The question is, which of them is your driving force when you sit
down to write?

## Christian Fiction *Should* Evangelize

The arguments in favor go like this:

Christian writers are Christians first. We've been told by Jesus to make disciples, to
teach them what He taught the Apostles. That gives us the responsibility to write
novels that glorify God and communicate the Gospel of Jesus Christ as a source of
hope and salvation for the world.

We can't be satisfied by simply weaving an entertaining story. Our novels must do
more. First and foremost, they must have a redemptive theme and introduce God to
nonbelievers. We believe in a God that entered in history to save lost humanity. Our
novels must testify to that event. That's how our books become tools that God can
use to change lives.

**Chapter and Verse** _____

Our word **evangelize** grew out of a Greek noun that means "good news." The Middle English word *gospel* means "good tale," a literal translation of the same Greek word.

Secular novelists chiefly seek to edify and entertain their readers. *Evangelization* is what sets the Christian novelist apart. The capacity to evangelize is what makes a Christian novel Christian.

Karen Ball, a leading Christian novelist and editor of Christian fiction, echoed this notion when she said, "I'm not at all against telling a great story, but there are a lot of great stories out there already. What we have to offer that's different is truth and hope. And not just any truth and hope, but the eternal truth and hope that comes only through Christ. If we're not bringing that into our stories, then what's the point?"

And Christian author Deborah Raney recently wrote, "My greatest fear is that Christian fiction, in an effort to appeal to the masses, will become too much like every other genre, with the message of hope in Christ being hidden to the point of not being recognized by the very souls who need to understand it most."

Many Christian readers of Christian fiction are likely to agree. Even though they're believers when they start reading, most enjoy the "battery recharging" that's accomplished by good novels that emphasize the Gospel. Few Christians seem to tire of rehearing "The Greatest Story Ever Told."

## Great Christian Fiction Starts with Great Stories

The alternative perspective (it's not truly an opposing viewpoint) insists that people and story must come first in a novel, because the Christian messages will ultimately be communicated through them. Simply put, Christian fiction must start out as good fiction that a reader is willing to read.

Christian author James Scott Bell, no slouch at delivering high-voltage Christian messages in his bestselling suspense novels, observes: "At the very least, the Christian artist must hold a positive vision of what life can and should be. This has traditionally been the *sine qua non* of great writing. But it all has to be wrapped up in a crackling good story. If I don't have readers turning pages, nothing else will matter because nothing more will be read."

Some Christian writers think that the notion of novelist as minister is pompous—an implication that authors who see fiction writing as a ministry are somehow more spiritual than "ordinary" novelists. They insist that saving people is God's job, and that our responsibility as Christian authors is to write the best possible stories we can. By incorporating explicit Christian messages, we make it possible for God to use our novels in the ways He sees fit.

A related concern I introduced in Chapter 1 is that fiction with a deliberately evangelistic message may alienate the very nonbelieving readers it's intended to reach. These people may, to use the Apostle Paul's word, see the Christian Gospel as "foolishness." At worst, they'll stop reading a novel designed to evangelize; at best, they'll ignore its Christian content.

### Wisdom and Knowledge

While you may hear that some Christian publishers seek novels that evangelize and others look first at story and characters, the simple truth is that well-written novels in both categories are published every day.

Susan Howatch, a bestselling writer of Christian-themed secular novels, has said, "I think it is extremely dangerous for any novelist to set out to evangelize, because you end up writing a Christian polemic. A novelist's first duty is to write a story. A novelist's second duty is to write a readable story, and without a readable story, nothing is possible. If you get the story right, the Christian themes will emerge from the interaction of the people, and they can be completely understated."

# Not an Alternate Route to Publication

It used to be true—though it isn't any longer—that it was easier for an unpublished author to sell a manuscript to a Christian publisher than a mainstream publisher. And so, in years past, some authors bolted Christian messages to their secular novels and offered them to Christian houses as an alternate route to publication.

This really isn't practical anymore, for three reasons:

1. The quality of Christian fiction has improved to the point that a manuscript not good enough to sell to secular publishers won't find a home at a Christian publisher.

2. Christian fiction has become sufficiently different from mainstream fiction that a few tweaks won't transform a secular novel into a Christian novel.

3. The expectations of editors and readers is that the explicit Christian content will be woven seamlessly through your story. You can't tack it onto a secular plotline and hope to sell your manuscript.

If you've read this far in this book hoping to learn the secrets of transforming your secular novel into a Christian novel, all I can say is, sorry—it's not going to work.

# The Role of Money

The success of Christian fiction—its fast-growing sales—has meant increased royalty payments to the bestselling authors. This makes some ministry-focused writers uncomfortable.

I've been part of several group discussions at writers' conferences that questioned whether a Christian novelist can have two masters. Simply put, can a Christian writer overcome the temptation to write "popular Christian fiction" that makes lots of money rather than create "small Christian novels" that communicate powerful, but possibly challenging, Christian messages that convict readers?

I'm confident that most Christian writers I know would say that enlarging the Kingdom is a more important goal than financial success. But as Jesus noted, "The worker deserves his wages." (Luke 10:7 NIV) Moreover, high royalties happen when a novel reaches a large number of readers. This makes money a kind of scorecard of the effectiveness of a Christian novel—the number of hearts and minds it can influence.

**Literary Sins** _____

Don't quit your day job when you begin to write Christian fiction. The *Left Behind* series, which earned royalties measured in many tens of millions of dollars, proves there's as much money to be made in Christian fiction as secular fiction. Keep in mind, however, that only a handful of novels—Christian or secular—become bestsellers. Most don't "earn out" the advance royalties paid to the author. The bottom line: don't rely on making piles of money before you start writing blockbuster novels.

# Writing with a Servant's Heart

Authors of Christian fiction need not be evangelists or ministers (in the pastoral sense of the word), but we should approach our fiction with a servant's heart. Jesus made the point (Mark 10:45 NIV) that he did not come to be served, but to serve.

B. J. Hoff, a bestselling Christian author of historical fiction and romantic suspense, recently made this important point on her blog. Her comments provide an excellent summary for this chapter:

> We have to realize that we're merely a part of a world and an entire community, and although what we write might have some impact on other lives, even lead a few to God, this is still a temporary run, and there are far more important

things on God's mind for us—and in his long-term plan for his world—than whether we're writing the best fiction around or if we're appearing on the best-seller chart or on the publisher's "star author" list.

I seriously doubt that God is keeping an account of the number of books we've published this year or how many book signings we've done or how many fan letters we've received. On the other hand, it's probably safe to assume that He does keep watch on the heart. … Never forget that in the past God has been known to use a donkey to make his point. In truth, He really doesn't need even the best of our abilities, although certainly He uses them if we don't hug them too tightly to ourselves.

May we keep a servant's heart. Christ didn't occupy Himself with taking bows, but instead washed his disciples' feet. He spent more time praying than performing, more energy feeding the hungry and healing the sick than drawing attention to himself. He devoted his time and effort to doing his Father's will and caring for his people instead of playing to the crowds or making a name for himself.

## The Least You Need to Know

- ◆ The Christian fiction you write may minister and evangelize—but it also must entertain.

- ◆ You tell the "truth" when you write Christian fiction, even though it's not "real," or "factual," or about people who actually existed.

- ◆ Never forget that *your* Christian fiction will have the power to change readers' lives.

- ◆ You must decide whether to make evangelizing or good storytelling your chief goal; whatever your decision, your novel must tell a good story and communicate an explicit Christian message.

- ◆ While a bestselling Christian novel can earn significant royalties for its author, don't focus on just making money.

- ◆ Approach writing Christian fiction with a servant's heart.

# Chapter 4

# An Overview of Leading Christian Publishers

## In This Chapter

- ◆ The fast-breaking changes in Christian publishing
- ◆ The two caveats about publishers
- ◆ Decoding the submission policies of leading Christian publishers
- ◆ An introduction to the leading Christian publishing companies and Christian imprints

A relatively small number of Christian publishers publish the lion's share of Christian novels in the United States. Their number shrinks each year as larger houses acquire smaller publishers and (one or two) others stop publishing fiction. At the same time, small publishers enter the marketplace; a few of these will succeed and grow into the significant publishers of the future.

This chapter introduces you to today's leading publishers and give you an overview of your target markets as a writer of Christian fiction. I've provided a thumbnail sketch of each house along with information on several publishers that will publish first-time novelists. Keep in mind "will publish" doesn't mean they're easy sells or have large lists of new novelists.

Rather, these houses are first-novelist friendly, in that that they will consider previously unpublished authors, encourage their acquisitions editors to attend major Christian writers' conferences, and are unusually open about their genres and editorial needs.

# If You Don't Like the Current Editors—Wait a Minute!

You could subscribe to every annually published writer's guide, read every magazine and newsletter about publishing, participate in every national writers' conference, and still not keep up with the torrent of changes at Christian publishing houses.

Hardly a day goes by—or so it seems—without a well-known Christian publisher merging with a larger (often mainstream) house. Or without a leading Christian publishing company revising its approach to fiction. Or taking on new genres. Or trimming a less-than-successful fiction line.

This isn't a criticism of Christian publishing; it's merely a statement of how things are. Significant consolidation—and rapid change—have impacted the entire book publishing industry in recent years, as large publishing conglomerates have snapped up most of the previously independent houses. Christian companies have "shared" in this overall trend.

From a writer's perspective, it rarely matters who actually owns a specific publishing company. The owners rarely make individual editorial decisions. The changes that are most significant to us are those that happen *inside* the editorial department. Each new acquisition of a Christian publisher seems to invite a fresh game of musical chairs—with experienced fiction editors coming and going—that revises the house's editorial policies and fiction-publishing strategy. The new editorial team identifies fresh target audiences. New genres replace the old. Editors revisit—and frequently reject—book proposals "in the hopper." Recently contracted books become orphans before they're published (some even may never be published). It can take months, even years, for publishing operations to become stable once again.

There's nothing novelists can do about the situation, except live with it—and pray that late-breaking editorial staff changes don't impact our proposals and our contracted manuscripts.

# Two Caveats About Publisher Information

The first caveat is that change happens too quickly for even annually published writers' guides to stay current in all dimensions. Treat the information in this chapter as a starting point for your research. Visit each publisher's website for its latest writer's guidelines, submission policies, and current contact addresses. I've included a list of website addresses in Appendix A; they usually don't change as often as other data.

The second caveat is that few publishers provide truly useful guidance about their long-range editorial strategy. Editors will admit "off the record" that deciding what kind of literary entertainment their readers will enjoy two or three years from now is mostly guesswork. To quote an editor I know, "It's impossible to define specific requirements for the future. I evaluate lots of proposals and know a good one when I see it."

**A Lamp Unto Your Feet**

The current novels published by a Christian publisher are not necessarily a good indication of what the company will publish three years from now. Publishing strategies are continuously changing and companies often experiment with different genres "to see what will happen."

This is another reason why it makes sense for a first-time writer to choose a "universal" genre that will never go out of fashion. No matter what changes happen, readers will continue to read—and Christian publishers will continue to publish—contemporary fiction, women's fiction, historicals, romance, and suspense. (I'll discuss the most popular genres in Chapter 6.)

# Those Exasperating Submission Policies

Most Christian publishers will not accept unsolicited proposals from unpublished authors. They'll only read submissions made …

- ◆ By a recognized literary agent.
- ◆ Through a manuscript submission service (The Writer's Edge or ChristianManuscriptSubmissions.Com (see Chapter 21).
- ◆ Via a recommendation from one of their current authors.
- ◆ By way of an invitation from one of their editors at a writers' conference.

These policies change from time to time, but they rarely become more liberal. Fewer and fewer publishers are willing to invest the time to read slush-pile submissions. This isn't surprising: plowing though several thousand unsolicited proposals and manuscripts over the course of a year takes mountains of time yet rarely yields more than *one or two* publishable novels. Consequently, most publishers have turned the initial quality "filtering" role over to those literary agents who are willing to consider queries from unpublished writers.

New writers often ask, "Do I really need an agent?" The simple answer is this: a recognized agent can open virtually every publishing door for a first-time novelist. There are no guarantees that editors will buy a manuscript, but it will get a fair reading—the essential first step in finding a home for a novel.

# Leading Christian Publishers and Imprints

The list of publishers I've assembled in this section are responsible for the lion's share of Christian fiction published in the United States. Some are independent companies; others are *imprints* (the publisher's brand name for a line of books, usually of a distinct genre or aimed at a particular market). A single publisher may have several imprints, each with its own editorial staff and publishing strategy. For example, Waterbrook Press and Multnomah Publishing are the two Christian imprints of Random House. An imprint can have its own imprints (sub-imprints).

## Avon Inspire (Christian Sub-Imprint of Avon Books)

Avon Inspire is a new imprint from Avon Books, an imprint of Harper Collins, which publishes contemporary and historical romance, chick lit, and romantic comedy, mostly written by well-established authors. It likes novels that feature the "things that matter most: family, community, faith, and love." The house will consider queries from first-time authors that are submitted by literary agents. Editors attend some major Christian writers' conferences.

## B & H Publishing Group (Division of LifeWay Christian Resources)

You may still find B & H Publishing listed in authors' guides under its previous name: Broadman & Holman. B & H is the book and Bible division of LifeWay Christian Resources.

B & H currently publishes Christian contemporary fiction. Its varied line includes a surprisingly high percentage of male-oriented Christian novels by male writers. The house has recently enlarged its fiction editorial staff and plans to place a greater emphasis on Christian fiction—including more novels by female writers.

B & H does not accept unsolicited submissions. Editors often attend major writers' conferences.

# Barbour Publishing

Ten percent of Barbour's Christian novels are written by previously unpublished authors—roughly ten each year, a higher number than most other Christian publishers. Barbour also publishes "anthologies" of three or four romance novellas (typically 20,000 words long). One novella in each anthology can be written by a first-timer—making them great "entry points" for unpublished writers.

Romance is Barbour's primary fiction genre. The independent Christian house publishes *trade paperbacks* in several romance subgenres, including contemporary, historical, prairie, and romantic suspense.

*Heartsong Presents* is a Barbour book club that publishes and distributes short *mass-market* romance novels (typically 45,000 words) directly to readers. *Heartsong Presents/Spyglass Lane Mysteries* is a newer Barbour book club that publishes 55,000 to 60,000 word romantic cozy mysteries. Both lines represent strong potential markets for first-time novelists.

### Chapter and Verse

**Mass-market paperbacks** are the compact books you see on sale almost everywhere—from airports, to supermarkets, to big-box stores, to traditional booksellers. The larger paperback books you increasingly find in bookstores are called **trade paperbacks.** They travel in the same "book trade" distribution channels as traditional hardcover books, although they are significantly less expensive. The majority of Christian novels published today appear as trade paperbacks.

Barbour prefers submission through an agent, but will read unsolicited and unagented queries. Editors attend some major writers' conferences.

# Bethany House (Division of Baker Publishing Group)

Bethany House is a true pioneer in Christian fiction. In 1979, Bethany published *Love Comes Softly,* Janette Oke's first historical romance. Since then, the house has published strong historical, nostalgic, and contemporary women's fiction lines. Bethany also offers some romance, romantic suspense, and male-oriented fiction and occasionally publishes fantasy and Bible-era historicals.

Bethany House takes pride in introducing new authors (it publishes a few first-time writers each year). Unique among Christian publishers, the company invites one-page queries from unagented writers, *sent via fax.* This is important; Bethany requires other kinds of submission through an agent and will not accept unsolicited queries or proposals via telephone, mail, or e-mail. Editors attend major writers' conferences.

## Faith Words (Christian Imprint of Hachette Book Group)

Faith Words (previously known as Warner Faith) has benefited from its parent company's ability to sell and distribute Christian novels in mainstream markets. The editors will consider most "faith-building fiction," including historicals, love stories, and romantic suspense, but are especially interested in contemporary fiction.

Faith Words won't read unsolicited submissions and is probably a difficult sell for a previously unpublished writer without a significant *platform*. Editors attend some major writers' conferences.

### Chapter and Verse

Your **platform** is your ability to reach a large number of target readers because they know about your previous accomplishments, have read your earlier books, or are part of your network of acquaintances or admirers. Celebrities have big platforms, which makes it remarkably easy for a celebrity to sell a novel (even if he or she needed a ghostwriter to help write it). Publishers like an author with a big platform because it simplifies the difficult (and expensive) job of promoting his or her book. Christian publishers are increasingly basing their buy/not buy decisions on the size of a writer's platform. Although this seems unfair—platform has nothing to do with the quality of a proposed novel—it's another way publishers can reduce the financial risk of publishing fiction.

## Guideposts Books

Guideposts Books is the new retail book-publishing arm of the large, well-known inspirational magazine publisher. (Guideposts has long distributed novels via mail order; most retail books begin life as mail-order novels.)

Guideposts Books publishes a small line of Christian novels, written mostly by previously published authors. They fall into the category of "continuity fiction": Guideposts owns the characters and the settings. The house commissions experienced authors to write short novels (35,000 words) that must honor a strict "bible" of details about characters and settings.

Guideposts Books will read unsolicited queries from authors who are familiar with the house's continuity fiction lines, but because the company values experience, first-time authors will find Guideposts a difficult sell.

# HarperSanFrancisco (Imprint of Harper Collins)

HarperSanFrancisco publishes a small line of Christian novels from well-established authors. An exceptionally difficult sell for a first-time novelist, unless he or she has a significant platform. Requires submission through agent.

# Harvest House Publishers

Harvest House sees its core market for fiction as Christian readers who like a good story without the inappropriate language, sensuality, and pessimistic outlook found in much contemporary fiction today. The house publishes women's contemporary and historical fiction, mysteries, and some male-oriented fiction.

Harvest House is open to publishing first-time novelists, but does not accept unsolicited queries. Editors often attend major writers' conferences.

# Heartsong Presents (Imprint of Barbour Publishing)

See Barbour Publishing.

# Howard Books (Christian Imprint of Simon & Schuster)

Howard is a medium-size publisher that is currently expanding its Christian fiction offerings. The house has recently enlarged its fiction editorial staff.

Howard publishes full-length novels in familiar genres, including contemporary women's fiction, historicals, and suspense, but is willing to consider high-quality character-based fiction that "bends" genres.

Most Howard authors are previously published, but the company is willing to publish a few novels each year by first-time novelists. Howard prefers submission through an agent, but will read unsolicited and unagented queries. Editors attend some major writers' conferences.

The relationship with Simon & Schuster creates an unusual opportunity for Howard authors to write novels for both Christian and mainstream imprints.

# Kregel Publishing

Kregel Publishing is a medium-size publisher that views its mission as an evangelical Christian publisher to "develop and distribute with integrity and excellence—trusted, biblically based resources that lead individuals to know and serve Jesus Christ."

The house offers a variety of fiction genres, but recently described its preferences as: mystery, suspense, and relationship-oriented stories that do not have traditional romance storylines, in both historical and contemporary settings.

Kregel is open to new writers, but doesn't accept unsolicited queries. Editors attend some major writers' conferences.

## Love Inspired (Imprint of Steeple Hill)

See Steeple Hill.

## Mountain View Publishing (Christian Imprint of Treble Heart Press)

A young, small Christian imprint that's open to first-time writers. Will look at unagented queries.

## Multnomah Publishers (Christian Imprint of Random House)

Multnomah publishes full-length novels in the following genres: romance, historical, suspense, biblical, fantasy, teen, science fiction, and futuristic. Multnomah only accepts proposals through literary agents. Editors attend some major writers' conferences.

## NavPress (Ministry of The Navigators)

NavPress, a ministry of The Navigators, defines its mission "to reach, disciple, and equip people to know Christ and to make Him known by publishing life-related materials that are biblically rooted and culturally relevant."

The house has been open to Christian novels in the contemporary, literary, and mystery/suspense genres, but is reportedly shifting its focus to fiction aimed at young adults. It occasionally publishes historical, biblical, and fantasy. All must display skilled writing, well-developed characters, and a compelling story.

NavPress does publish some first-time novelists, but it does not read unsolicited queries. Editors attend some major writers' conferences. The company will not publish novels that contain vulgar language or graphic sexuality. It will weigh the acceptability of other content and behaviors on a case-by-case basis.

# New Spirit (Christian Imprint of Kimani Press)

This is a new imprint of Kimani Press, a division of Harlequin, that publishes "compelling inspirational fiction and nonfiction for African Americans." New Spirit will offer "inspirational fiction featuring universal messages of loss, tragedy and redemption. New Spirit books will explore life's struggles and the path to reconciliation."

New Spirit accepts submissions with or without an agent (see Harlequin's website for guidelines and details).

# Revell (Division of Baker Publishing Group)

Revell is a medium-size publisher of contemporary and women's fiction. The house does not read unsolicited submissions and does not publish submission guidelines on its website. Editors often attend major writers' conferences.

# RiverOak (Imprint of Cook Communications Ministries)

RiverOak's motto is "The Good News in Fiction." The house goes on to promise "page-turning fiction with memorable characters and engrossing storylines that clearly illustrate God's interaction in our lives."

RiverOak publishes a variety of genres, including contemporary, suspense, fantasy, and westerns. The company does not read unsolicited proposals; its editors attend some major writers' conferences.

# Steeple Hill (Division of Harlequin)

Romance is at the heart of every book Steeple Hill publishes. Its primary fiction genres are romance (both historical and contemporary), relationship novels, mysteries, romantic suspense, and thrillers. Steeple Hill has several fiction imprints: Love Inspired, Love Inspired Historical, Love Inspired Romantic Suspense, Steeple Hill Women's Fiction, and Steeple Hill Café. The Love Inspired lines are series-romance mass-market paperbacks; the Steeple Hill lines are single-title trade paperbacks, and include many subgenres.

Interestingly, all lines are open to new writers. Steeple Hill's comprehensive website provides detailed writer's guidelines and submission information. The Love Inspired lines accept unsolicited submissions; the Steeple Hill line does not. Editors attend selected major writers' conferences.

## Strang Book Group

Strang Book Group publishes a small line of speculative Christian fiction—"mind stretching thrillers"—under the Realms imprint. Genres include fantasy, supernatural thrillers, time travel, spiritual warfare, and futuristic fiction.

Strang will consider unsolicited manuscripts from first-time authors. The publisher's unusual website provides extensive submission instructions.

## Tyndale House

Tyndale House is the Christian publisher responsible for the *Left Behind* series—perhaps the most successful crossover novels ever. The company sees its corporate purpose "to minister to the spiritual needs of people, primarily through literature consistent with biblical principles."

Tyndale seeks well-written, well-told stories with great hooks. The house will consider most genres, but has had the greatest success with historical, contemporary, suspense, romance, romantic suspense, and, of course, apocalyptic fiction.

Tyndale does not accept unsolicited manuscripts, but will consider agent-submitted manuscripts from first-time authors. Editors attend selected major writers' conferences.

## WaterBrook Press (Christian Imprint of Random House)

Random House established WaterBrook as a Christian imprint in 1996. It has become a major publisher of well-established Christian authors—a tough sell for a first-time novelist, unless he or she has a significant platform.

WaterBrook does not read unsolicited queries. Editors often attend major writers' conferences.

## Thomas Nelson

Thomas Nelson is a major Christian publisher that offers a variety of genres, including contemporary, suspense, and thrillers, by well-established, multi-published authors. Thomas Nelson does not read unsolicited queries or publish submission guidelines on its website.

## Zondervan (Christian Imprint of Harper Collins)

Zondervan is a major publisher of mostly well-established, multi-published novelists, although the company does try to hold open a slot or two each year for first-time authors. The house strives to publish novels in line with its mission: "To be the leader in Christian communications meeting the needs of people with resources that glorify Jesus Christ and promote biblical principles."

Zondervan publishes a variety of genres; the two most common are contemporary fiction and suspense. You'll also find some romance, historical, and fantasy on its list.

Zondervan does not accept unsolicited queries. Editors attend major writers' conferences. The company evaluates language, content, and behavior on a book-by-book basis, although it will not publish novels that contain foul language or graphic sexuality.

## The Least You Need to Know

- ◆ Many Christian publishers have undergone significant change in recent years—change that has significantly impacted Christian writers.

- ◆ Few publishers provide truly useful guidance about their long-range editorial strategy—a reason for first-time novelists to write in genres that will always be popular among readers.

- ◆ Because few publishers will read unsolicited manuscripts anymore, it's become increasingly important for Christian novelists to have literary agents.

- ◆ Many leading publishers are still accessible to unagented writers at Christian writers' conferences.

- ◆ There are significant differences among major Christian publishers that writers should research and understand.

- ◆ Many Christian "publishers" are actually imprints of larger secular publishing companies; most follow traditional Christian publishing guidelines.

# Part

# 2

# Writing Publishable Christian Fiction

My goal in this part of the book is to give you the foundational information you need to write a Christian novel that will stand tall enough among the competition to attract the interest of a literary agent and editor.

In today's competitive marketplace, *publishability* is the key to your success as a Christian novelist. The first and foremost aspect of publishability is that your novel generate—and maintain—a fictional dream for readers. This is job one for any novelist, Christian or secular. We'll also take close looks at genres, storytelling, and the boundaries of topics and language in Christian fiction.

# Publishability and the Fictional Dream

## In This Chapter

- ◆ The novelist's pyramid
- ◆ Getting past the gatekeepers
- ◆ The concept of publishability
- ◆ The key to publishability
- ◆ The five requirements of publishable fiction

Publishability is a concept that lives in the minds of agents, acquisitions editors, and publishing company executives. Your manuscript is publishable when they all agree it will become a novel that readers will buy.

Publishability is hard to pin down, frustrating, and not always fair. But it's crucial that you understand the rules of the game. This chapter will teach you the basics, and also introduce the key factors that make a novel publishable.

# Your Journey Up the Novelist's Pyramid

It goes without saying, but I'll say it anyway, that you want to write publishable Christian fiction. That's the chief reason you're reading this book. How far are you along on your journey to a published novel? To use a different metaphor, how high have you climbed on the novelist's pyramid?

*There are four major milestones on the journey from beginning to write a Christian novel to achieving success in the Christian fiction marketplace.*

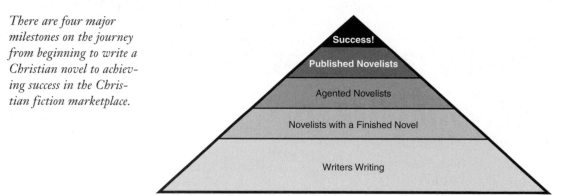

Every novel begins with a writer writing. Getting those first few ideas into a word-processing document novel is an exciting event—the stuff dreams are made of.

Alas, many would-be novelists never get past the first level of the writer's pyramid. They write four or five thousand words of a 90,000-word novel, then keep rewriting—actually torturing—those words over and over again. They never move beyond the first few chapters of their "books" to produce complete manuscripts.

This is one reason why editors and agents typically insist on seeing a complete manuscript from an unpublished novelist. They have learned to their regret that three overly polished chapters does not a finished novel make. I tell you this not to frighten you, but to emphasize that finishing a complete manuscript is the indispensable first step of writing a publishable novel.

## You're a *Real* Novelist When You Finish a Manuscript

If you've climbed to the second level of the writer's pyramid—if you've actually completed a novel-length manuscript—take a moment to pat yourself on the back. Writing a full-length novel is a significant achievement. At this point, you can begin to call yourself a Christian novelist. True, you're still unpublished—but you now have the "product" you need to move forward on your journey to success.

### Wisdom and Knowledge

How many words does a novel-length manuscript contain? Well, the smallest Christian novels I know of are 45,000-word Christian romances. Anything shorter than that would class as a novella. So-called category romance novels are 60,000 to 65,000 words. Full-length novels in many Christian genres seem to range from 80,000 to 100,000 words, with 90,000 words a good target number. Larger word counts drive up the cost of book production, so publishers are not eager to buy doorstop-size manuscripts.

## Passing Through Gate Number One

The novelist's journey to success is not an easy one. Along the way, you must get past three eagle-eyed gatekeepers who are anything but pushovers. The first gatekeeper is your literary agent.

The traditional role of a literary agent is to *represent* manuscripts to editors. Agents still do that job today, but they also serve as "publishability filters." One or more agents will likely give your manuscript its first publishability evaluations. The agent who tells you "I'm willing to represent your manuscript," is also saying, "I've concluded that you've written a publishable novel."

If you are having difficulty passing through gate number one and finding an agent to represent your work, it's a safe bet that your manuscript is not quite publishable yet. This is a common problem. Publishability problems can be difficult to identify and analyze—especially for an author, who may be too close to his or her work to recognize that something is wrong.

Publishing companies like agents to serve as initial publishability filters, because the work done by agents saves them enormous time and effort. That's why most major publishers are not willing to consider unagented manuscripts.

However, a few Christian publishers still maintain "slush piles" (the unflattering name for the stack of unsolicited manuscripts sent to a publisher) and editors who attend writers' conferences will often agree to look at unagented manuscripts.

### A Lamp Unto Your Feet

Many writers don't appreciate that reading an unsolicited manuscript can represent a significant cost to editors and agents—time worth many hundreds of dollars. Alas, most of this time and money is wasted, because so few "over the transom" manuscripts are publishable. A better bet is to meet an agent or editor at a writers' conference and "pitch" your project. But be sure it's publishable first.

## The Fabulous Phone Call

One of the most joyful days in any unpublished novelist's life is the day when your agent (or an editor) calls with the good news: "We're going to offer you a publishing contract."

When a publishing company says yes, it means that your manuscript has passed muster with two other gatekeepers. First, an acquisitions editor has determined that you've written a publishable manuscript. Second, a committee of publishing company executives has agreed to take the risk of investing money in the expectation that readers will buy your published novel. (I'll discuss the roles of gatekeepers in more detail in Chapter 20.)

## What Happens Next?

Once your novel is published, it joins the hundreds of thousands of other novels "out there" in the marketplace. Many first-time novelists quickly discover that their dreams of becoming a published Christian novelist did not extend to this part of the journey. Having a published novel on bookstore shelves and being a *successful* novelist are two very different things.

The hard and sad truth is that only a handful of published Christian novels go on to become bestsellers. Most do merely okay with readers. Sales of 10,000 to 15,000 copies are typical—numbers necessary to "earn out" the royalty advance given to the author, but far from blockbuster status.

### Wisdom and Knowledge

Do low sales mean that agents, editors, and publishing execs made bad decisions about the publishability of a novel? Not at all! Deciding that a manuscript is publishable does not mean that readers will transform the published novel into a bestseller. Identifying the next blockbuster is more art than science, more luck than process.

# Inside Publishability

Publishability can be a highly subjective concept. Publisher A may reject your manuscript as unpublishable, while Publisher B may buy it and produce a bestseller.

But it's sadly true that many, many manuscripts are wholly unpublishable in their current form, and deserve to be unpublished. Simply put, they don't meet the essential requirements of a readable, enjoyable novel.

Agents and editors rarely have the time to diagnose publishability problems of the manuscripts they read. They simply return unpublishable novels with vague rejection letters:

- ◆ "Your manuscript is not up to our standards."

- ◆ "We sensed that your story had too many characters."

- ◆ "We don't find your novel sufficiently compelling."

- ◆ "Your protagonist, while appealing, seems somehow distant and unapproachable."

- ◆ "We didn't fall in love with your book, but can't say why."

These are snippets, by the way, from the large collection of rejection letters that Janet and I received during the days when we wrote unpublishable fiction.

Karen Ball, a senior editor who also writes Christian novels, explains her Top Three Reasons for Instant Rejection:

1. **Amateurish writing.** Say it with me: "Send no proposal out before its time!" I can't tell you how many proposals I received that weren't anywhere near ready to be considered for publication. Sadly, I still see manuscripts like this. Just turned down a couple of them this week.

2. **Been there, published that.** It happens all the time: proposals have storylines too similar to something my house had recently published. I think this happens because writers look at what publishers are doing so they can know what that publisher might want.

3. **What were you thinking?** Someone sends me a proposal that's not even close to anything we'd publish. My company made it clear that we didn't do SciFi or Speculative fiction, but scores of SciFi proposals made their way to my desk. And I won't even go into all the steamy romances that were sent our way.

"Amateurish writing," to use Karen's term, is another label for unpublishable fiction. It's not ready for prime time—or publication.

Agents and editors can discern the publishability or un-publishability of a manuscript after reading a single page. They will often read more, but rarely need to, because the publishability mistakes made on page 1 will be repeated throughout a manuscript.

## Forget the Glorious Past!

There was a time when agents and editors would work with a writer to refine a "not quite soup yet" manuscript and make it publishable. Those days are long gone. Few editors—and fewer agents—have a charter to bring promising writers along. It's a time-consuming process that doesn't make much sense given the many hundreds of published Christian novelists who are clamoring to write more novels, and the ample supply of publishable manuscripts available from unpublished novelists.

Even though only a small percentage of manuscripts from unproven writers are truly publishable, the huge number of new writers turning out fiction means there are plenty of first-time novels for editors to choose among.

## The Paradox of Publishability

At the same time that editors and agents are rejecting your manuscript, your friends, family, and members of your writing critique group may be telling you how good your work is. (You'll understand how and why this can happen when I talk about the key aspect of publishability in the following section.)

This can be a confusing period in a writer's life. One temptation is to get mad at agents and editors—to assume that they are overly critical. Another is to opt for self-publishing (see Chapter 24), on the theory that a "real" paper-and-ink publisher will never be interested in his or her manuscript.

If you see yourself in either of these places, take heart! Producing a publishable manuscript is really a matter of applying specific *craft* to fiction writing. Once you understand the requirements of publishability, you'll be on your way to writing publishable fiction.

Somerset Maugham, the British dramatist and novelist, said, "There are three rules for writing the novel. Unfortunately, nobody knows what they are." I'm delighted to report that Somerset was wrong. Get ready to hear what I believe is the first and foremost rule for writing the novel.

# Here It Is! The Key to Publishability

You already know what makes a manuscript publishable, although you may not have put the principal reason into words. The key to publishability lies in the answer to this simple question: Why do you enjoy reading Christian fiction? (Every successful writer of fiction I've known is also an avid reader. They go hand in hand. It's hard for me to imagine a lukewarm reader writing a publishable novel.)

When I ask that question at the start of the workshops I teach at writers' conferences, I invariably hear some variation of the following answer: "I enjoy reading fiction because it delivers an out-of-body experience. A good novel takes me to times and places I've never been before, puts me into the heads of people I'd never otherwise get to know, and exposes me to aspects of living that are far different than my everyday life."

John Gardner, a novelist who also became well known as a teacher of creative writing, coined a label for this kind of experience: the fictional dream, which I introduced in Chapter 3. Quite simply, a publishable novel produces a sustained, vivid, memorable fictional dream in the minds of its readers. A well-written novel drops a reader into the fictional dream easily and quickly—usually on the first page.

When an editor or agent picks up your manuscript, he or she expects to fall into an exciting fictional dream. If that doesn't happen almost immediately, your manuscript will be rejected, unless the editor or agent spots an easy way to fix the problem. It makes no difference if you have a nifty story, interesting characters, or a fascinating setting. Words that don't create a fictional dream are nonfiction.

Equally important, a well-written novel rapidly *restores* the fictional dream whenever the reader returns to the book after an absence. (Few readers consume a novel in one sitting; most read chunks of story when they can.)

Finally, a well-written novel *sustains* the fictional dream—it keeps the reader in faraway places page after page, with no interruptions. It's like going to the movies. You don't want the film to break every two minutes. The lack of a sustained fictional dream is a sure sign of amateurish writing that's not yet ready for publication.

### A Lamp Unto Your Feet

Think of yourself as an architect of fictional dreams. That's every novelist's primary responsibility. If your manuscript doesn't deliver vivid fictional dreams, you haven't written a novel.

### Literary Sins

Sustaining a fictional dream can be difficult, because a fictional dream is fragile. It's like an optical illusion that seems to exist, but really doesn't. Readers willingly go along with the deception because they want to be entertained. But any minor problem in the text—errors in grammar, spelling, content, point of view, or story continuity—will shatter the dream for most readers. Errors that repeatedly knock an agent or editor out of the fictional dream early in your story will be enough to propel your manuscript toward the rejection pile.

# The Five Ingredients of Publishability

That brings me to the four other ingredients of publishability. Interestingly, each can stand on its own as a requirement of good fiction. And all play key roles in creating, sustaining, and restoring a fictional dream—which is ingredient number five on my list.

## 1. A Publishable Genre

I almost hesitate to point out that it does no good to create a fictional dream that readers don't want to experience. The notion seems so simple—and yet countless writers choose Christian genres that readers may ignore. If you want to write a publishable novel, it truly makes no sense to swim upstream against the genre wishes of potential readers.

I'll talk about genres in detail in Chapter 6. For now, let me make this point: it's easy to identify the genres that the readers of Christian fiction prefer. Browse through the fiction shelves at any Christian bookstore, read the titles of Christian novels that receive awards each year, check out which books achieved bestseller status at online booksellers.

## 2. Good Words, Strung Together Well

We often forget how powerful good words are. Ann Tatlock, a well-known Christian novelist, observes:

> When God created men and women in his own image, that included the ability to use language. The God who spoke the universe into being gave to humankind alone the ability to communicate with words. That's an amazing gift and an immense responsibility. With words we not only express ourselves in seemingly innocuous ways, but we build up and we tear down, we heal and we destroy, we bless and we curse, we tell the truth and we tell lies. Think about it. Words—both spoken and written—are the building blocks of ideas, and ideas, once ingested, become a part of us.

The phrase "good words, strung together well" probably conjures up thoughts in your mind of good grammar, proper spelling, intriguing metaphors, and other facets of good writing you learned in school. All of these things are important to a novelist, but when we talk about publishability, the most important aspect of "good words, strung together well" is to write fiction that has a compelling *authorial voice*. Be warned: it's not easy to get a handle on authorial voice from books about writing. Your best approach is to develop a good ear for voice when you read Christian fiction, and then make use of it when you write. I'll cover authorial voice in detail in Chapter 7, including extracts from the works of many Christian authors.

**Chapter and Verse**

Your **authorial voice** is the voice that readers "hear" in their heads when they read a novel—the voice that speaks to readers when they enter a fictional dream. Your voice emerges from the countless decisions you make, such as choice of words, grammar, punctuation, point of view, sentence length, and many more.

## 3. Accurate Content

I'll bet you're thinking, *Fiction is make-believe, so why is accuracy important, and what does accurate content have to do with a fictional dream?*

Imagine you're deep inside an enthralling suspense story. You're turning pages so fast, the breeze is making you feel cold. The hero—naturally, you've identified with him—is in peril. You can feel his fears; you ache to have the tension resolved. And then, you read, "Ahead was freedom. His only chance to escape. He looked through the window at the sun setting in the east."

*Mweeep!* The alarm in your head goes off and your mind switches to neutral. You're jolted awake from the fictional dream. The sun does *not* "set in the east." You are unhappy—and angry at the author (although you should be equally mad at the editor who let such a blatant mistake get into print).

Obvious errors spelling in spelling and grammar, trite language, even too-familiar clichés will also produce the same jarring effect in the minds of most readers. Editors know, however, that most of these will be removed during the editing process; they are likely to be more forgiving about careless typos in submitted manuscripts than about the content errors they manage to identify.

Editors and agents know that the most serious content errors are specialized in nature. They are mistakes in geography, weaponry, cars, fashion, sports, arcane hobbies, and other specialized fields that can often slip past an editor. But they will impact the small group of readers who know enough about the subject matter to recognize that the author has made a serious mistake. I'll review the problem—and present the solutions—in Chapter 8.

## 4. A Gripping Story

Why would anyone want to experience a dull fictional dream? Of course, they wouldn't, which points to the need for a gripping story in the novel you're writing.

The makings of a good story—and an exciting fictional dream—are lush dramatic conflict, rich characterization, and a festival of problems to drive the primary character(s) forward through the events of the story. On the other hand, sudden loss of story energy or an error in story *continuity* will usually knock a reader out of the fictional dream.

I'll teach you surefire techniques for creating a gripping story in Chapter 9.

> **Chapter and Verse** _____
>
> **Continuity** means that people, places, objects, and other aspects of a story remain consistent as the story unfolds. Readers can't sustain a fictional dream when the heroine's hair color changes mysteriously, or there are two Saturdays in one week, or the villain's gun starts as a revolver and finishes as an automatic.

## 5. Paragraphs That Engage the Reader's Imagination

We're back to creating a fictional dream for readers. And to three obvious questions: How do you create a fictional dream with words? How do you get readers dreaming on page 1 of your novel? How do you maintain the dream across 300+ pages and ensure that readers will drop back into the dream when they start reading again after a brief absence?

The answer to all three questions is that you construct—and judiciously place—paragraphs that will engage your reader's imagination. I call them "magic paragraphs"; they have the ability to drop the reader inside a character's head, which is how most fictional dreams begin.

Incidentally, magic paragraphs can also help you keep point of view straight in your writing—a nifty side effect, because POV errors are among the powerful fictional-dream killers. I'll show you how to build magic paragraphs in Chapter 10.

# You Can Master Publishability

I'm sure you've noticed that publishability produces lots of balls for you to juggle successfully when you write a Christian novel. Mistakes in any area can torpedo your manuscript.

The most encouraging thing I can say is to remind you that every published novelist went through the process of mastering publishability. If you have a writing critique group, ask the members to focus on the key ingredients of publishability. If friends and relatives read your manuscripts, bring them up to speed on publishability. Above all, learn to evaluate your own writing for publishability.

### It Is Written ...

Christian novelist Angela Hunt recently gave her own definition of publishability: "... Good writing. An attention to craft. Plots that hold together. Believable characters. Accurate details. Unique settings. Believable, human villains. And a spiritual element that is woven in, not tacked on like the tail on a cardboard donkey. Finally, a Christian novel should offer hope. Because that's what Christ offers us."

## The Least You Need to Know

- Your goal is to climb the novelist's pyramid; your first milestone is to finish a book-length manuscript.

- Your manuscript must get past three gatekeepers: a literary agent, acquisitions editor, and committee of publishing company executives. Your manuscript is publishable when all three agree it can be transformed into a novel that readers will buy.

- The key to publishability is the know-how to create—and sustain—a vivid fictional dream that engages the reader's imagination.

- You must also get the other aspects of publishability right, including strong authorial voice, a gripping story, and accurate content that won't knock readers out of their fictional dreams.

# Chapter 6

# The Most Popular Christian Fiction Genres

## In This Chapter

♦ Why genre is important

♦ Write in an "official" genre

♦ The four most popular Christian fiction genres: contemporary, historical, romance, and suspense/mystery

♦ Other less marketable genres

Christian fiction offers an interesting paradox. Viewed from the outside, many industry observers still see Christian fiction as a single genre. But from the inside, you'll find a broad array of different genres, including contemporary fiction, romance, historical fiction, biblical fiction, suspense, mystery, thriller, adventure, science fiction, and others.

Which view is correct? That's easy! From your perspective—the viewpoint of a Christian novelist—you must divide Christian fiction into specific genres. The reason is that every novel you write needs to fit one of them. This chapter tells you why, and explains the essential characteristics of the most popular Christian genres.

# Playing the Genre Game

I've had this discussion a thousand times in my workshops at writers' conferences:

*Me:* "It's really important that your Christian novel fit into one of the 'official' Christian fiction *genres*."

*Student:* "Whoa! I don't like the idea of being pigeonholed. I want to write Christian fiction, period! My current novel fits *several* genres—why do I have to squeeze it into a specific category?"

*Me:* "Because booksellers care about genre, readers care about genre, reviewers care about genre, publishers care about genre, editors care about genre, and agents care about genre."

### Chapter and Verse

We say a book fits into a specific **genre** when it honors the conventions—the rules, so to speak—of the genre. These include length, the kinds of storylines, the preferred authorial voice, the settings, the kinds of characters, and many more. Readers have well-defined expectations for the genres they enjoy. To write a successful genre novel, you must fulfill them.

## Don't Jumble Your Genres

Marketing studies have found that the majority of readers who enter a bookstore to purchase a Christian novel do not have a specific title in mind. Rather, they plan to browse among the genres they like to read. How will readers see your novel? Is it a romance, a mystery, an adventure—or a jumbled genre of your own invention that mixes a bit of this with some of that? It makes little sense to ignore reader preferences and devise your own mixed genre or otherwise disappoint reader expectations.

Perhaps even more important to a first-time novelist, how will the bookstore characterize your book? Specifically, on what shelf in the store will they put it? Shelves have labels; jumbled genre novels don't fit any of them.

Book reviewers, too, specialize in different genres. Which reviewer should write the critique for your novel? The history wizard, the mystery maven, or the romance expert?

And where should your novel be placed in the publisher's catalog? Among contemporary Christian novels, romances, historicals, mysteries, or science fiction Christian fiction? Here again, your novel has to conform to a small set of labels.

And which editor should help transform your submitted manuscript into a finished novel? The know-how to edit a Tudor historical is different than the expertise to edit an apocalyptic saga.

And which agent should represent your manuscript in the first place? Like editors, their competence tends to be genre-specific. Chances are, an agent who specializes in romance novels may not want to tackle a prophecy/end-times tale.

The simple truth is that no one in the chain that leads from agent to bookseller knows

> **Wisdom and Knowledge**
>
> Most secular bookstores have a "general fiction" shelf that holds so-called uncategorized novels. The closest Christian parallel is the somewhat ambiguous category "Christian contemporary fiction," which I'll discuss later in the chapter. Uncategorized novels are just that: they don't follow the conventions of any specific genre. They are *not* jumbled genre novels.

what to do with a jumbled genre novel—a book that doesn't fit a distinct category. You don't have to write a genre novel—Christian contemporary fiction is a perfectly acceptable category—but if you confuse agents, editors, and booksellers by jumbling genres, you probably won't sell your manuscript.

## Who Decides the Genre?

You do—*before* you start writing. I've been shown manuscripts by unpublished writers, who then asked me to assign their novels to an appropriate category. That's not the way the process works. You need to know your genre when you begin to plan your novel.

Genre is not merely determined by the content of the story. A mystery, a western, an historical, a romance, a science fiction novel, or even a Christian contemporary can tell the story of a murder. But each will produce a distinct "sound" inside a reader's head and create a distinctive fictional dream. Different conventions produce different reading experiences.

## Choose a Popular Genre

If you look hard enough, you'll eventually find one or two recently published Christian allegorical novels. But I don't advise an unpublished author to write an allegory. (An *allegory* uses fictional characters as symbols to represent spiritual, moral, or other abstract concepts. The most famous Christian allegorical novel is *The Pilgrim's Progress*, by John Bunyan. The lead character finds himself carrying a heavy burden after he reads a book—an allegorical representation of someone feeling convicted of sinful behavior after reading the Bible.) The same is true for Christian westerns. And for Christian science fiction. It's not *impossible* to sell first novels in these categories, but it's mighty difficult.

When I give this kind of advice, a common response is: "But I recently listened to an inspirational speaker who encouraged me to write the kind of books I love! What's more, I feel called to write Christian allegory (or Christian westerns, or Christian science fiction)." Okay—but expect an uphill battle to find an agent or editor who shares your love, or who can advance your call. If you want to write a novel that stands a reasonable chance of finding a home at a leading publisher, you should aim for one of the popular Christian genres. Editors are actively looking for new authors in these categories.

**Literary Sins**

A genre novel follows specific genre conventions, not a "formula." Moreover, genre novels are not lower-quality works than uncategorized fiction. A publishable genre novel will have an original storyline, compelling characters, and riveting dialogue—while it honors the conventions of the genre. Anything less will earn your manuscript a rejection letter.

By contrast, the handful of "author slots" for less popular genres are filled with established novelists who write new novels each year and are eager to get them published. They've won the support of agents, editors, and sales personnel. A newcomer in these categories has to displace a proven performer—an exceptionally difficult thing to do.

# The Big Four Genres

Let's take a closer look at the four most popular Christian fiction genres. I'll give you an overview of each and its distinctive features.

## Christian Contemporary Fiction

Christian *contemporary* fiction is, like "general fiction," a broad category that encompasses novels that don't fit specific genres. I want to emphasize at the start that contemporary fiction is *not* a catchall category for jumbled genre books. Rather, it is the grouping for "uncategorized" novels that do not follow the conventions of well-defined genres such as romance, mystery, suspense, or historical.

Christian contemporaries are usually full-length novels, typically between 85,000 and 110,000 words. (In fact, few 110,000-word Christian novels are published these days;

the practical maximum word count is closer to 100,000 words. Publishers seem to prefer smaller books, perhaps because they cost less to produce.) Many Christian contemporaries are reviewed by mainstream publications, and some become crossover novels with significant sales to secular readers.

**Chapter and Verse**

The **contemporary** in Christian contemporary fiction indicates that the action takes place in more-or-less modern times. The definition varies from publisher to publisher, but is generally post-1950. Anything older is typically categorized as an historical novel.

"Christian women's fiction" is often considered part of contemporary fiction. You'll sometimes see "Contemporary/Women's Fiction" as the name of the category. These are contemporary novels that deal with issues of special interest to women, including such angst-filled topics as poverty, spousal and child abuse, family breakdown, and abortion. They often contain love stories, but present romantic elements more introspectively and possibly less optimistically than a romance novel.

Sprawling categories like contemporary fiction will often have "subgenres"—smaller groupings carved out of the main genre. For example, "Christian chick lit" is a recently developed contemporary subgenre that tells humorous stories of twenty-something (and possibly thirty-something) unmarried women. Because the plots typically revolve around their heroines' efforts to get married, some observers view chick lit as a subgenre of the romance category. Others don't, first because a chick-lit story doesn't necessarily lead to a "fully realized" romance and wedding, and second because chick lit often invites readers to laugh at other issues shared by single women, including their careers and their family relationships.

Chick lit started as a secular subgenre that often includes fairly loose-living heroines who think materialistically, drink a lot, and engage in recreational sex. These elements are not included in Christian chick lit.

Another contemporary fiction subgenre—one that waxes and wanes in popularity—is the so-called "Christian character novel." The hallmark of a character novel is that the characters are more important than the plot. The actual story will be simple; so simple that some readers may say, "Nothing happens as the story unfolds." In fact, one or more of the characters is changing—usually in response to a combination of external and internal forces.

## Christian Historical Fiction

Historical fiction, one of the most popular Christian fiction genres, tells stories set in the past. The dividing line used by many publishers is 1950; anything later is considered contemporary fiction.

Almost any historical time period is fair game, but certain eras seem to intrigue readers—and editors—more than others. In the United States: Civil War, post–Civil War, Ragtime era (1895–1900), the Great Depression, and World War II. In Great Britain: Tudor (1485–1603) and Elizabethan (1558–1603), Regency (1811–1820), Victorian (1837–1901), and eighteenth-century Scotland.

Some historical novels include actual historical events and may give famous people of the day cameo roles in the story. Others tell a story divorced from actual history; the historical times and places serve as period stage sets that enable purely fictional characters to interact with each other. In either case, readers take a trip through time and enjoy the opportunity to experience a vivid sense of life in a different era. Depending on the publisher, the length of Christian historicals ranges from 75,000 to more than 100,000 words.

Many first-time authors who set out to write Christian historical novels discover a more challenging task than they expected. Getting the details of history right demands extensive research to learn what historical figures wore, what they ate, how they dressed, how they talked, how they lived, how they thought, how they prayed—there's no end in sight to the myriad of information a successful historical may demand.

Plotting an historical novel can also be a thorny task. You must find a compelling way to "retell" historical events that are significant, but may lack the dramatic tension of a good storyline. You must create subplots that fit into the chronology of events that history gives you. You must present real people of the day accurately and realistically. And you must invent fictional characters who are credible participants in a significant historical event.

## Christian Romance

Half of the mass-market paperback novels sold each year are romances—secular and Christian. Romances are so popular, in fact, that most Christian publishers produce some—and a few make romance novels the heart of their offerings.

All romance novels are about love, but some may not be considered traditional love stories. The vital distinction is that many love stories have sad endings—think *Romeo and Juliet*, or the movie *Casablanca*—while romance novels end happily and optimistically, with a live hero and heroine, and a fully realized romance. If the pair aren't married by the end of the novel, the reader feels confident that they're on their way to the altar.

Christian romance may well be the easiest genre for a first-time novelist to enter, because romance publishers have a voracious appetite for manuscripts. Some will still consider unagented manuscripts. Also, so-called "category romances" are only 45,000 to 60,000 words long, depending on the publisher. Many romance novelists report that they are easier to write than the longer novels demanded by other popular genres. Category romances are published in a variety of subgenres, or categories—such as romance, romantic suspense, romantic intrigue, and historical romance. Publishers of category romance produce a few books in each category each month. The books are often numbered for easy identification and are available for a short period of time—typically until next month's romances push them off the shelf. The two leading Christian category romance publishers are Steeple Hill (an imprint of Harlequin) and Barbour Books.

No other Christian genre has more subgenres than romance. The list includes historical romance, gothic romance, romantic suspense, romantic mysteries, prairie romance, western romance, fantasy romance, humorous romance, mature romance, and ethic romance—to name a few possibilities. Full-length romances range from 75,000 to 95,000 words.

There are conventions in the romance genre that are important for you to recognize:

- Because most readers are women, stories are usually told from the heroine's point of view (or at least begin and end from her point of view).

- The hero and heroine meet in the first chapter—this is the romance novel equivalent of beginning the story *in media res*, in the middle of things.

- The shifting relationship between hero and heroine is the heart of the story (the reason why readers read romance novels); readers don't appreciate backstory or extraneous detail that gets in the way.

- The lead characters are often stereotypes—the beautiful female with a mind of her own, the handsome alpha male used to getting his own way.

- The story takes place over a compressed time period—a few days or weeks, which means that the heroine and hero's relationship must develop more quickly than a real relationship.

Most Christian romances follow a well-known story plan: girl meets boy, girl falls for boy, girl loses boy, girl gets boy again—where some sort of misunderstanding, personality conflict, or external force drives them apart after their relationship has begun. This storyline is so familiar that it may strike you as a cliché. In fact, it can serve as the frame for an unlimited number of different stories, because there are so many possible variations for each of the elements.

## Christian Suspense and Mystery

Christian suspense and Christian mystery novels both focus on crime, but in different ways. Suspense novels keep the reader guessing, wondering if the lead character, usually the heroine, will survive the onslaught of evil deeds directed against her. Mystery novels pose a puzzle, challenging the reader to figure out "who done it?" as the detective—the heroine or hero—works to identify the perpetrator. Both kinds of novel ratchet up the tension with each passing chapter.

Suspense and mystery novels typically have highly "internal" voices—readers experience the heroine's fear, uncertainty, and race against time, and participate in the detective's thought processes as she solves the crime.

Both suspense and mystery are popular genres in their own right, and both have important subgenres:

◆ Romantic suspense

◆ Romantic mystery

◆ Cozy mystery

The romantic suspense and romantic mystery subgenres don't need much explanation. They are novels that have fully developed romances as part of their plots. Cozies are "kinder, gentler" mysteries where clever plot twists are more important than graphic, in-your-face violence, where action takes place in an unusual setting that's fun to read about, where cats, dogs, and other pets are significant characters, and which may involve an elaborate *MacGuffin*, about a detail-rich topic such as bell-ringing, fishing, painting, sailing, or museum management.

There seems to be a growing interest in cozy mysteries, with some Christian publishers actually starting new cozy lines. However, Christian cozies face an interesting challenge: they must compete with mainline cozy mysteries, which are typically gentle reads that meet most of the rules and conventions of Christian fiction. They don't carry explicit Christian messages, but they can be read without offense by most Christian readers.

**Chapter and Verse** _____

The **MacGuffin,** a term credited to famed moviemaker Alfred Hitchcock, is the object around which the plot revolves—the item that the characters in a story are worried about, the thing that makes them act and react. One of the most famous MacGuffins is the packet of "letters of transit" in the movie _Casablanca_. A key point is that the characters care about the MacGuffin, while the readers care about the characters.

As all writers of suspense and mystery novels know, it's often easier to put your characters in hot water than to get them out. Christian novelists are sometimes tempted to resolve plotting difficulties via improbable miracles, astonishingly answered prayers, or other last-minute acts of God. This approach is often nothing more than a Christian variation on the Ancient Greek dramatic technique of introducing a well-known god into the story at the end to untangle difficult plot problems. A pulley system lowered the god's statue to the stage and into the action. The term _deus ex machina_—god from the machine—is now used to label all artificial or improbable plot devices that "miraculously" resolve problems and bring a story to a close.

God must play an important role in every Christian novel, but readers of suspense and mystery novels expect heroes and heroines to get out of hot water mostly by their own devices. A bit of God's help is fine—but God should not do their work for them.

Suspense and mystery novels offer a reasonable chance of success to the first-time novelist. Most Christian publishers have a few in their catalog, and some publishers produce several each year. Length depends on publisher and subgenre, and can range from 55,000 words to about 95,000 words.

Among the most popular secular mystery novels are "police procedurals" (stories that depict the gritty realities of police work) and hard-boiled private eye novels (stories about knight-like private detectives who walk the mean streets alone). A few Christian novels in these categories are published each year, but they appeal mostly to male readers. A first-time novelist won't find it easy to break in. Still, it can be done—if you have highly polished writing skills.

Christian thrillers are often treated as a subgenre of suspense, and like suspense novels, they keep the hero or heroine in continuous peril. The difference is that the stakes in a thriller are usually much higher. The protagonist is driven to do more than save him- or herself—the storyline may involve a threat to the country, to our way of life, to Christianity, or even to the whole world.

Legal thrillers are thrillers set in courtrooms, or involving strong legal themes. They probably should be called legal suspense novels, because many revolve around the legal challenges faced by one character. Similarly, medical thrillers build suspense in a hospital or laboratory setting. Christian intrigue is a fairly small category that is often grouped with suspense. This is the home of the spy novel—and similar flights of fancy—set in international locations and filled with secret-agent derring-do.

Because there are several successful Christian thriller writers, and because the market is limited, I don't recommend first-time novelists tackle this subgenre—unless you're confident that you have especially good writing skills and can tell an extra-compelling story.

# A Few Other Genres

I've included the genres in this section for completeness, even though it would be an uphill battle for an unproven author to sell a novel in these categories. The barriers to entry are too high—even if you write an eminently publishable manuscript. For these genres, mere publishability isn't enough; you have to write a book good enough to push an established novelist off his or her perch.

## Christian Biblical Fiction

Many Christian writers are surprised to learn that Christian biblical fiction—the fictionalization and retelling of a Bible story—is not an especially popular genre with Christian readers. Nonetheless, a few biblical novels are published each year, virtually all from well-known writers.

Biblical fiction is sometimes labeled as a subgenre of historical fiction. Others argue— and I agree—that biblical fiction is its own genre, because the chief challenge is to be faithful to the Bible. Reconstructing the historical setting of the ancient Middle East is a secondary requirement.

Writing biblical fiction demands a lively imagination—and the creativity to expand a few dozen words into 75,000. Some well-known Bible stories are a few verses long, and most are shorter than a chapter. The well-known parable of the Prodigal Son, for example, spans only 21 verses: Luke 15:11-32.

## Christian Science Fiction and Fantasy

An oft-used indicator that a novel should be classified as science fiction is that some aspect of science or technology is absolutely essential to the storyline—take it away, and the plot crumbles. Another gauge is that the story takes place away from Earth or in future times. Similarly, a key characteristic of fantasy fiction is that magic or some other supernatural device is a vital component of the storyline. Another sign is that the action takes place in a strange invented world.

In addition, both Christian science fiction and Christian fantasy will have explicit Christian themes or be written from a Christian worldview. Simply put, in fictional worlds that may be radically different than our own, Christianity remains true. Christian science fiction is a hard-sell genre, because it has a relatively small readership. Published novels typically range from 75,000 to 90,000 words.

**Wisdom and Knowledge**

Science fiction and fantasy fiction are two of the genres included in "speculative" fiction, a label for fiction about worlds that are significantly different from our own. Other genres in speculative fiction are supernatural fiction, alternate history fiction, some horror novels, and fiction that presents magic as reality.

## Christian Westerns

In the United States, western fiction is our mythology—tales of rugged, bigger-than-life men and women coping with a lawless land. Westerns are highly stylized; like mythology, neither the people nor most of the settings really existed in history. But factual accuracy is beside the point; western novels present morality stories that teach the power of sacrifice, the importance of committing to values, and the potential impact of one person doing the right thing.

Readers who enjoy westerns point out that they are filled with dramatic conflict—man against nature, good guy versus bad guy, hero forced to overcome his own shortcomings to survive. Moreover, Christian themes of sacrifice and servanthood fit comfortably into western storylines. Despite these positives, the readership for Christian westerns is small—and seems to be shrinking. The notable exception is romance fiction that has a western or prairie setting. Word count requirements vary significantly among the few publishers of Christian westerns, but 65,000 to 80,000 words is a good initial estimate.

## Christian Adventure

Christian adventure novels tell tales that fascinate male readers, but often leave women readers cold. The storylines are typically quests involving small teams of soldiers, adventurers, or mercenaries who must complete a vital mission despite vicious villains, daunting settings (jungles, deserts, wilderness regions, uncharted islands, deep oceans, arctic tundra), and unexpected hazards (from dinosaurs and man-eating lions, to the treachery of "friends"). This is another difficult genre for first-time novelists—mostly because male-oriented novels have a smaller potential audience and there are several established novelists who fill the available Christian adventure slots. A good target word count is 85,000 to 95,000 words.

## Christian Horror

The scary elements of a suspense novel or thriller are created by a man or a woman—specifically, by a well-drawn villain. A horror novel makes readers confront wholly irrational and unexpected dangers: monsters, natural disasters, man-eating sharks, out-of-control animals, dinosaurs, asteroids plummeting from space, mutated viruses and bacteria, and other mindless foes. These things typically have no malicious reason to attack us—they just do.

It's sometimes said that secular horror novels—and movies—force people to confront their fear of death by exposing it in a way they can examine from a safe distance. Perhaps this is why Christian readers, who don't see death as the end of their existence, have not made horror a popular genre. If you're committed to writing a Christian horror novel, check out the few published each year and get specific guidelines from their publishers.

## The Least You Need to Know

- Decide which genre you want to use before you start writing; agents, editors, publishers, booksellers, and readers all use genre to "define" the manuscripts and books they handle.

- The most popular—and marketable—Christian genres are contemporary fiction (including women's fiction), historical fiction, romance, and suspense/mystery.

- Don't write a jumbled genre novel that might confuse agents, editors, booksellers, or readers.

- The genres aimed at male readers tend not to be popular, and established writers write the few novels published each year. Both facts make it difficult for first-time novelists to break into these categories.

# Chapter 7

# Establishing a Strong Authorial Voice

## In This Chapter

- ◆ What authorial voice is made of
- ◆ Why voice is so important
- ◆ You develop voice by writing and reading
- ◆ How to analyze voice
- ◆ "Listen" to the voices of different novelists

Voice is one of those things that's hard to define and even harder to explain—although every reader and writer knows it exists. From a reader's point of view, voice is the "sound" the reader "hears" while reading a novel. From a writer's point of view, voice emerges from the way the writer strings words together.

To develop your authorial voice, you must learn to hear and work with the "music of language"—the rhythmic flow of words, the "beats" that separate thoughts, the changes of pace that convey different emotions.

I designed this chapter to help you do just that. On the pages that follow, you'll find short excerpts from novels written by leading Christian authors.

All are under 200 words long, to demonstrate that voice can be communicated by a surprisingly brief block of text. Reading—and comparing—the excerpts is a great way to begin your study of voice.

# Hearing Authorial Voice

Christian authors often tell similar stories and deliver similar Christian messages. Yet a handful of Christian novels will become bestsellers—often because readers prefer one authorial voice to another.

Good voice is the result of countless decisions a writer makes, including diction, choice of words, punctuation, point of view, sentence length, frequency and kinds of figures of speech, amount of humor, past or present tense, balance between narrative and dialogue, use of flashbacks, and many more.

## A Critical Aspect of Storytelling

Voice establishes who is currently telling the story. A dynamic businesswoman. A brash private investigator. An abused homemaker. A small-town pastor. A sassy "chick-lit" heroine. An overworked nurse. A hero from the Bible. A prairie home-steader. A cowboy. An Amish wife. A God-like narrator. Different kinds of characters should create different sounds in a reader's head.

Voice establishes the psychic distance between reader and character. A distant-sounding voice is right for a character you want the reader to look at from a distance. A close voice is perfect when you want the reader to feel completely within the character.

Voice also helps to establish genre. Think back to the novel you read most recently. Did it strike you as serious? Scary? Grim? Suspenseful? Funny? Cheerful? Romantic? Or smart-alecky? Did it carry you back to first-century Judea or send you into the future, to a distant galaxy, far, far away? Much like movie music, the right authorial voice can set the stage by communicating emotion, locale, and even time frame.

## Is Authorial Voice Unique?

Despite conventional wisdom, it's not true that all successful writers have unique voices that readers can identify merely by perusing excerpts of their latest novels. One bestselling Christian author told me, "I wouldn't recognize my authorial voice if it called to me." Another said, "When it comes to authorial voice, I've always believed that I have laryngitis."

This is probably a good thing, because novelists need different voices for different books—or even different characters in the same book. Much more important than striving for a unique voice is writing each of your novels with a strong, compelling voice that's right for the specific genre, characters, and setting. That's what editors and agents look for.

Voice comes naturally—as you write and as you read. If I want to write with a voice appropriate to a brash, self-confident private investigator, I'll prime my ear by reading several PI novels written by authors who achieve that kind of voice. The reverse is also true. When I want to write in a specific voice, I never read novels that present significantly different voices. They will confuse my inner ear—and upset the cadences of my work-in-progress.

# The Best Way to Study Voice

Read lots of novels, then read some more. Listen when you read and try to correlate the specifics of the writing with the sound effects you hear. The voice excerpts that follow will get you started. Each will show you a different authorial voice; each illustrates different techniques to create good voice. I've provided a few questions after each excerpt to get you thinking about voice, along with space to jot down your responses.

## From *Doesn't She Look Natural* by Angela Hunt

A grieving woman, I've decided, is like a crème brûlée: she begins in a liquid state, endures a period of searing heat, and eventually develops a scab-like crust.

By the time we sell the house I am pretty much crusted over, so I'm honestly surprised when the real estate agent slides a check toward me and tears blur my vision.

Ms. Nichols doesn't seem to notice my streaming eyes. "That's a tidy little profit, even if it is only half the proceeds," she says, eyeing the bank draft as if she can't bear to let it slip away. "If you're in the market for another property..."

"I'm sure we'll be renting for a while." I lower my gaze lest she read the rest of the story in my tight expression: This money is all we have.

The Realtor babbles on. "Our agents also handle rental properties. If you're interested, I have a nice listing inside the Beltway."

"Anything I could afford near the District wouldn't be big enough for me and my boys."

… I can't deny the truth any longer. I am now not only divorced, but homeless as well.

Good thing I've developed that crust.

## Your Turn

◆ What kind of person is "talking" to you?

_____

◆ What kind of story does this "sound like"? (Women's fiction? Romance? Mystery? Suspense? Something else?)

_____

◆ Is the lead character in control of her situation? What did you "hear" that conveyed this information?

_____

◆ What is the effect of present-tense writing on voice?

_____

## From *Welcome to the Empire* by James Scott Bell

The valet was dressed in a toga and gold braids, his muscular body honed to Herculean proportions. Sam got out and left the keys in the ignition.

"Need help with your luggage?" Hercules said.

Sam shook his head and only then thought about what he didn't have with him— a change of clothes. He didn't expect to be here more than twenty-four hours anyway. He wouldn't be able to sleep, except maybe in a chair for an hour or two.

Hercules handed him a ticket and said, "Anytime you want your chariot, we'll bring it up. Enjoy your stay."

Sam walked toward the front doors. Lights assaulted him from every direction. It lit up the walk like high noon. Blinking gold bulbs popped all around the ornate but automatic front doors, which were fashioned out of glass and imitation brass. The entry could have been from one of those Italian sword-and-sandal movies of the 60s starring Steve Reeves. You didn't quite buy that it was real, but you went along with the fakery to experience the movie.

That's Vegas all over, Sam thought. You go with the fake and the phony to live the fantasy.

## Your Turn

◆ Whose voice did you "hear" when you read the excerpt?

_____

◆ What kind of story does this "sound like"? (Women's fiction? Romance? Mystery? Suspense? Something else?)

_____

◆ Which words chosen by the author for this excerpt seemed "loudest" in the voice you "heard"?

_____

◆ Have you formed an opinion of Sam? How does voice help to convey the information you need to figure him out?

_____

## From *Remember to Forget* by Deborah Raney

Again Maggie declined the offer of a ride. Did these people really think she was such a fool that she'd accept a lift from a man—a complete stranger—on a deserted country road?

But as twilight pulled a cloak over the landscape, she started to wonder if she was a fool. Whirling in the road, she looked back toward Salina. A haze of light rode the horizon where the town sprawled. She'd probably walked thirty or forty city blocks and there wasn't a building or a light in sight, save for a couple of white grain elevators that occasionally peeked over the rolling terrain. Maybe she would be better off going back into town for the night.

Go west.

That voice again—or whatever it was. She couldn't go back.

# Your Turn

♦ Whose voice did you "hear" when you read the excerpt?

_____

♦ What kind of story does this "sound like"? (Women's fiction? Romance? Mystery? Suspense? Something else?)

_____

♦ How old is Maggie? What did you "hear" that conveyed this information?

_____

♦ What is Maggie's state of mind? What did you "hear" that conveyed this information?

_____

# From *Secrets on the Wind* by Stephanie Grace Whitson

The acrid scent of burned grass and scorched earth clung to the still air. Fire had blackened the hillside above the half-ruined dugout. He felt his stomach clench. Arrows clung to the dugout's sod face like quills from a porcupine. Dismounting, he pulled one from between the earthen bricks. He could feel the hair stand up on the back of his neck as he touched the tip of the arrow, envisioning what it must have been like in this place only hours ago—the wild rush of painted ponies, the unearthly yelps and cries, the raised war lances, all synchronized into a horrible beauty.

# Your Turn

♦ Whose voice did you "hear" when you read the excerpt?

_____

♦ What kind of story does this "sound like"? (Women's fiction? Romance? Mystery? Suspense? Something else?)

_____

♦ Which words chosen by the author for this excerpt seemed "loudest" in the voice you "heard"?

_____

◆ Did the voice work with the words to establish time and place? If so, how?

## From *Double Blind* by Hannah Alexander

The movement on the desert attracted Sheila once again, closer this time, and larger, but still several hundred feet ahead of her. The sun's glare again kept her from seeing the figure clearly, but when she looked away she could see it in her peripheral vision, the same way her nightmares caught her sometimes when she woke up in the mornings. The figure was too small to be a horse. A large dog, perhaps?

She kept her attention on the road and allowed the approaching animal to develop along the side of her vision. It drew nearer. For as long as she could remember, she'd been afraid of dogs, though she didn't know why.

Suddenly, the dog disappeared, and a cloud of dust rose where it had been. She glanced that way, but saw nothing. Was she imagining things now?

The right front tire of the Jeep sank into the soft shoulder of the road. She jerked the steering wheel to the left. A loud pop startled her.

She caught her breath, fighting the wheel, but the deep sand would not relinquish its hold. The Jeep coasted to a quick stop.

She'd blown a tire.

## Your Turn

◆ Whose voice did you "hear" when you read the excerpt?

◆ What kind of story does this "sound like"? (Women's fiction? Romance? Mystery? Suspense? Something else?)

◆ Did Sheila's state of mind change during the excerpt? What did you "hear" that conveyed this information?

◆ Do you feel close or distant to Sheila? What aspect of voice made you feel that way?

## From *Glory Be!* by Ron and Janet Benrey

Emma had just begun to shape croissants on a large buttered pan when Peggy Lyons burst into the kitchen and shouted, "There's a bug on the porch."

Emma willed herself not to scream at Peggy. She had seen this same panic-stricken look on her housekeeper's face many times before. Peggy was a fine worker but easily flustered by minor problems. Emma unstuck her fingers from the slick, buttery dough.

"Tromp on the bug, Peggy," she said, evenly, "whap it with a newspaper, spray it with insecticide, or catch it in a jar. Pick one of the above, but do it quickly. I need your help."

"You don't understand, Emma. There's a *Bug* on the porch. A car! A silver Volkswagen Beetle convertible."

## Your Turn

◆ Whose voice did you "hear" when you read the excerpt?

_____

◆ What kind of story does this "sound like"? (Women's fiction? Romance? Mystery? Suspense? Something else?)

_____

◆ Is Emma in control of her situation? What did you "hear" that conveyed this information?

_____

◆ What language choices give you information about Emma's personality?

_____

## From *Night Light* by Terri Blackstock

The rain had cooled the summer heat, and a breeze blew a fine mist into Aaron's face. He wished he could walk out into the middle of it and let the warm water pour down over him, pool at his feet, then rise to his knees, his waist, his shoulders, his face. He wished he could drown in the clean warmth of it, leaving all his cares behind.

It would be so cool if there really was a heaven, if he could just close his eyes and drift up to some beautiful place, where the lights were on and there was food hanging from trees, where his sister and brothers could be safe, where a nice God welcomed him and loved him.

But if a God like that existed in a real heaven, he wouldn't want the likes of Aaron Gatlin there. Not after all he'd done.

You made your bed, now sleep in it. His mother had said that so many times, as if her own bed wasn't a filthy mess.

No, a real God wouldn't have a bunch of snot-nosed orphans dirtying up his heaven. He'd be scared they'd steal some of those fancy pearls off the gate.

## Your Turn

◆ Whose voice did you "hear" when you read the excerpt?

_____

◆ What kind of story does this "sound like"? (Women's fiction? Romance? Mystery? Suspense? Something else?)

_____

◆ How old is Aaron? What did you "hear" that conveyed this information?

_____

◆ Do you feel close or distant to Aaron? What aspect of voice made you feel that way?

_____

These excerpts illustrate different voices—each one right for a specific kind of novel. I can't speak for other authors, but I know that Janet and I don't hold strategy sessions to decide the appropriate voice for our novels. With us, voice "happens" when we begin to write. That's why I want to reemphasize the point I made earlier: voice comes naturally as you write and as you read. The more you read, the more you write, the more distinctive (and "right") your own authorial voice will become.

## The Least You Need to Know

◆ Voice is the "sound" a reader hears when he or she reads a well-crafted novel.

◆ Editors seek novels that have strong, compelling voices.

◆ Your own authorial voice will emerge you write fiction—the more you write, the stronger your voice will become.

◆ Reading the work of novelists with voices similar to your own can help to strengthen your voice.

◆ Think about voice whenever you edit your own writing. Remember that one of the first characteristics an agent or editor evaluates is your authorial voice.

# Chapter 8

# Handling Content Well

## In This Chapter

- ◆ Detail feeds the fictional dream

- ◆ Meeting the challenge of authenticity

- ◆ Content errors are fictional-dream killers

- ◆ The 12 most common sources of content errors

- ◆ How to get the details right

- ◆ Including trademarked content

Fiction is the opposite of fact, and yet the Christian novels you write will be full of factual content. A full-length novel is likely to contain *hundreds* of distinct facts and details.

In this chapter, I'll explain why the factual aspects of Christian fiction must be accurate and I'll tell you how to ensure they are.

## Details Strengthen a Fictional Dream

A good fictional dream can become even better when the reader experiences "true" sights, sounds, smells, tastes, and feels. Small facts and details help to build the fictional dreams that put readers into the characters' heads. To prove my point, here's an excerpt from *Fire Dancer* by Colleen Coble:

Water (from the hose she held) sprayed toward the barn, but it was like dropping a thimble of water on the fires of hell. The fire laughed at her attempts and flared higher. She screamed for help again and saw several ranch hands running toward her from the back pasture. Then with a deafening roar, the roof collapsed. Flames licked their way toward Tess, and she had no choice but to back away. The scent of kerosene was stronger now, choking her.

"Mom," she sobbed, sinking to her knees. Cinders fell from the sky in a swirling black rain that singed the hair on her arms and marked her forever with the scent of fire.

And here's a second excerpt, this one from *Gone to Glory*, a cozy romantic mystery that Janet and I wrote:

She took a step.

*Clink.*

Daniel saw Lori freeze. She looked at him wide-eyed. "I think the sound came from under the floorboard I'm standing on."

"It did," Daniel agreed.

"I've heard that weird metallic noise before."

"Me too."

She took a deep breath. "A treadle switch for a booby-trap."

"Could be."

"If that's what it is, I armed the device when I stepped on the floorboard."

He nodded. "I suggest that you keep absolutely still until we figure this out."

"I'm not going anywhere, believe me." She laughed, but her laugh sounded suddenly hollow.

Both of these story moments depict characters living through dangerous situations:

◆ In the first, small details about the fire—its sound, its look, its smell, its ability to reach out to Tess with cinders—enable the reader to "be there" as Tess makes a futile attempt to fight back.

◆ In the second, the steady flow of details transform a simple "clink" into a threat—and help the reader join Lori and Daniel on the booby-trapped porch.

The spectrum of vivid and truthful content possibilities is as wide as the world we live in. In recent Christian novels, I've experienced details such as these:

- A strident word of current slang heard by the hero

- A character's grim appearance brought about by a chronic disease

- The ominous *snick-snack* as the villain cocked his automatic pistol

- The cloying taste of over-sweetened preserves

- The worrisome smell of a musty house

- The comforting feel of a cat's fur

As in many aspects of art, less is often more when you provide details to help your reader experience new sights, new sounds, and the other sense reactions you build into your story. This is another area of novel-writing craft best learned by reading successful novels of the kind you want to write.

Go through your favorite novel with a yellow marker and highlight the vivid details that feed the fictional dream. I predict you'll find that authors have rationed the quantity of facts, and have provided essential details in well-turned phrases to create the vividness that John Gardner wrote about. One elegantly worded detail can enable a reader to imagine a complete scene, whereas as a dozen weak descriptions won't have any effect.

A fine example is Colleen Coble's simple sentence from the earlier excerpt from *Fire Dancer:* "The scent of kerosene was stronger now, choking her." No adjectives. No lengthy explanations of what kerosene smells like (we all know what it smells like). Nothing more than what readers need to add reality to their mental re-creations of Tess's circumstances.

 **It Is Written ...**

> In all the major genres, vivid detail is the life blood of fiction.
>
> —John Gardner, novelist and teacher

# Facts That Advance the Story

All of the facts in a good novel enter the reader's mind via a fictional dream. But not all the facts you find a novel were put there to create a fictional dream. Many—perhaps most—details are intended to advance the story.

You may decide to have your hero walk through the Denver International Airport, or the Metropolitan Museum of Art in New York City. Your heroine may drive a car along the Blue Ridge Parkway in North Carolina, or across the Golden Gate Bridge in California. He and she may fall in love watching a glorious sunset over the Rocky Mountains, or while sailing a small boat on the Chesapeake Bay.

Readers will be delighted to accompany them on their fictional journey. Moreover, they will enjoy being introduced to new places in the company of interesting characters.

The following excerpt comes from Austin Boyd's technology-filled novel, *The Return*:

> John had never experienced a space launch quite like this one. More like leaving on a vacation with the van loaded and all the kids on board. No crowds, no lengthy procedures with contractors and armies of NASA engineers and technicians. Just a detailed checklist, a final wave goodbye from the folks at the lab—and the big red switch.
>
> John pointed to a glowing mushroom-shaped button, Rex Sr.'s engineering humor at work. One prominent button to start the engines, releasing a massive load of methane and oxygen to burn in three nozzles and lift the craft off Mars. Methane and oxygen they'd made from the Martian atmosphere and Martian water, with enough of a kick to propel them all the way to Earth.
>
> "You're the captain, Rex," John said. "It's all yours."
>
> Rex reached toward the button, then hesitated. "No, sir. This should be your honor."
>
> John shook his head. "Can't do it, Rex. Your rocket. Take us home."

As you can see, the facts in this excerpt do more than support the fictional dream—they also propel the story forward and create suspense: will the rockets fire and bring the astronauts home?

## How Many Facts Are Enough?

That can be a tricky question to answer. Too little detail can weaken the fictional dream; too many will bore the reader.

Writers often fall in love with facts that advance their stories. I've read a historical romance set in the 1940s that described half the significant events of World War II.

I've perused a murder mystery about a hero who applied code breaking to identify the murderer. It read, in parts, like a textbook on cryptography.

Note how Austin Boyd successfully fought the urge to include unnecessary detail in the previous excerpt. We're told everything we need to know about the technology of the flight home from Mars—and not much more.

Janet and I have been guilty of putting more detail than necessary in some of our books—as our editors frequently told us. We've gotten better with each succeeding novel. The best advice I can give you is the approach we follow: keep an eye out when you revise your manuscript. Strike out any fact that the reader doesn't need to know, or that doesn't contribute to the fictional dream.

## The Related Challenge of Authenticity

Sometimes facts are like the props on a stage set: they help to furnish a scene. *Dead as a Scone*, one of the Christian cozy mysteries that Janet and I wrote, takes place in the fictional Royal Tunbridge Wells Tea Museum, an institution full of antiquities and artifacts. The plot turns on an elaborate set of antique wooden "Tunbridge Ware" tea cozies (Tunbridge Ware—wooden boxes and other objects decorated with mosaics made of contrasting wood veneers—is real; Janet and I invented the set of tea cozies at the heart of our story.)

The setting of a cozy mystery is important, because it becomes a character in its own right. Consequently, the museum we created had to seem real to readers. This, in a nutshell, is the *challenge of authenticity*. We had to invent credible, imaginary antiquities that would seem real to readers who are knowledgeable about museum-quality artworks.

We were especially concerned about accidentally creating "serious *un*-authenticities"—the kind of errors that prompt well-informed readers to throw a book across the room, and then warn their friends not to read it. Our faux paintings, sculptures, antiquities, or whatever must pass the "they could have been real!" test in every reader's mind.

 **Chapter and Verse**

Challenge of authenticity is the term we coined for the requirement that fictional antiques, art work, and other artifacts must seem plausible to readers who have the knowledge and experience to spot obvious mistakes.

Consider the two large oil paintings of American Revolutionary "tea parties" on display at our fictional museum. We came up with two nonexistent paintings by

Lilly Martin Spencer, a real American painter who worked during the nineteenth century. One painting is of the renowned Boston Tea Party of 1773, the other of the less well-known Edenton Ladies Tea Party of 1774 (an historical event that occurred in Edenton, North Carolina).

Why Lilly Martin Spencer? She was an English-born American artist of sufficient fame to be included in art encyclopedias, yet not famous enough to be familiar to most readers. However, the relatively few readers who have heard of Lilly Spencer will know that she might have tackled paintings on this subject. Her still-life paintings and portraits became quite popular in Europe and America. It's wholly plausible that she would produce two large oil paintings about Revolutionary tea parties.

In much the same way, we invented the plausible set of antique wooden tea caddies I described earlier. We made them the work of Robert Russell, a well-known maker of Tunbridge Ware. He might easily have made such a set for a wealthy collector during the mid-nineteenth century.

# Errors Can Kill a Fictional Dream

Because vivid details can be so important—the stuff of fictional dreams—errors in facts and details will kill a fictional dream faster than you can write "the sun rose in the west." A reader who comes across a blatant error and wakes up is likely to stop reading your novel there and then. This includes both kinds of details: facts that support the fictional dream and facts that advance the story.

A popular mainstream mystery novelist, one of my favorite authors, wrote an historical mystery that involved nineteenth-century sailing ships. She talked about ships with such confidence—and such apparent accuracy—that I came to believe she knew as much about sailing as I do. But then, she let a "falling halyard" break someone's arm. Alas, a *halyard* is a rope, not a heavy wooden spar. I was catapulted out of my fictional dream and I began to doubt the other nineteenth-century "facts" about daily life in England that she'd presented in the story. I finished the book, but it wasn't as enjoyable a read for me as it might have been.

Another term I've found misused in several novels is "high tea." Writers who don't know their Assam from an Oolong seem to think that the "high" in high tea is a synonym for elegant, that high teas are enjoyed by wealthy Englishmen in their palatial manor homes. In fact, a high tea is a workingman's meal, what we might describe as a robust supper. It's called "high tea" because it's served on a high dining table, rather than a low tea table. "Afternoon tea" is the classier event—a time for estate-grown teas, scones and clotted cream, and teacakes and savories.

**Literary Sins** _____

It's certainly true that many, perhaps most, readers won't experience my dream-shattering reactions. Not a lot of readers will be familiar with nautical terminology or the proper names of English teas. That practicality doesn't justify carelessness. It's not okay to be sloppy about facts and details because only a few of your readers will spot those particular errors.

# The Dirty Dozen

I've amassed the following list over the years by chatting with editors, paying attention at critique groups, and keeping track of the mistakes I spotted in novels. Here's my tally of the 12 most common sources of content errors in Christian fiction:

- **Legal details**—for example, terminology and legal mistakes involving wills, estates, and lawsuits; incorrect adoption procedures; confusion about legal ethics and how opposing attorneys can interact.

- **Courtroom and trial procedure**—for example, wrong procedures for selecting juries, examining witnesses, handling objections, and giving opening and closing statements.

- **Medical details**—for example, incorrect symptoms of specific diseases; errors in causes of death, quickness of death, the pain caused by different traumas, the amount of blood loss produced by particular injuries, and the effects of poisons.

- **Women's fashion**—for example, incorrect style of clothing worn during a specific decade, makeup and hairstyling gaffes ("No woman would ever do something like that!"), the wrong clothing colors to match a characters complexion and hair color. Broadly speaking, female readers are more likely than male readers to spot these mistakes.

- **Police procedure**—for example, investigation and crime scene procedures, police chain of command, job descriptions and day-to-day responsibilities of police personnel, and constitutional limitations on what law enforcement personnel can do.

- **Descriptions of firearms**—for example, misnaming of firearm components, errors involving which weapons have "safeties" and which don't, the naming conventions of weapons from different manufacturers, the "stopping power" of various calibers.

- **Geography of real cities**—for example, mistakes involving two-way versus one-way streets, wrong locations and appearances of city landmarks, use of defunct restaurants and hotels, ignoring the effect of rush hour on traffic, incorrect locations of suburbs and nearby communities.

- **Technological anachronisms** —for example, color TV in the wrong decade, cell phones before they'd been invented, interstate highways before they were built, medical procedures, antibiotics, vaccines, and diagnostic tests used before they were actually available.

- **Technological miracles**—for example, easy-to-hack computers and easy-to-discover passwords, trivial-to-tap telephones, impossibly small transmitters, diabolical devices that always work, the magic ability of computers to provide anyone's biography at the press of a key.

- **Historical details**—for example, mistakes involving countries that didn't exist at the time, political leaders assigned to the wrong country or decade, battles fought during the wrong wars, religious conflicts over the wrong issues or during the wrong century.

- **Sports details**—for example, attending a game before the team actually moved to town, assigning famous players to the wrong teams, errors involving the years when teams won national championships, mistaken names and locations of stadiums, and incorrect golf and tennis terms.

- **Music and movies**—for example, releasing movies and recordings in the wrong year; assigning actors and actresses to the wrong movies, crediting specific hit songs to the wrong performer, giving Academy Awards to real movies that never earned them.

# Getting the Facts Right

There was a time when novelists would spend months in research libraries collecting facts and details for a new novel. And if the novel was set in a faraway place, the writer would visit the location to soak up the atmosphere and capture the kind of details necessary to enhance the fictional dream.

Some bestselling novelists still work that way, but the rest of us usually have to settle for collecting—and verifying—facts by surfing the Internet, by browsing through books, magazines, and travel guides, and by chatting with people who have "been there, done that." Unfortunately, all of these methods can introduce serious errors into our novels.

# The Internet Is Full of Errors

Treat the content you find on websites and blogs gingerly—there are generally no checks for accuracy, no guarantees that the information is correct. Because I've noted countless errors over the years, I make it a practice to verify every detail I collect on the net. I insist on at least two independent sources for each fact.

I belong to several Internet writing "loops" and I've noticed a trend: loop members increasingly post requests for facts and information they need for their current works in progress. I see several problems with this "research technique":

♦ You don't always receive an immediate answer—it's often faster to do your own research.

♦ The quality of the responses is uncertain; there's no way of knowing if the well-intentioned answers are accurate.

♦ Asking for help can become an "easy way out"—a quick way to avoid the hard work of personal research that soon turns into a habit.

♦ You lose the benefits of personal research, especially the broader knowledge you gain in a specific topic area.

**Wisdom and Knowledge**

The best content resource is probably a good research library—and the knowledge to use it. An enormous advantage of a brick-and-mortar library are the reference librarians that can point you in the right direction. If you are fortunate enough to live near a friendly college or university, you may be able to use its library—possibly for a fee. Most big-city libraries have well-stocked reference rooms.

# Stocking Your Own Research Shelf

Most of the Christian writers I know have amassed their own collections of research material. For example, those who write twentieth-century historical novels have stacks of old magazines, each a "time capsule" full of information about what people wore, how they looked, what they cared about at the time, and what products they bought.

One writer who specializes in prairie romances buys nineteenth-century books at local auctions. She especially seeks out cookbooks, health guides, and books that provide advice to homemakers. They provide the kind of information her heroines would have had on hand.

Because we write mysteries, Janet and I own books about police procedure, investigative techniques, poisons, firearms, famous crimes, and legal procedure. I've found that an old set of encyclopedia can also be very useful. We own a 1972 edition of Encyclopedia Britannica. It's a pain to store, but the articles are remarkably complete and often provide interesting detail I've not found anywhere else.

# Trademarked Names

You can use trademarked names and products in your novel, but be sure to use them correctly. It's incorrect usage to have your hero enjoy a glass of *coke* or make a photocopy on a *xerox* machine. Both of these famous trademarks must be capitalized.

If your hero spends the night at a real Marriott hotel, your heroine dines at an actual Outback Steakhouse, and they go for a drive in a rented Ford Explorer, the owners of the respective trademarks will probably be delighted about the free publicity. But their attitudes would change quickly if your hero found his mattress full of bedbugs, the heroine came down with food poisoning, or a flaw in the vehicle managed to cause an accident. This could make you (and your publisher) liable for publishing false and disparaging things about a trademark.

The bottom line: include a few trademarked places and products to add color to your manuscript, but don't make them "villains" in your story.

## The Least You Need to Know

- Use facts and details to create a "real" world for your fictional characters to live in and strengthen your novel's fictional dream.

- Don't include unnecessary facts merely because you enjoy the particular subject; too many details will bore a reader.

- Eliminate any content errors that will shatter a reader's fictional dream.

- Check twice if you use a fact you find on the Internet.

- Take appropriate care when you include trademarked products and places in your novel.

# How to Tell a Gripping Story

## In This Chapter

- Choose your approach to storytelling
- The basics of good storytelling
- Charging your novel with dramatic conflict and dramatic energy
- Using plotting models to outline your story
- Weaving together subplots to form a cohesive story
- Dividing the story into scenes

If you want to write successful Christian fiction, you have to tell gripping stories. That's what this chapter is all about. I'll teach you an effective way to design and build a good story—a story-modeling approach that goes back to the ancient Greeks, and has created compelling stories for more than 2,500 years.

## Two Approaches to Storytelling

There's really no alternative to telling a gripping story. No one will buy your novel if you don't. But there are two ways you can get the job done.

1. **Work out your story as you write it.** This is called the "seat-of-the-pants" approach to plotting. You write—and rewrite—your manuscript until a good story emerges. I know many successful authors who write novels this way, and they insist it's perfect for them.

2. **Plan your story before your write it.** This is called the outlining approach to plotting. You develop the structure of your story before you start writing. Here again, I know many published Christian authors who outline first. Janet and I are among them; we switched to this technique when we developed the first novel we sold.

A good way to start a fistfight at a writers' conference—either Christian or secular—is to claim that one storytelling approach is better than the other. Both sides of the issue have determined advocates. I've learned from painful experience not to take part in these debates. I don't recommend either approach as the one best way to write a successful novel. As I'll point out later, though, the plotting techniques described in this chapter probably work best when combined with *some* outlining.

# What Makes a Gripping Story?

To answer this question, ask yourself what kind of stories you like to read. Chances are, your favorite novels have heroes (or heroines) who are opposed by people (villains) or natural forces. It is this battle between hero and villain that creates dramatic conflict in the stories you enjoy. I'll use "hero" to stand for hero, heroine, protagonist, and every other appropriate term for the leading character in a story. Likewise, I'll use "villain" to represent the character or forces that oppose the hero.

# Generating Dramatic Conflict and Dramatic Energy

Dramatic conflict is the stuff of a good story. To create lots of conflict, the hero needs a reason for pushing ahead—an overarching need or a problem so serious that he can't quit. A story becomes wimpy if the hero has no *motivation* to press on and can merely walk away from the challenge.

As the hero moves toward his goal, he is opposed by the villain, who does his best to stop—or possibly reverse—the hero's progress.

Will the hero get what he's after? Or will the hero fail? When those questions are answered, the story is over. But, while the answer remains uncertain, the reader keeps turning pages.

Uncertainty of what will happen is the primary generator of dramatic energy. Write a Christian novel truly charged with dramatic energy and it will probably become a bestseller. The number-one rule for creating dramatic energy is *Keep your hero in hot water.* This is true no matter what kind of story you're writing, although the meaning of "hot" will change depending on genre. A novel aimed at women might challenge the heroine with the increasing heartache of an abusive relationship, whereas a male-oriented adventure story might pit the hero against an army of terrorists.

"Pile on the problems" is a simple concept, something we recognize in the novels we enjoy reading. And yet, it can be difficult to achieve in our own stories.

## Fuel for the Fire

When I analyze participant work during the plotting workshops I teach at writers' conferences, I find that the following suggestions solve many common lukewarm story problems:

- Don't fall in love with your hero. Don't be reluctant to make him suffer. Even though it seems kinder to have him observe other people's problems, pour on the pain.

- Be sure to balance drive against opposition. Your villain needs to be as strong as your hero, or else your hero won't be stressed to the maximum.

> **It Is Written ...**
>
> I start with a tingle, a kind of feeling of the story I will write. Then come the characters, and they take over, they make the story. But all this ends by being a plot.
>
> —Isak Dinesen

- You can increase the level of dramatic energy by foreshadowing challenges— making your readers worry what might happen to the hero next—and steadily raising the stakes of failure as the story moves forward.

- Recognize that one overarching problem is usually not enough to sustain a high level of dramatic energy throughout a novel. Most successful stories also include an array of short-term problems, challenges, and dilemmas—each usually lasting a scene—that add further uncertainty and dramatic energy.

- Adjust the pacing of your story to give your hero (and the reader) a breather now and then. This can set the stage for a fresh jolt of angst for your hero—and increase the perceived impact.

## "Real Life" vs. Fiction

The everyday stories we experience "in real life" tend to lack drama. That's because we live them event by event, in chronological order.

When we plot a fictional story for a novel we aren't constrained by time or place. We can cunningly organize the events to increase their dramatic, thematic, and emotional significance. Simply put, we can maximize dramatic energy to keep the reader reading.

# Using Models to Plot Your Story

A model can be defined as a "representation that shows the construction of something." A model airplane, for example, illustrates how the various components—wings, fuselage, and tail—are arranged to create a structure that will fly. A plotting model does much the same thing. It shows how the various elements of a story work together to generate dramatic energy. Plotting models are useful, because as a novelist, you are a manager of dramatic energy.

## The Stair-Step Model

Perhaps the simplest plotting approach is the so-called stair-step model. You'll find a stair-step plot in many mystery novels—especially those that have a private investigator as the hero. However, the same approach can work in other genres, too, including romantic suspense.

The idea is to continuously increase the pressure on the hero—the temperature of the hot water—by raising the stakes with each passing chapter. Depending on the story line, you may decide to increase the character's peril, or angst, or personal disability, or other challenge. Eventually, the hero either triumphs or fails—the action ends and the tension disappears.

Although simple to implement, the stair-step model lacks flexibility and has fairly limited application. A more useful approach is the classic three-act story model.

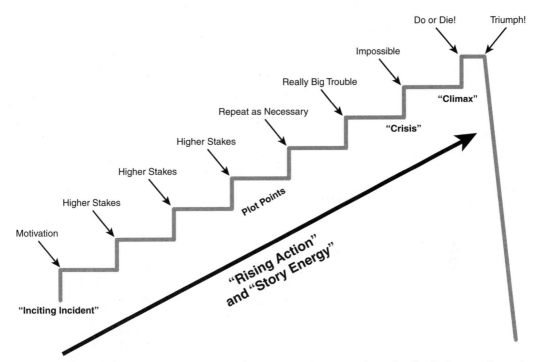

*The stair-step model builds dramatic energy by continuously raising the stakes for the hero as the story moves forward.*

## The Classic Three-Act Model

Talk about time-proven: this plotting approach goes back to ancient Greece, to a primer on writing epic poetry and plays authored by Aristotle in 350 B.C. He based his work on successful poems and plays written centuries earlier.

Because this model can seem more complicated than it really is, I'll build it from scratch to show you the simplicity of what's inside.

The three-act model divides a story into three pieces, each called an "act." This is appropriate even though the story will be part of a novel rather than a play.

The acts are divided by two events or happenings called plot points. Each plot point is an important aspect of the story: it impacts the hero and sends the story off in another direction. Aristotle used the word *peripeteia* to describe the rapid shifts that influence the hero.

**Chapter and Verse**

Aristotle wrote that a good story will have **peripeteia**. This means a sudden change of direction in a story at a key point—an event that creates strong emotional impact for the reader.

A plot point is a point of irreversible change for the hero; he can't get back to where he was before the event took place. An oft-used example of a plot point is Romeo's killing of Juliet's cousin—an event that can't be undone. Romeo is subsequently banished from Verona, laying the foundation for the tragedy that follows.

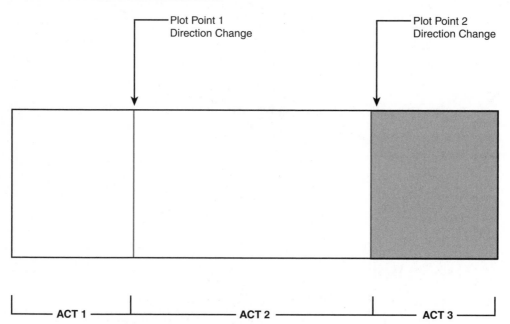

*The three-act model divides a story into three parts: Act 1, Act 2, and Act 3.*

Besides the two major plot points, there are four other transition points in the classic story model. Think of them as milestones as the story progresses:

1. A point in Act 1 when the hero's motivations are clear to readers—they know what he wants and why he will press forward to get it.

2. The midpoint of the story—a point when something in the hero's life changes significantly.

3. A point later in Act 2 when the hero reaches the low point in his journey—I call this the point of maximum angst.

4. The point somewhere in Act 3, near the end of the story, when the reader learns whether or not the hero will succeed or fail. You may hear the fourth transition point called the *dénouement* of the story; the point when the outcome is no longer in doubt.

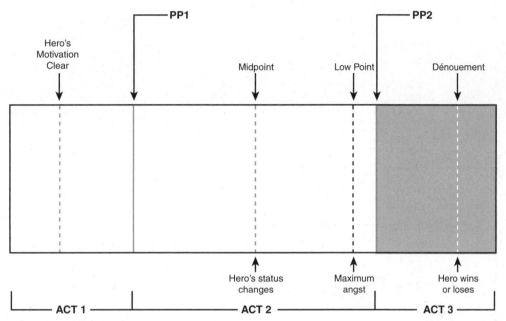

*Four other transition points represent significant milestones in the hero's journey through the story.*

## The Complete Four-Act Story

Whoops! Where did "four-act" come from? Well, the midpoint of the three-act model divides the long second act in half. It's really more convenient to talk about four equal-length acts, so that's what I'll do.

I can read your mind. You're thinking: *That model looks mighty complicated!* In fact, the model is quite straightforward once you become familiar with what it does. What's really important to observe is that we've divided a complete story into 13 small "chunks" or elements. You build an effective story by thinking about these story elements one at a time.

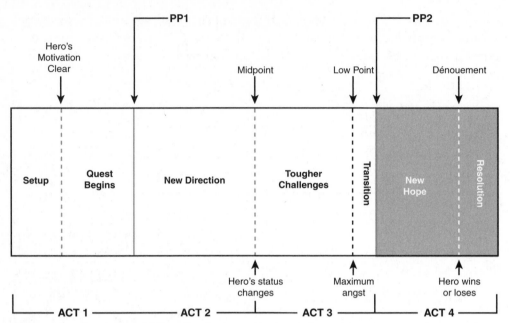

*The complete four-act model describes the major elements of a good story.*

# The 13 Plot Elements in Action

Enough theory. Let me show you the 13 plot elements of a real story in action:

1. **Set up the plot.** My story is about the younger son of a wealthy father, who is not at all happy living at home. I'm not sure why he's unhappy. Perhaps he doesn't like life in a small town? Or maybe he finds living with his father and older brother to oppressive.

2. **Make the hero's motivation clear.** After thinking about the problem for a while, the younger son comes to the conclusion that it's time to leave home. He decides to make his own way in world.

3. **Begin the hero's quest.** Because he recognizes that he'll need resources to survive, our hero convinces his father to give him his inheritance now. The young man leaves home and goes off into a world he's heard about, but never seen.

4. **Change the hero's direction.** Our hero decides to settle in Sin City, a metropolis known for its immoral living. This is the first plot point; his decision has triggered an enormous change in his life.

5. **Challenge the hero with problems.** He runs with a fast crowd and, not unexpectedly, gives in to sin.

6. **Change the hero's status.** We've reached the midpoint of the story. Our hero soon is out of money—a significant change in his status.

7. **Give the hero tougher problems.** Because he's become destitute, the young man is forced to accept menial jobs to survive.

8. **Let the hero suffer maximum angst.** His jobs become more and more menial. Our hero is finally reduced to feeding pigs—the lowest job of all in Sin City, and an affront to his faith. He wishes he could eat as well as the pigs do.

9. **Offer the hero a transition.** The young man realizes that he has hit bottom. His only hope is to go back home—but how? He knows that he cut himself off from his father and his older brother when he demanded his inheritance while his father was still alive.

10. **Change the hero's direction.** The young man decides to slink home and become his father's servant. At least he will eat regularly and no longer have to feed pigs.

11. **Give the hero new hope.** His father spots the young man walking along the road toward home. The father, overjoyed, runs to meet him on the road.

12. **Achieve a win/lose conclusion.** The father welcomes the young man back—as his son.

13. **Tie up the loose ends.** The father arranges a symbolic feast for his return son. The guests dine on the "fatted calf." The father explains his joy to the older son, who is rather annoyed by the way the father welcomes his "prodigal son" back into the fold.

I'm sure you recognized my story as soon as I began to retell it. Clearly, I borrowed the well-known parable of the prodigal son. Jesus knew how to build a good plot!

# Using the Plot Model

It's important that you recognize from the start that the plot models I described are not story formulas. Both the stair-step and four-act models define the structure of a good story—they don't tell you what kind of story to write or suggest appropriate content for any of the elements. Use the models as a guide to your creativity, to give shape to your work, and to simplify the job of creating a gripping story. Because the four-act model is the most useful, I'll use it throughout the rest of this chapter.

# Every Story Begins with a Premise

I'll sometimes dive right into the story model when I begin to plan a novel, but most of the time I come up with a premise for the story first. A story premise is often expressed as a "what-if" statement. For example, *"What if* a younger son, determined to succeed on his own, leaves home, fails, and concludes that he is 'lost' to his father?"

When Janet and I planned our novel *Glory Be!* we began with this story premise: "What if a clever killer takes advantage of a spate of practical jokes in a small town to disguise a murder?"

# Create the Main Plot First

If your novel will have subplots, start with the main plot first. The best way to employ the four-act model is to capture the 13 elements for the plot. Stay at a high level. Don't flesh out minor details. Don't write much dialogue. Don't include character *backstories*.

**Chapter and Verse** _____

**Backstory** is the history and experiences of a character *before* the events described in the novel. Providing some backstory in your novel will help readers understand the wants, motives, and shortcomings of key characters.

Your goal is to produce 13 brief statements that fully summarize the plot. Try to do it in no more than three double-spaced pages. Use the simple statements I wrote for the story of the prodigal son as guides.

# Then Build the Subplots

When you finish the main plot, produce 13 brief statements for each of your subplots. Try to summarize each subplot in less than two double-spaced pages. The Christian cozy mysteries that Janet and I write usually have four or five plots and subplots:

- Main plot—that propels the hero forward through the story

- Murder plot—why and how victim was murdered

- Romance plot—most of our cozies are romantic

- ◆ Christian plot—the story that communicates a Christian message

- ◆ Other plot (optional)—a brief subplot involving family issues, pets, hobbies, or another peripheral topic

We summarize the 13 elements for each of the subplots, making each statement succinct and specific. We've found that the time we spend up front—typically a few hours for each story—saves us countless hours of work when the writing begins, because the exercise helps us to fully understand each storyline.

## Let the Weaving Begin!

At this point, your main plot and subplots will be independent storylines. You probably don't know where, or how, they will interact. Well, your next step is to weave the plot statements together to create a single, coherent summary of your complete novel. Add brief transitions as necessary to smooth the flow between the various statements. I've provided a short example from our novel, *Glory Be!*

Saturday afternoon. The choir practice room at Glory Community Church …

**Main Plot**—The first choir rehearsal since the big fight among the choir members. The battle over how to spend the gift the church received seems to have quieted down. Rafe Neilson is in a good mood when he takes his place among the other singers.

Rafe is aghast when …

**Murder Subplot**—Emma McCall decides, on her own, to "bait" the murderer. She tells the other choir members that Lily Kirk's death was not an accident. The other members listen intently.

Rafe is equally surprised when Rafe becomes concerned about Emma.

**Romance Subplot**—Rafe recognizes that he cares about Emma, that he's beginning to fall in love with her—despite the many arguments they've had.

Rafe worries: If the killer is a member of the choir, he or she may make Emma a target.

One enormous advantage of weaving together the complete novel in this way is that you create a "ready to go" story synopsis to include the proposals you send to agents and publishers. It's not much of an exaggeration to say that many authors find it more difficult to build a synopsis than to write a full-length novel.

You can also see why I like to combine plot modeling with outlining. Interweaving a main plot and four subplots as Janet and I frequently do requires us to juggle 65 different plot elements when we write our novel—far too many to keep straight in our heads. Our summary of woven-together plot elements is the starting point of a good outline. All that remains to do is divide the complete storyline into appropriate scenes and chapters.

# Scene by Scene

The basic "unit" of the novel is not the chapter, or the paragraph, or the sentence. Your novel should be divided into scenes. The simple definition of a scene in a novel is "a unity of time and place." For example, "Saturday afternoon; the choir practice room at Glory Community Church."

A typical novel will have 60 to 80 scenes. Once you apportion the plot elements among the scenes, you can group scenes together in appropriate chapters. You don't have to put a story element in every scene—you may decide to include a scene to achieve the pacing we talked about earlier, or to provide a convenient opportunity to tell backstory. Each scene should give the character a problem, challenge, or dilemma to resolve. Scene problems can be related to the hero's overarching desire or problem, but they don't have to be. Your villain can have a problem to solve; so can secondary characters. In any event, the scene ends when the character solves—or doesn't solve—the problem.

## The Least You Need to Know

- A gripping story drips with dramatic conflict and is full of dramatic energy.

- As a Christian novelist, you are a manager of dramatic energy.

- Your hero or heroine must be opposed by people or natural forces—this is a primary source of dramatic conflict.

- It's a good idea to give your hero or heroine other problems along the way to constantly keep him or her in hot water.

- Plot models are not formulas—they are guides to creativity that have been proven over thousands of years of writing plays, poems, and novels.

- Plan your novel as a series of scenes, each a unity of time and place.

# Engaging Your Reader's Imagination

## In This Chapter

- ◆ Vivid fictional dreams sell novels
- ◆ Finding and analyzing magic paragraphs
- ◆ Where point of view (POV) fits in
- ◆ Writing in first-person POV
- ◆ Writing in omniscient POV
- ◆ Writing in third-person POV

It's a simple truism that the Christian novels you love to read—and editors love to buy—generate vivid, continuous, fictional dreams. A manuscript that produces a weak, erratic fictional dream will seem "dead" by comparison. It deserves the quick rejection it will receive.

In this chapter, I'll talk about the surprisingly simple craft you can apply to engage a reader's imagination. I'm going to start my explanation with a bad example:

Connie was nestled in bed, breathing deeply. Standing inside the bedroom door, Donna Angelo stopped worrying in her heart. Connie, her stepdaughter, looked warm and cozy. Donna hadn't felt warm and cozy for a long time.

Yes, I wrote this "dead" paragraph. And yes, it's okay English (although I won't argue if you think it isn't). But *no*, it doesn't work as fiction, because it doesn't create a fictional dream when you read it.

# How Do You Create a Fictional Dream?

Janet and I asked ourselves that question again and again during our early days writing fiction. Surprisingly, we never found a book on the subject—or a writing class—that explained how to do it. So we turned to published fiction and tried to figure out the technique. That should have been an easy thing to do—after all, nothing is hidden in a novel; the words the author wrote are there in open view. But the secret ingredients kept eluding us.

I finally took a dozen novels that I enjoyed and "reverse engineered" the writing. Slowly, I began to see a pattern. Successful fiction authors all seemed to use the same simple technique to launch fictional dreams. I called it the magic paragraph.

In fact, there are probably a zillion different magic paragraphs, but most of them follow the same simple outline. Because magic paragraphs vary some with point of view (POV), we'll look first at the magic paragraph for the common third-person POV.

## A Magic Paragraph Invites the Reader to Dream

Here are the four components of a magic paragraph:

1. *Signal* which head to enter.

2. *Twang* a sense or start a thought process.

3. *Show* what the character experienced.

4. *Start* the character thinking.

To see an effective magic paragraph at work, read this brief excerpt from *Finding Christmas* by Gail Gaymer Martin:

Donna Angelo stood inside the bedroom door and looked at her stepdaughter nestled in bed. Connie's deep breathing assured Donna she was asleep. Her heart eased at the sight of the child so warm and cozy. Donna hadn't felt warm and cozy for a long time.

This is the magic version of the *un-magic* paragraph you read on the previous page. I turned the original inside out—sorry Gail!—to illustrate the differences.

Gail wrote a classic magic paragraph. Let me dissect it to show you the four different components:

1. *Signal* which head to enter: "Donna Angelo ..." the first thing the reader needs to know is the chief point-of-view character in the scene—the owner of the head the reader should "jump" into.

2. *Twang* a sense or start a thought process: "... stood inside the bedroom door and looked at her stepdaughter nestled in bed." Obviously, the twanged sense is sight. But the phrase also tells us where Donna is and *how* she's looking at her stepdaughter. When we enter Donna's head, we expect to see the bed from a slight distance—perhaps from 10 feet away.

3. *Show* what the character experienced: "Connie's deep breathing assured Donna she was asleep. Her heart eased at the sight of the child so warm and cozy." Clearly, the author implies that Donna saw the child breathing deeply. The reader—now inside Donna's head—will understand that she probably also *heard* the child breathing.

4. *Start* the character thinking: "Donna hadn't felt warm and cozy for a long time." The reader immediately grasps that this a negative thought. Donna is contrasting her own discomfort with the good feelings experienced by her sleeping stepdaughter.

The four parts of this short magic paragraph work together to plunge the reader into a fictional dream. We learned a lot about Donna via *showing* rather than *telling*.

If you re-read my "dead" paragraph now, it might seem a bit better than it really is. This is because you've become used to seeing the world through Donna's eyes. But read it again tomorrow, and you'll find—once again—that it doesn't put you into a character's head.

Why not? For starters, you don't know *whose* head to enter. There are two characters present. My paragraph doesn't issue a clear invitation; it forces you to guess. An equally serious shortcoming is that I don't present a sensation you can savor or a thought you can experience. I merely tell you from a distance what one character thought.

## Another Magic Paragraph

Here's an excerpt from *Summer* by Karen Kingsbury:

> Jenny closed her eyes and sucked in the cool spring air. *God … send the answers. Please …* She let the silent prayer sit for a while, echoing in the hallways of her heart. Somehow direction and wisdom would come, because God would bring them. He would walk them down the unknown path before them and give them the answers that seemed so elusive.

Here are the different components of this magic paragraph:

1. *Signal* which head to enter: "Jenny …"

2. *Twang* a sense or start a thought process: "… closed her eyes … *God … send the answers. Please …*" Karen might have written, "Jenny began to pray without speaking …" but having Jenny close her eyes—and think a silent prayer—tells the reader the same thing.

3. *Show* what the character experienced: "She let the silent prayer sit for a while, echoing in the hallways of her heart."

4. *Start* the character thinking: "Somehow direction and wisdom would come, because God would bring them. He would walk them down the unknown path before them and give them the answers that seemed so elusive."

**Literary Sins** _____

The mistake that's easiest to make with a magic paragraph is to leave out item 1 and not clearly signal the owner of the head the reader should enter. The result is a "muddled paragraph" that can confuse the reader and interrupt the fictional dream.

This magic paragraph is a little more complex than the first example, because the reader also learns that Jenny "… sucked in the cool spring air." An experienced writer like Karen Kingsbury can include more information in a magic paragraph without damaging it.

## Super-Simple Magic Paragraphs

The examples I've just shown you came early in their respective chapters. Wise authors insert fresh magic paragraphs after blocks of dialogue or description to maintain the fictional dream. These don't need to be as elaborate. Once readers get used to being in a particular character's head, occasional use of super-simple magic paragraphs will keep them there. They require only two elements:

1. *Signal* which head to enter in a single sentence that has the character acting or reacting.

2. *Show* the character thinking, or sensing, or both.

For most readers, the best parts of the novel are the thoughts and sensations bouncing around inside a character's head. They want to fear, suffer, ache, love, hate, laugh, and cry along with the hero or heroine. It's usually enough to signal which head to enter and provide the thoughts and sensations—the reader can fill in the missing details.

# Start Reading

The best way to increase your understanding of magic paragraphs is to identify—and analyze—them in your favorite novels. You can expect to find full magic paragraphs near the beginning of every scene and chapter. Many will look like the examples I presented, but sometimes the structure will vary. You'll find all four elements, but they may be out of order, or implied, or possibly disguised.

Here's an excerpt from *In Shady Groves* by Yvonne Lehman:

> He did not reach out for her hand as she ascended to the brow of the hill. Dancing eyes met his and breathless laugher escaped through parted lips. Even the graying light could not shade her beauty. "What do you find so amusing, little dove?"

And here's another from *All Together in One Place* by Jane Kirkpatrick:

> Her wooden spade cut the soil. Mazy thought of the fat rattlers that moved lazily in summer sun, pleased they'd still be sleeping in the limestone rocks and caves and not surprising her. She disliked surprises. She knelt, planted and pressed dirt around her precious love apples. Tomatoes, some called them now. They'd be fat and plump earlier than ever before.

I leave it to you to identify the four elements of a magic paragraph in each excerpt.

# Establishing Point of View

Engaging the reader's imagination is closely related to point of view (POV), because besides dropping the reader into a character's head, a magic paragraph establishes a particular POV. This makes POV errors especially deadly fictional-dream killers—and why I need to give you a short course in POV.

Point of view is actually a *convention*. The reader "agrees" to be told a story by different characters in each POV:

**A Lamp Unto Your Feet**

If you ever find point of view confusing, imagine you are making a home movie rather than writing a novel.

- ◆ First-person POV—by the character who lived it
- ◆ Omniscient POV—by a God-like narrator who sees all and knows everything
- ◆ Third-person POV—through one or more characters who lived it

A good way to visualize the different points of view is to imagine a magical flying camera that can move around the imaginary world created by novelist. Think about what the camera can see, what it can't see, and how it moves from location to location.

# First-Person Point of View

In first-person POV, the narrator is a personally involved storyteller. The flying camera is fixed inside the narrator's head for the entire novel. It *never* shifts, unless the author decides to switch to a different POV for a chapter or two.

The camera sees everything that the narrator sees—and can't see anything that the narrator can't. For example, the narrator can't see him- or herself unless there's a mirror in the room.

The first-person POV is useful when a story revolves around one character. When well-executed, the reader feels exceptionally close to the narrator.

Here's an excerpt from *Humble Pie*, a novel that Janet and I wrote:

> I slammed my long-suffering front door with enough force to make the pine board flooring in the foyer quiver, then threw the envelope full of legal papers the length of our hallway. "I've had a truly rotten afternoon, James," I bellowed. "Hardesty Software is a brood of vipers! And I'm ready to flog that silly twit of a woman!"

First-person POV has several major shortcomings. The story is limited to the narrator's personal experience—the fixed camera can't capture sights and sounds unless the narrator is there to experience them. The narrator can *infer* what other characters think and feel, but can't convey their emotions and thoughts in a way that the reader can experience them. And of course, the narrator must survive the action of the novel. If the lead character dies, there's no one left to tell the story.

In the first-person magic paragraph, the word "I"—rather than a name or a pronoun—signals the reader to enter the one available head. The other elements are the same as you'll find in a third-person magic paragraph.

Here's a magic paragraph that Janet and I wrote for *Little White Lies*:

> I double-parked my red sports car, with its engine running, a half block from the Police Headquarters' "official vehicle" lot. I didn't know what kind of car Reilly would be driving, but I had a good view of the exit through the Miata's squat windshield. A few minutes later an unmarked blue sedan nosed into the street. The sky was still light enough for me to spot Reilly at the wheel. I shifted into gear and slipped into the flow of traffic behind him. With luck he wouldn't recognize me—though I didn't much care if he did. *The arrogant clod!*

"I" signals the head to enter. The 44 words that follow—to the end of the second sentence—represent a long twang of the character's sense of sight. We then began to see what the character sees, and we finally get her thoughts at the very end.

## Omniscient Point of View

The essential characteristic of the omniscient POV is a Godlike narrator who tells the story to the reader. It's easy to spot an omniscient novel; it's full of information that characters don't know.

Here's an excerpt from *Enigma*, a secular novel by Robert Harris:

> Cambridge in the fourth winter of the war: a ghost town. A ceaseless Siberian wind with nothing to blunt its edge ... whipped off the North Sea and swept low across the Fens. It rattled the signs to the air-raid shelters in Trinity New Court and battered on the boarded-up windows of King's College Chapel ... By nightfall, without a light to be seen, the university was returned to a darkness it hadn't known since the Middle Ages. ... It was to the bleak spot in the flatlands of eastern England that there came, in the middle of February 1943, a young mathematician named Thomas Jericho.

We know someone is talking to us, but we don't know who. An omniscient narrator rarely introduces himself or herself to the readers. The only character is mentioned at the end of this excerpt, and we know almost nothing about him.

In omniscient POV, the flying camera is *above* the action. The narrator can point it inside any character's head to reveal thoughts, feelings, and emotions. Omniscient POV can be a good choice for sprawling stories, adventures, quests, and family sagas.

The trouble is, unless the novelist is exceptionally skillful, readers may feel closer to the narrator than the lead characters. Although some Christian novelists use omniscient POV for prologues that "introduce" first-person and third-person novels, there are few wholly omniscient novels written these days. Because it's difficult to pull off successfully, inexperienced writers should avoid an omniscient POV.

For this reason, I won't give any omniscient magic paragraph examples. I will say, however, that the best way to begin an omniscient magic paragraph is by twanging a character's thought process, rather than sense.

## Third-Person Point of View

The third-person POV has no apparent narrator. This surprises many writers (and readers), but take a closer look at a novel written in third-person and you'll see what I mean.

In first-person and omniscient POVs you can "hear" a person talking to you as you read. But in third-person, you experience the sensations, emotions, and thoughts of the different viewpoint characters. You learn the story by watching the action and listening to the dialogue. There shouldn't be any "omniscient" information that comes from outside the head of a character.

The flying camera moves from head to head in third-person POV. It continues to capture the sensations, emotions, and thoughts of one character until the author moves it into another head. Third-person POV is useful for all but the "biggest" stories, which is why it's the most popular point of view.

Third-person POV has one significant shortcoming that results from the lack of a narrator. It's difficult to tell a good backstory and write interesting exposition because everything must be "filtered" through a character's consciousness.

**Chapter and Verse**

The owner of the head you want the reader enter is often called the **focus character.**

I discussed third-person POV magic paragraphs in detail earlier in the chapter. One common writing mistake I didn't talk about is the failure to re-invite readers into the *focus character's* head often enough. My motto is, keep writing magic paragraphs until your word processor quits. I use them after blocks of dialogue and narrative, but I'll also put two or three together at the start of a scene, and then again in the middle of the scene to refresh the reader's memory.

## Shifting POV

Another question sure to start arguments among novelists is whether or not it's okay to "jump heads" within a single scene. Conventional wisdom says no, but I believe that's simply because so many novelists write faulty point-of-view shifts.

A manuscript full of confusing POV shifts will earn a well-deserved rejection for "head hopping." And yet, more than a few successful novelists manage to pull off the trick without bouncing readers out of their fictional dreams.

Having said this, it's probably a good idea to stick with a single POV in each scene. Janet and I follow the rule in our third-person POV novels, and so do the majority of the Christian writers we know.

# One Story, Three Different POVs

Because it's useful to compare magic paragraphs in different points of view, I wrote the following three examples. Each of them tells the same little story, but from a different POV. Take the time to compare these three little stories, identify the magic paragraphs, and see how they differ in each POV. See what you think of the POV jumps in the omniscient and third-person examples.

## A First-Person Example

I had just finished typing the last chapter of *Building Fictional Dreams for Fun and Profit* when she pushed open my office door. No bell or knocker for this lady; I could tell she was in a hurry. The angst she felt filled her expression; I could tell she was hurting.

"Are you the Dream Wizard?" she asked, her big brown eyes taking in the clutter of paper around my computer.

"In the flesh."

"My name is Carolyn. I need your help."

I imagined the annoyance racing through her mind: *Here's a novelist who knows the difference between third-person and omniscient points of view. Life isn't fair.*

"No sweat, Carolyn," I said. "I love helping writers in distress, but it'll cost you." I winked at her. "You know what I mean."

Anyone could have heard the gears in her head grinding. Should she agree to my terms? Or should she try to grab a few relevant chapters off my messy desk and run like a rabbit? She finally made her decision:

"Okay, Wizard—you win. I'll listen to your blasted lecture on the magic paragraph. It'll be worth it, if you can help me figure out the difference between third-person and omniscient points of view. I need to find the right magic paragraphs for my novel."

## An Omniscient Example

The Dream Wizard led a lonely life. Not many writers came to visit, because the price of a friendly chat was too high. He would offer a chair—maybe a meal—then deliver a tiresome lecture on the magic paragraph. Some writers, though, felt they had no choice.

Carolyn came calling in the middle of March. She stood outside the Wizard's door and heard the sounds of heavy fingers pounding a keyboard. She figured he was perched at his desk—probably working on his book, *Building Fictional Dreams for Fun and Profit*. Should she disturb him? You never knew how to deal with self-appointed wizards.

The clicking stopped. She decided to move.

Carolyn turned the knob and pushed. The flash of light as the door swung open made her blink. There he sat, surrounded by stacks of paper. A novelist who knows the difference between third-person and omniscient points of view. *Life isn't fair.*

She moved into the room, baffled that he merely stared at her. Why doesn't he say something? she wondered.

"Are you the Dream Wizard?" she finally asked.

"In the flesh."

"My name is Carolyn. I need your help."

"No sweat, Carolyn. I love helping writers in distress, but it'll cost you." He paused. "You know what I mean."

She half-nodded, not sure how to respond to his taunting attitude.

The Dream Wizard arranged a Mona Lisa smile on his face and winked at Carolyn. He had decided to wait for her to make the next move. Of course, she knew what he meant. Writers are a transparent lot. He found it amusing to watch her stare back at him, to imagine the gears in her head grinding. Should she agree to his terms? Or should she try to grab a few relevant chapters off the messy desk and run like a rabbit?

The Wizard said nothing. Give her time—she'll come around.

"Okay, Wizard—you win," Carolyn said. He could tell she wasn't happy. "I'll listen to your blasted lecture. It'll be worth it, if you can help me find the right magic paragraphs for my novel."

## A Third-Person Example

Carolyn tipped her ear close to the door and heard a keyboard clicking. The Dream Wizard was sitting at his desk. Probably working on *Building Fictional Dreams for Fun and Profit*.

The clicking stopped. Time to move.

She turned the knob and pushed. The flash of light as the door swung open made her blink. There he sat, surrounded by stacks of paper. A novelist who understands the difference between third-person and omniscient points of view. Life isn't fair.

She moved into the room. Why is he just staring at me? Why doesn't he say something?

"Are you the Dream Wizard?" she asked.

"In the flesh!" His voice signaled his enthusiasm.

"My name is Carolyn. I need your help."

"No sweat, Carolyn. I love helping writers in distress, but it'll cost you. You know what I mean."

She felt herself half-nod. What could she say in response to his taunting grin?

The Dream Wizard winked at Carolyn and waited. Why not savor the moment? he thought. *Of course*, she knew what he meant. Writers are a transparent lot. It was almost funny watching her stare back at him while the gears in her head ground away. Should she agree to his terms? Or should she try to grab a few relevant chapters off the messy desk and run like a rabbit? Give her time—she'll make a decision.

"Okay, Wizard—you win." Her voice seemed resigned. "I'll listen to your blasted lecture. It'll be worth it, if you can help me figure out the difference between third-person and omniscient. I need to find the right magic paragraphs for my novel."

Once you get the hang of crafting effective magic paragraphs—it's a simple skill to master!—you'll be well on your way to writing compelling fiction that grabs a reader's imagination.

## The Least You Need to Know

◆ You must continually re-engage the reader's imagination; this is the key to sustaining a fictional dream throughout your novel.

◆ Writing magic paragraphs is a simple, effective way to engage a reader's imagination.

◆ Write magic paragraphs at the beginning of a scene and after blocks of dialogue and narrative.

◆ Learn how to write magic paragraphs by identifying—and analyzing—magic paragraphs written by your favorite Christian authors.

◆ Your magic paragraph will vary depending on the point of view you choose: first-person, omniscient, or third-person.

# Chapter 11

# Coping with Limitations on Language and Content

## In This Chapter

- Where the limits on language and content come from
- Some writers like the "rules," some hate them
- Why you need to know where you stand
- Writing so that language no-no's don't impact your novel
- Do boundaries around painful subjects still apply?

How do you feel about profanity? Are you offended when you read it in a secular novel? Do you expect the fictional characters in your Christian novels to take God's name in vain from time to time? I can frame similar questions about sexuality, "edgy topics" (such as abortion, addiction, spousal abuse, incest, and racism), and many different kinds of so-called "non-Christian behavior," ranging from adultery, to drinking, to gambling, to playing cards.

Some Christian novelists feel strongly about surmounting the limitations on language and content that are alive and well across much of Christian publishing. Others are comfortable to write within the well-defined boundaries. Hate them or love them, every writer must understand his or her position on the "rules." This chapter explains how your stand will impact the kind of Christian fiction you write, the specifics of how you write, and the publishers willing to consider your manuscript.

# The "Rules" of Christian Fiction

The limitations on language and content vary somewhat among Christian publishers, but every one enforces rules that fall into two broad categories:

1. **Prohibited language**—chiefly profanity and familiar expressions that take the Lord's name in vain, other coarse language, other religious expletives, anatomical terms, intimate clothing, and an assortment of other words. A fairly rigorous list of no-no words would include such entries as blimey, breast, butt, crap, damn, devil (except in religious context), fiend, for Heaven's sake, for Pete's sake, geez or jeez, gosh, golly, heck, hell (except in religious context), miracle (unless describing one), pee, priest, poop, passion, sex, shucks, words for undergarments (e.g., bra or panties), and whore.

**Wisdom and Knowledge**

You may be surprised to see "gosh" and "golly" on the no-no list. Several Christian publishers refuse to include even so-called "mild oaths" or "euphemisms for curses" in the novels they publish.

2. **Prohibited content**—explicit sexuality, graphic violence, divorce, and certain behaviors, activities, and circumstances that are generally considered to be off-limits in Christian fiction. These include drinking, dancing, smoking, gambling, bodily functions, nudity, Halloween celebrations, Christian characters lying to each other, and potentially compromising situations (for example, the heroine and hero spending the night together alone in the same house).

Some publishers have formal no-no lists they can provide to their authors. Others give editors the discretion—and enough latitude—to consider questionable words and actions on a case-by-case basis.

## Ignoring the Rules Can Have Bleak Consequences

In Chapter 2, I urged you not to fight the system, because challenging these "conventions" of Christian publishing will limit the number of publishers who might be interested in your novel. It's important to point out that editors didn't invent the rules merely to give aspiring novelists a hard time.

Publishing, as I've noted before, is a risky business. Editors try their best to control risk—and like it or not, there's considerable risk in publishing a Christian novel that includes a "damn" or two, or a "My God," or a scene that has a presumably Christian couple engaging in premarital sex. The fact that believing Christians talk—and act—this way in real life has nothing to do with the significant possibility that some readers will be offended and trigger a backlash:

- The upset readers will probably complain to their Christian bookseller, the publisher of the book, and maybe even the author.

- The bookseller is likely to return all unsold copies of the novel.

- If word gets around, other Christian bookstores may do the same.

- Even secular bookstores may refuse to stock a specific Christian novel—or the publisher's whole line—if they conclude that Christian readers don't like the content and are unlikely to buy the books.

**Literary Sins** _____

Many first-time novelists assume that an editor at a publisher without a defined no-no list can bend the rules. It doesn't work that way. Editors are well aware of the risks of offending Christian readers. They will often be more scrupulous about language and content than those editors who have a formal list as a guide.

Because this scary chain of events *could* happen, many Christian publishers choose the prudent course of strictly following the conventions of Christian fiction. Some companies are willing to waive the rules for well-established novelists who have track records of writing bestsellers. But they generally won't budge an inch for a first-time author—unless he or she shows up with a spectacular manuscript.

Don't count on this happening at the start of your career. The time to push the envelope is when tens of thousands of readers are clamoring for your next novel.

## Some Writers Applaud the Rules ...

Many Christian novelists would honor the prohibitions, even if their publishers didn't insist on them. Their arguments go something like this: Everyone knows that Christians sin. Why waste space in a novel with dreary details of the squalid side of Christian behavior—especially if the depictions of sinful behavior are gratuitous and do nothing to advance the story? Illicit sexual situations, vulgar language, violence, and the rest are usually included in secular novels to titillate their readers; they don't enlighten anyone, or point the reader toward God. These things can have shock value, but they rarely increase dramatic tension or improve a plotline.

The people who buy Christian novels expect uplifting stories that illustrate Christianity as God wants it to be. Moreover, they expect to enjoy a "safe" read without the in-your-face sex, profanity, gruesome violence, and other content they associate with secular novels.

As you see, this is a perfectly reasonable position for a Christian novelist to take, because it turns a spotlight on reader expectations and reflects the writer's own values. As a reader, I'm not troubled by coarse language, but I can remember several occasions when secular violence offended me and shattered my fictional dream (see Chapter 5). As Christian writers, we have to recognize that we often write for readers with lower thresholds than our own.

Following the rules also simplifies your life as a first-time novelist because you have nothing to explain to an agent or editor. Your agent can send your manuscript to *every* Christian publisher, certain in the knowledge that it won't be rejected because of language or content.

### It Is Written ...

If we want to garner respect in the arena of secular fiction and use that respect as a bully pulpit for the Lord ... we must do it with the undeniable quality of our writing. And for goodness sake, we must demonstrate the difference Christ makes in our lives by doing it without superficial descents to the level of the pagan authors everyone outside Christianity is already reading.

—Athol Dickson, Christian novelist

## ... Other Writers Boo Them

But maybe you're determined to kick against the goads of the Christian publishing conventions. Maybe you, like many published novelists—and more than one critic— consider the rules antiquated and silly.

◆ Does it make any sense that the villains in Christian novels can kill people but not curse?

◆ Would anyone other than a character in a Christian novel say "Oh my" after hitting his thumb with a hammer?

◆ Isn't it irrational that a hero—a perfectly sound Christian—coming home from a hard day at work can't enjoy a cold beer?

◆ Why can't a Christian woman assure her friend that her dress doesn't make her look fat—even though she knows it's a little white lie?

◆ Where's the logic in a rule that prevents an honorable Christian man and a righteous Christian woman from dancing—even at their own wedding?

◆ And hasn't the prohibition against divorce in Christian fiction created an impossibly large number of young widows and widowers in Christian novels?

Clearly, I could go on for pages poking fun at many of the other prohibitions—they all, after all, seem to stop us from portraying "real" behaviors and activities. In many cases, characters can't do the things that many of us do routinely—including a range of activities that are sponsored by solidly Christian churches.

I could argue that the rules tend to be denominational in nature, and proscribe behavior that many—perhaps most—Christians don't find offensive.

I could point out that the rules aren't enforced uniformly from publisher to publisher, that you will find the occasional Christian character who has a cocktail, or says "Damn!" or was divorced.

And I might even cite the literary critics who assert that mainstream readers will never take Christian fiction seriously as long as these artificial restraints damage the realism of the novels we write. The critics claim that by avoiding honest depictions of sinful behavior, Christian novelists create synthetic, half-developed characters who don't display the full range of human traits. Our heroes and heroines are often too virtuous, and our villains wildly inauthentic.

> **A Lamp Unto Your Feet**
>
> A few Christian publishers will let novelists bypass some of the conventions. However, if you're determined to include streams of profanity and explicit sex scenes in your novel, you probably should be writing for a secular publisher.

If you feel this way, you'll find editors and agents out there who'll agree with you—enough to get an excellent manuscript published (although far fewer than if you honor the rules). But keep in mind that even the most tolerant Christian publishers have boundaries they won't cross.

The editorial director at a leading publisher of Christian novels told me that his company doesn't have a written no-no list, although it does take into account the conventions of Christian publishing: "Providing offense-free entertainment is not our primary goal when we publish Christian fiction," he explained. "However, we do operate on the belief that care must be exercised with regard to sexuality and violence. We take a dim view of depictions that are gratuitous, graphic, or for the purpose of titillation. And we look closely, as well, at language. We never allow true profanity—the taking of God's name in vain—and we carefully consider words that are vulgar or just plain coarse. We know that we publish to a reading audience that has certain expectations of prudence as well as quality."

## The Middle Ground: Getting Along with the Rules

Many Christian writers—I'm one of them—take a middle position. We don't like all the rules, but we understand their purpose and we recognize that we have to live with them. The question I ask when I sit down at my computer is this: "How can I write my novel so that the conventions of Christian publishing don't negatively impact the effectiveness of my story?" This isn't always an easy question to answer, but I know that hundreds of published Christian writers come up with successful responses every day.

A funny thing about the Christian publishing conventions is that most of the timeless secular novels we read in great literature courses had to meet many of the same rules. Consider how many "famous" novels written during the nineteenth and first half of the twentieth centuries are without profanity, vulgar language, or explicit sexuality— and yet present complex and realistic characterizations, convey the full spectrum of emotions, and often seem to drip with sensuality. I often make the point to rule-haters that Janet and I can write mystery novels that have much of the same content and language as the classics written by Agatha Christie, Ngaio Marsh, Dorothy Sayers, Raymond Chandler, Rex Stout, and our other favorites.

Creativity is sometimes defined as problem solving in the face of constraints. A well-known example is Michelangelo, who tried to "free" the statue trapped inside a block of marble, rather than transform the block into a statue. Thought of this way, Christian publishing's limitations on language and content can be stimulants to creativity—not barriers.

Let's look at a few of the ways you can make yourself, your readers, and your editor happy about language and content.

# Alternatives to No-No Words

I wouldn't be surprised to see an edgy novel about a Christian alcoholic prostitute on sale at a Christian bookstore, but I'd be amazed to find an industrial-strength four-letter word inside its pages, or an expression that takes the Lord's name in vain. Profanity and coarse language are at the top of the no-no lists because eagle-eyed readers seem to complain about them more than any other violation of Christian publishing conventions.

The Christian publishing embargo against foul language raises an obvious question. If your story includes characters who in real life would have a pungent vocabulary, how do you write effective dialogue for them? The answer is that you have to communicate the use of coarse language without filling your manuscript with bad words. Therein lies a skill that you as a Christian writer must take time to develop.

### It Is Written ...

The convention [to avoid profanity and obscenity] seems to raise more hackles than anything else and I don't understand why. ... Profanity is, well, profane to anyone who believes in God and obscenity is offensive to most people of faith. Does that mean that we hide our head in the sand and pretend bad language doesn't exist? Of course not. Our characters can and do curse, but we have to be more creative because we have to show and illustrate this without using the actual words. Sometimes it's as simple as writing, "He cursed." Or, "He uttered a word that made her blush."

—Angela Hunt, Christian novelist

An abundance of four-letter words in a secular novel is usually a symptom of lazy writing. A little effort to go beyond "quick and easy vulgarity" can pay dividends in richer, more interesting, more compelling characterizations. It pays to remember that most of the best-drawn villains in literature and theater didn't curse.

In each of the following examples, I've provided a practical alternative for a no-no word. Read through the whole list to get your bearings and then think about each sentence. In the space provided, try to craft an even better workaround that captures the original thought, yet eliminates the prohibited word.

1. She caught him staring at her breasts.

   *Alternative:* She caught him ogling her figure.

   *Comment:* I began with a toughie. It's difficult to come up with an equivalent that has the same impact as the original. Another possibility is, She caught him staring at her in a way that made her angry.

2. He fell on his butt.

   *Alternative:* He fell on his bottom.

   *Comment:* This is an easy switch that few writers would find objectionable. Most publishers will also let you write, He fell on his derriere; although few writers I know would be willing to type such a sentence.

3. "Your theory is a load of crap," he said.

   *Alternative:* "Your theory is nonsense," he said. "Pure drivel."

   *Comment:* You may be tempted to write, "Your theory is a load of manure." It might pass muster, but it sounds artificial. I prefer the "double hit" using non-scatological language.

4. "Damn!" he shouted.

   *Alternative:* "Blast!" he shouted.

   *Comment:* A strong single-word expletive can quickly express an unhappy state of mind. "Blast!" is an alternative that will get a nod from many editors. So will "Rats!" Sometimes, though, it's better to approach from a different direction: "He took a deep breath and fought to contain the anger he felt."

5. "You're as evil as the Devil," she said.

   *Alternative:* "You're pure evil, through and through."

   *Comment:* There's not much need for the word "devil" in a nonreligious context, though some of your older characters might have the word in their vocabulary.

6. "For Heaven's sake," she said.

   *Alternative:* "For goodness sake," she said.

   *Comment:* Not much of a change; both expressions are familiar to readers and express pretty much the same feelings of surprise and mild annoyance.

7. "Geez! That was a stupid thing to do."

   *Alternative:* "Sheesh! That was a stupid thing to do."

   *Comment:* Most publishers will allow "Sheesh!" to replace many different four-letter expletives. Unfortunately, it sticks out as an unusual word, so don't use it too often and don't have more than one character sheeshing.

8. "Gosh! I wish I could take back my words."

   *Alternative:* "Oh my! I wish I could take back my words."

*Comment:* "Gosh" and "golly" are not acceptable—which never bothered me, because I can't imagine creating characters who would speak either one. You can often replace a so-called mild oath with an appropriate action. For example: John made a face. "I wish I could take back my words," he said.

9. "The hell you will!" she screamed. Or, "It's cold as hell," he said. Or, "My car is fast as hell," she said.

*Alternative:* "No way!" she screamed.

*Comment:* "Hell" has become a universal comparator—and consequently conveys little information. Apparently, *everything* can be contrasted to hell. Whenever you're moved to write "hell," rewrite the sentence.

10. "This whole experience has been a miracle," she said.

*Alternative:* "This whole experience has been wonderful," she said.

*Comment:* The *second* definition of "miracle" is "a superb example of something; a wonder; a marvel." It's an unnecessary word to use unless you're writing about a real miracle, because "wonder" (as in *wonder drug*), "wonderful" (as above), and "marvel" and "marvelous" are complete equivalents.

11. She walked across the room in her bra and panties.

*Alternative:* She walked across the room and slipped into her dress.

*Comment:* The alternative captures the original thought without naming specific undergarments.

12. He walked across the lawn, carefully avoiding the dog poop.

*Alternative:* He glared at the dog, then walked across the lawn, picking his way from one clean patch of grass to another.

*Comment:* A few more words add to the humor of the situation and eradicate a no-no.

# No-No Behaviors and Activities

There aren't any workarounds if a Christian publisher flatly prohibits drinking, dancing, smoking, gambling, divorce, and the like. Sometimes, editors are willing to "forgive" such activities when they're performed by non-Christians (usually secondary characters) or pre-Christians (possibly one of the lead characters who becomes a believing Christian during the story).

"But," you ask, "what about those 'edgy' novels you told us about earlier?" Don't they violate the no-no rules?"

Well, not necessarily—because a well-crafted edgy novel will challenge Christian readers without causing the kind of offense that brings a flood of complaints.

# Christian Novels That May Surprise You

The following novels deal with decidedly edgy topics, and some highly un-Christian behaviors. They were published because the authors told compelling stories in a way that challenged—but didn't offend—the great majority of Christian readers.

**Abortion:**

*Tears in a Bottle*, Sylvia Bambola
*The Atonement Child*, Francine Rivers

**Alcoholism/Drug Abuse:**

*Beyond the Shadows*, Robin Lee Hatcher
*Looking for Cassandra Jane*, Melody Carlson

**Deception:**

*Little White Lies*, Ron and Janet Benrey

**Domestic Violence:**

*A Nest of Sparrows*, Deborah Raney
*Sadie's Song*, Linda Hall
*Serenity Bay*, Bette Nordberg
*Ain't No River*, Sharon Ewell Foster

**Drunk Driving:**

*The Living Stone*, Jane Orcutt
*Waiting for Morning*, Karen Kingsbury

**Homosexuality/AIDS:**

*A Season of Grace*, Bette Nordberg
*Spring Rain*, Gayle Roper
*Tiger Lillie*, Lisa Samson

**Infertility:**

*Ashes and Lace*, B. J. Hoff
*In a Heartbeat*, Sally John
*The Long-Awaited Child*, Tracie Peterson

**Infidelity/Divorce:**

*Breach of Promise*, James Scott Bell
*Footsteps*, DiAnn Mills
*Redeeming Love*, Francine Rivers
*The Breaking Point*, Karen Ball
*The Forgiving Hour*, Robin Lee Hatcher

**Mental Illness/Depression/Suicide:**

*Becoming Olivia*, Roxanne Henke
*Songbird*, Lisa Samson
*The Novelist*, Angela Hunt

**Pornography:**

*Last Light*, Terri Blackstock
*Ain't No Mountain*, Sharon Ewell Foster

**Unplanned Pregnancy:**

*A Moment of Weakness*, Karen Kingsbury
*Child of Grace*, Lori Copeland

**Rape/Incest/Sexual Abuse:**

*Antonia's Choice*, Nancy Rue
*In the Still of Night*, Deborah Raney
*Mending Places*, Denise Hunter
*What She Left for Me*, Tracie Peterson
*Why the Sky Is Blue*, Susan Meissner

**Sexuality/Attraction:**

*The Hidden Heart*, Jane Orcutt
*A Quarter for a Kiss*, Mindy Starns Clark

**Racism:**

*Trial by Fire*, Terri Blackstock
*All the Way Home*, Ann Tatlock

There's a big difference between, say, a novel about a prostitute and a novel that shows a prostitute at work. Handled properly by an experienced novelist, Christian fiction can be "about" lots of topics that involve behavior and activity on the no-no list. If a book is a compelling read, some editors may allow the lead characters to have adulterous affairs, commit murder, live immoral lives, get divorced, commit suicide, do cruel things to their children, or have thoroughly un-Christian thoughts zipping through their heads—at least for part of the story.

I cheerfully acknowledge using several weasel phrases in the previous paragraph: "experienced novelist," "compelling read," "some editors may allow." They're important—because, as I've emphasized throughout the book, edgy novels are best left to multi-published authors.

**It Is Written ...**

> I'm aware that some readers are uncomfortable when they find [unpleasant] issues in fiction written from a Christian worldview. But by *not* including these issues, I believe we do a terrible disservice to our readers. ... We can't even read a newspaper without our heart breaking at the pain and horror being inflicted on human beings worldwide, so how can we even *think* of writing stories that ignore some of these same tragedies? If our fiction doesn't reflect the truth, if it doesn't ... explore the need for mercy, compassion, healing, and hope—then it's sadly lacking in value to those who read it.
> —B. J. Hoff, Christian novelist

Most unpublished Christian novelists want to write a first novel that can find a home at *many* Christian publishers. To do that with an edgy topic, you have to know what different editors will find acceptable in an initial manuscript from a first-time author. That's not easy information to gather, because publishing decisions are highly situational—and highly subjective.

You can get some data by attending Christian writers' conferences and asking the editors you meet (as I'll discuss in Chapter 14). You can learn some more by joining a critique group that includes a few published novelists who have experience with different houses.

The safest course, however, for an unpublished writer is to avoid no-no-list behaviors and activities in your first novel. After you're published and have begun to build a readership base, you and your editor can discuss—and negotiate—limits for future novels.

## The Least You Need to Know

- ◆ No-no lists exist—some on paper, some in editors' heads.
- ◆ The limitation on language and content reflect strongly held expectations by many readers.
- ◆ You won't win arguments about profanity or foul language.
- ◆ You can "write around" language no-no's in ways that won't significantly impact your story.
- ◆ Let experienced Christian authors challenge content and topic limitations— first-time novelists should write books that can find homes at most Christian publishers.

# How to Integrate Christian Theme and Christian Messages

## In This Chapter

- ◆ The role of theme and message in your novel
- ◆ The most popular "families" of explicit Christian messages
- ◆ How to extract themes from Scripture
- ◆ Building your explicit Christian message into the plot and subplot
- ◆ Ensuring that Christian characters don't "accidentally" engage in non-Christian behavior

How would you answer if someone asked you, "What is your novel about?" You could say, "It's women's fiction about life in nineteenth-century North Carolina," or "It's about a man and a woman who fall in love despite their great cultural differences," or even "It's about 300 pages long."

If an agent or editor asks you this question, don't be flip and don't merely outline the plot. He or she also wants to know the *theme* of your novel—and perhaps a rundown of the different Christian messages your story delivers. In this chapter, I'll teach you how to build an effective theme *and* a meaningful message into your Christian novel without merely nailing these things to your storyline.

# Theme vs. Messages

You'll find lots of conflicting definitions out there for *theme*, but here's the one I like best and find most useful: the theme of your novel is the unifying idea of the story—the concept that ties its various insights and values together.

Theme tends to be abstract; many readers may not even notice the theme (although literary critics will usually assume they have the skill to spot a novel's theme). For example, Janet and I define the theme of *Little White Lies* as the willingness of otherwise honest people to tell "harmless" little white lies to advance their own interests—even Christians who sincerely believe that lying is sinful. Many readers recognize the novel is about the downside of lying, but no one we've spoken to at book signings or writers' conferences has ever zeroed in on our complete theme.

> **Wisdom and Knowledge**
>
> To add more complications to the topic of "theme," you may hear the word used in a related, but different, context to talk about novels. A series of novels set in a specific town in North Carolina can be said to have a common theme. So can romantic murder mysteries link crimes to food recipes, or historical novels that feature different kinds of pets. This usage is much like the word *theme* in "theme park."

In contrast, *messages* are the more concrete concepts that you believe—and that you hope readers will accept after they've finished your novel. The chief message we wanted *Little White Lies* to deliver is that Christians should recognize that the so-called "harmless" lies they tell so freely can have lethal consequences, to themselves and to others. Readers tend to "get" messages more than they do themes.

Don't worry too much about keeping theme and message separate in your mind; they often overlap. This can happen when theme is especially prominent in a story and is similar to the principal takeaway—the most important message—of the novel. A good example is a theme behind many evangelistic novels: "Sinners find it difficult to gain salvation by trusting Jesus Christ as their Lord and Savior." Often the principal message is a variation on this theme: "A sinner gains salvation by trusting Jesus Christ as his or her Lord and Savior."

# Finding a Meaningful Theme

Many writers let theme happen automatically; they don't intentionally think about theme. I prefer to identify theme early in the writing process, because even a partially developed theme can be a handy filter that helps me determine many different facets of my novel, from title, to character names and personalities, to plot details, to scene locations, to the tone of the dialogue. I'll illustrate once again with *Little White Lies*.

We began the novel with a heroine—Pippa Hunnechurch, a British-born "head-hunter" (executive recruiter) living and working in Maryland—and a simple idea: many of the job hunters submitting resumés to Pippa would lie about their accomplishments and credentials. A popular resumé falsehood in the real world is claiming a university degree that was never earned. (Our working title was *An English Trifle*, although neither of us remember why.)

Our initial theme was fairly vague: we told members of our critique group that our novel was about the problems caused by people who told lies on their resumés. But even this loosey-goosey theme gave us useful guidance:

**It Is Written …**

I start my novels with theme. [Many authors] probably say they start with "character," but I find myself much more interested in exploring ideas as they relate to people, so I start with the ideas and make up people and situations to fit what I want to think about.

—Athol Dickson, Christian novelist

- ◆ We invented several characters who might feel the need to lie on their resumés.

- ◆ We devised a motive for a murder that flowed from a deceitful resumé.

- ◆ We figured out how Pippa might "accidentally" find out that she had been lied to by a really promising client.

- ◆ We created several excuses that different clients might offer to explain why they submitted falsified resumés.

- ◆ We thought about different ways Pippa might react when faced with a client who lied to her.

**It Is Written …**

I never think in terms of "theme." It's my readers (and sometimes my editors) who seem to enjoy pointing out the "themes" in my stories. I don't deliberately attempt to weave themes or "messages" into any of my books. My sole purpose is to tell a good story about interesting people—to depict their struggles and their successes, their trials and their tragedies, their frustrations and their overcomings. … If certain themes come into play, it's not because of anything I've planned.

—B. J. Hoff, Christian novelist

As we moved ahead, our story developed and so did our theme. About one third through the novel, we realized that our initial idea to have clients submit resumés that contained heavy-duty falsehoods wasn't quite right. We decided that our story would be far more interesting if the lies clients told were minor exaggerations about their experience and past successes. After all, few people are willing to invent phony college degrees, but most of us have no problem telling "harmless" little white lies about ourselves.

Our new working theme—otherwise honest people will tell "harmless" lies on their resumés to get ahead—immediately triggered a barrage of new content for the novel:

- A scene in the beginning of the story where Pippa herself benefits from a little white lie

- Improved dialogue as major characters justify the telling of "harmless" little white lies

- A scene that has Pippa telling a "harmless" lie to a police detective

- Pippa's strategies for identifying the killer and for turning the tables on the clients who told her little white lies

- And, of course, the final title: *Little White Lies*

Interestingly, we wrote two other Pippa Hunnechurch novels based on a common series theme—the power of minor sins to cause major grief. *The Second Mile* (we originally planned to call it *Good Enough for Government Work*) examined the problem of doing an adequate job, rather than a thorough job. *Humble Pie* showed how "harmless" pride could have fatal consequences.

# Delivering the Message

When Sam Goldwyn, the famed moviemaker, was asked his opinion of "message movies," he purportedly answered, "If you want to send a message, call Western Union." Novelists often receive similar advice. A workshop leader at a writers' conference I attended a decade ago said, "If you have something you're burning to say, stand on a soapbox in the park—don't write a novel and bore readers silly."

The problem, of course, is that messages in novels are often delivered clumsily, in ways that shatter fictional dreams and exasperate readers. This was certainly true of the Christian messages in many early Christian novels. They were tacked on—and blatantly apparent—like the spare tire holders on the backs of some SUVs. These days, editors expect the explicit Christian message in a Christian novel to be seamlessly integrated within the storyline. It should seem a completely natural component of the story—not an add-on or an afterthought.

## Messages on the Fly

I've heard many successful novelists say that the messages in their books emerge—and becomes clear—like people walking out of a fog, that they don't know the messages until this happens. I agree—with an important caveat. The *deeper* messages you'll deliver are often illusive—they won't show up until much of your novel is written. But as with theme, you should begin writing with a tentative message in mind and use it to guide your efforts while you're waiting to discover the "true" message embedded in your novel.

Building a message into a story may involve designing several parts of the plot to support your message. In *Little White Lies*, we had to "salt" the story with "harmless" lies that caused problems throughout the plotline, some in resumés and some in common business situations. We had to provide enough plausible examples that the reader would get the point—understand the message—without anyone preaching a sermon against little white lies at the end of the book.

 **A Lamp Unto Your Feet**

While most writers would like to begin a Christian novel with a clear Christian message in mind, things generally don't work that way. Rather, we spot the more significant messages as we develop the manuscript. This often means revising early work to strengthen the emerging message.

Doing this right requires some forethought. At the very least, a Christian novelist should figure out early in the process of writing a novel:

- ◆ The tentative Christian message his or her book will communicate to readers
- ◆ Whether the message will be a major component part of the main plot, built into the novel as a subplot, or conveyed "incidentally" throughout the story

I urge even "seat-of-the-pants" writers (who don't outline their stories) to take the time to research and develop a coherent, scripturally sound Christian message—and figure out the best way to deliver it. I say that because I suspect that a novelist who can wait for a message to materialize along with a storyline has a rock-solid grasp of Biblical theology. The rest of us need to help the process along because the explicit Christian message in a Christian novel is too important to leave to chance.

## Walk by Faith and Rely on God's Grace

In Chapter 1, I described the spectrum of spirituality you can incorporate into your Christian novel. I suggest you reread the examples as an introduction to the following brief discussion about specific message content.

When Janet and I decided to write Christian fiction, we began to catalog the explicit Christian messages we found in the novels we read. We expected to see a broad range of messages that spanned the different pronouncements of Christianity—from love your neighbor, to feed the poor, to go and make disciples throughout the world. We discovered instead that two short phrases could summarize most of the messages we studied: *walk by faith* and *rely on God's grace*.

*Walk by faith* encapsulates much of the Gospel in three words. It urges nonbelievers to become believers; it tells "cultural Christians" to reaffirm that Christ is their Lord and Savior; it encourages believers to deepen their relationship with Jesus. In short, trust in the living Christ and the promises he has made. These, of course, are fundamental teachings of Christianity that have long been at the core of evangelistic sermonizing.

*Rely on God's grace* encompasses a surprisingly large variety of messages aimed chiefly at believing Christians (or seekers who have some knowledge of Christianity):

- Accept God's grace alone for your salvation; "good works" are worthwhile because of the benefit they provide for others, not because they'll help you pay your way into heaven.

- *Let go* (of your own will), *let God* (take control your life).

- Abandon the guilt or shame that are holding you back.

- Understand that you a new creation, that your sinful past has been forgiven.

- Forgive those who trespass against you, in the same way that God forgives your trespasses against him.

- Recognize the truth of John 15:5: "Apart from me you can do nothing."

Now, I'm not suggesting that you must deliver a *walk by faith* or *rely on God's grace* message in your novel. Not all stories will support them. Rather, consider these phrases convenient starting points when you sit down to create your Christian message.

# Extracting Themes and Messages from Scripture

I've listened to many first-time novelists complain that they have difficulty generating explicit Christian themes and messages for their novels. I usually ask a simple question: Did you look inside your Bible? Their sheepish grins tell me that they didn't.

A "study Bible" with a concordance and extensive footnotes is a great resource for both themes and messages—especially a "Life Application Bible" that applies relevant biblical concepts to everyday challenges and situations.

Over the years, I've found another useful source of ideas for Christian themes and messages: the illustrations—the anecdotes—in sermons and other biblically based talks in church, during Bible studies, and during radio or TV broadcasts. I jot down illustrations and biblical references in the small black notebook I carry with me (the same notebook I use to capture plot ideas and descriptions of interesting people I see).

I also visit sermon websites designed for pastors (I've provided some links in Appendix A). You can download sample sermons, each one a self-contained "package" that expounds on Scripture, explains theology in everyday language, presents pertinent illustrations, reflects a popular theme, and includes a well-written message. A good sermon can be a wonderful source of inspiration and ideas when you plot a Christian novel.

# Plotting Your Christian Content

The explicit Christian content in your novel can be designed before you begin to write—much like the other aspects you outline at the start of the process. Although you can build Christian content into the main plot of your novel, there are two reasons why it's more productive to create a separate Christian subplot:

1. A defined subplot—a separate "Christian story"—will keep you focused on the essential requirement of delivering a relevant Christian message.

2. Building a complete subplot makes it easier to seamlessly integrate the Christian content within your storyline.

I'll illustrate my suggestion with the 13-point Christian subplot from *Dead as a Scone*, one of our cozy romantic mysteries set in England. My descriptions of the plot elements are somewhat longer than the brief summaries I recommended in Chapter 9, because I provided additional details to help you understand the subplot.

## 1. Set Up the Plot

Flick Adams, an American, is the new Chief Curator of the Royal Tunbridge Wells Tea Museum, in Kent, England. Nigel Owen is the British-born Acting Museum Director. Their ivory-towered world is upset when the museum's oldest trustee, Dame Elspeth Hawker, dies at a board meeting seemingly of natural causes. Her death means that most of the museum's collection of paintings, ceramics, maps, books, ship models, and other tea-related artifacts will be returned to her heirs.

Both Flick and Nigel describe themselves as Christians, but they don't consider themselves "religious." Both have drifted away from their childhood faith; neither has been inside a church in years. They don't have a Christian worldview.

## 2. Make the Hero's Motivation Clear

Flick and Nigel are the only two people in England who believe that Dame Elspeth was murdered at the board meeting. They join forces to save the museum's collection of tea-related artifacts and also to solve the murder.

On the afternoon before she died, Dame Elspeth met with Nigel and told him that one of the trustees was "a clever thief." She also quoted a verse from the Bible that Nigel didn't pay any attention to, something about a crook repaying more than the amount he stole. Both Flick and Nigel recognize that the verse could be significant. But what did Elspeth say? They decide to find out, on the theory that it might be significant to their investigation.

## 3. Begin the Hero's Quest

Flick and Nigel use an Internet search engine to locate Bible verses that sound like the fragment that Nigel remembers. They finally settle on Exodus 22:7-8 as the verse Dame Elspeth spoke: "If a man gives his neighbor silver or goods for safekeeping and they are stolen from the neighbor's house, the thief, if he is caught, must pay back double."

The pair have no idea what Dame Elspeth meant when she quoted Exodus 22:7-8. Perhaps chatting with a Bible expert would help sort things out. They settle on an obvious choice: the Reverend William de Rudd, Vicar of St. Stephen's Church, in Tunbridge Wells, a member of the Board of Trustees.

## 4. Change the Hero's Direction

Flick and Nigel make a startling discovery when they visit Vicar de Rudd. He shows them a bronze plate that reads: "St. Stephen's Church is the gift of a thief who made every effort to pay back double." It turns out that Commodore Desmond Hawker founded the church during the final years of the nineteenth century. His favorite Bible verse was Exodus 22:7-8.

## 5. Challenge the Hero with Problems

Flick and Nigel realize that Commodore Desmond Hawker—the fabled nineteenth-century tea merchant—is somehow linked to his granddaughter's death early in the twentieth century. They begin to find out all they can about the commodore. The tea museum has extensive materials about his life and times, including many cartons of personal papers and effects stored in the tea museum's archives. They doubt any of these "account books and miscellaneous receipts" will be useful.

When the pair talk to St. Stephen's historian—a woman who had been a friend of Dame Elspeth—she shows them the manuscript of a biography of Desmond Hawker that the Hawker family had commissioned three decades earlier, but never allowed to be published. It affirmed that Desmond Hawker deserved his shoddy reputation as a nineteenth-century "robber baron," and hinted at a host of sins that Desmond Hawker committed against Neville Brackenbury, his original partner in the tea trade.

And yet toward the end of his life, Desmond apparently became a committed Christian. His many friends at St. Stephen's attested to the fact that Hawker turned his life over to God. Moreover, Desmond used the lion's share of his fortune to fund the charitable Hawker Foundation.

Nigel is willing to accept Desmond's late-in-life conversion, but Flick is skeptical. She knows that "business is war" and doubts that Christianity has the power to soften the hard heart of a wealthy businessman.

Flick visits the author of the unpublished biography (Philip Oxley, a professor of industrial history at Oxford University) and learns that Desmond cheated Neville Brackenbury. He allowed him to fall into bankruptcy because of other investments, and then bought his share of the partnership at a low price. Brackenbury subsequently committed suicide.

## 6. Change the Hero's Status

Oxley provides a truly startling bit of information: Desmond admitted, in letters he wrote near the end of life, to "stealing from Neville Brackenbury." The stolen goods include most of the collection of tea-related artworks that are currently on display at the museum.

Flick and Nigel are thrown for a loop. If Desmond acquired the artworks under false pretenses, who really owns the fabulous collection that's worth 40 million pounds? They need to know before the museum buys the artifacts from the Hawker heirs.

## 7. Give the Hero Tougher Problems

Flick and Nigel search for more information, but wherever they look, the evidence seems conclusive: Desmond Hawker behaved badly during his years as a tea merchant. Even Nigel begins to doubt that a man as wicked as Desmond could change stripes and become a sincere Christian.

## 8. Let the Hero Suffer Maximum Angst

Flick and Nigel find themselves troubled that their tea museum heaps honor after honor upon Commodore Desmond Hawker. One major display is a replica of his office, another details his many successes. Shouldn't the museum also describe the unsavory side of Desmond's accomplishments?

## 9. Offer the Hero a Transition

The pair realize that one key will unlock all of the mysteries about Desmond Hawker: they need to understand what happened late in his life to "push" Desmond toward Christianity. Everyone who knew Desmond Hawker is long dead; the only source of information about him are the voluminous records in the museum's archive. Nigel decides to launch a search.

## 10. Change the Hero's Direction

Nigel has an idea. Because he's looking for something away from routine correspondence, he browses through boxes of miscellaneous items, rather than Desmond's business files.

## 11. Give the Hero New Hope

Nigel strikes pay dirt. He finds a nineteenth-century copybook that Desmond intended for his son Basil. In it, Desmond explains his conversion to Christianity and repents for the sins he committed against his old partner.

After ruining Neville financially, Desmond agreed to make a "sham purchase" of Neville's prized artworks collection, to keep the items away from creditors. Neville received a tiny sum for the valuable collection, assuming that he would eventually buy it back from Desmond. But when the time came, Desmond refused to sell it back. Neville's bankruptcy and the loss of his prized collection eventually drove him to suicide.

As a sincere Christian, Desmond recognized the wrong he had done to his old partner and sought to make amends. Desmond tried to find Neville's family, but the detectives he hired were never able to locate them. Desmond asked his son Basil to continue the search—but Basil ignored the request.

## 12. Achieve a Win/Lose Conclusion

Although Desmond committed a despicable act, he did in fact buy the tea-related artwork from Neville Brackenbury. Consequently, his family does own the collection—and can sell it to the museum.

Desmond's sin echoed through the generations. One of the trustees was Neville's great-grandson. His "stealing back" of what he considered family property eventually led him to murder Dame Elspeth.

Both Nigel and Flick come to understand Desmond's transformation to a believing Christian. They acknowledge that he recognized his own sins, repented, and did the best he could to undo the damage he'd done. He did try to make restitution in part to the aggrieved family—but despite his best efforts, he failed.

## 13. Tie Up the Loose Ends

Nigel and Flick, both impressed by the power of Christianity to change lives—and by Desmond's late-in-life return to Christianity—decide that they will start attending church once again.

Flick and Nigel are able to use the information they gathered to identify the murderer.

# Maintain a Consistent Christian Worldview

As a Christian novelist writing Christian fiction, you will write from a Christian worldview. That means that Christian values should circumscribe *good* and *bad* throughout your novel. Not surprisingly, this doesn't always happen automatically. I described the concept of worldview in Chapter 1. Worldviews tend to be complex; few of us are uniformly Christian in our outlook, which can lead to confusing inconsistencies in the behavior of some characters.

Writing from a Christian worldview means that Christian characters should honor biblical principles in everything they do—not merely in what they say in dialogue. They can't switch back and forth between Christian and secular worldviews. And that can easily happen if you don't pay close attention to your story.

In a first submitted draft of one of our older cozy mysteries, for example, Janet and I had a scene in which a lead character who had returned to being a committed Christian engaged in deception to help advance the plot. Our editor pointed out the inconsistency. The character's behavior—her boldface lying—didn't match her recent profession of faith. We realized that our editor had made a great catch: our secular plot solution had overpowered our novel's Christian worldview when we wrote the scene in question. We'd focused on the technical details of resolving a story issue and ignored the potentially negative message that our solution sent to readers. Naturally, we revised the story to eliminate our character's less-than-Christian behavior. Not doing so might have confused many readers—and sent the wrong message to many others.

My point is, don't assume that everything you think—and write—will inevitably reflect a Christian worldview. Pay close attention to the small things you allow characters to do.

## The Least You Need to Know

- If you can, identify Christian theme and Christian messages early in the writing process.

- Theme is the unifying idea of your novel—it may not be apparent to readers.

- Messages are more concrete concepts that you believe, and that you want readers to take away from your novel.

- Scripture and sermons are good places to find Christian themes and messages.

- Take care to not send conflicting messages by accident.

# Part 3

# Sitting Down to Write Christian Fiction

Now that you know the essential ingredients of a publishable Christian novel, you must sit down and actually write one. Many people have described the writing of a full-length novel as one of the most difficult tasks a person can undertake. It is tedious, hard work—that offers no guarantees of success should you actually finish your manuscript.

Over the years, many successful novelists have been quoted as saying, "I don't enjoy writing; I enjoy having written." It's not surprising that so many hopeful authors start writing novels but never finish them—including many Christian novelists who feel called to write Christian fiction.

This part details the nitty-gritty aspects of writing Christian fiction, from getting the most out of a Christian writers' conference to dealing with the darker aspects of authoring a novel—including your jealousy when other writers succeed faster than you do, and the "bad behavior" you may run into among Christians you meet during your novel-writing journey.

# Chapter 13

# When You Start to Write Your Novel ...

## In This Chapter

- ◆ Start each writing session with a prayer
- ◆ Finding the right place to write
- ◆ Mastering the essential tools of the trade
- ◆ Does creative-writing software help?
- ◆ What to do when you don't want to write
- ◆ Keep your developing story to yourself

You've finished your planning. You have a great story in mind and a blank page on your word processor. The time has come start writing your Christian novel.

Before you dive in, consider the practical recommendations I've gathered together in this chapter. They represent a potpourri of suggestions for writing Christian fiction—a collection of proven ideas that I've found useful over the years.

# Don't Forget to Pray

I often do. And then I remember the vast creative power I haven't taken advantage of. Here's a simple prayer that I speak before I write:

> Lord ... I thank You for the opportunity to be a writer of Christian fiction, and for the creativity that I know comes from You.
>
> I humbly ask You to be my guide and my counselor as I sit down to write. Focus my mind and heart on the story You want me to tell and help me ignore the many minor distractions that will otherwise interrupt my writing. Give me the strength to do the hard work of crafting fiction, the commitment to finish the novel I've begun, and the patience to wait upon Your timing.
>
> Finally, Lord, don't let me fall into pridefullness, jealousy, or envy. Help me deal with the disappointment and rejection that may accompany my efforts. And never let me forget that everything I write is for Your Glory.

I won't presume to advise you how or when to pray, but I will point out that Christian novelists have lots to pray about. Writing a novel is a complicated endeavor, with many different aspects, and countless ingredients that could benefit from God's providential oversight.

As Christian fiction writers, we should pray for the obvious:

- Writing that honors God's name and serves His purpose
- Inspiration
- Wisdom
- Discernment
- Patience
- Charity
- Fortitude to keep writing
- Elimination of any jealousy or pride
- Freedom from crippling self-doubt
- Effective use of the time we dedicate to writing Christian fiction

But there are lots of other concerns that deserve prayer. I've known a writer who prayed for quietude (so she could get over the panic of a close deadline), and another who asked for courage (he planned to pitch his novel at an upcoming writers' conference), and yet another who needed additional strength to throw away several flawed chapters and begin her novel again.

Do first-time novelists ever pray for an amiable agent, a friendly editor, or a publishing contract? *Hmmm* ... that's the first silly question you asked since you started reading this book!

# An Inspirational Place to Write

Novelists can be a funny bunch of folks. That's "funny" as in strange, rather than ha-ha. *Where* we write fiction can play an important role in our ability to write well. We seem to work best in a writing space that reflects our personality. I have no idea why this is true, but it appears to be a universal phenomenon that impacts both secular and Christian novelists. Consequently, when interviewers question published novelists of either stripe, they often ask them to describe their writing spaces. The answers authors give are as varied as the novels they write:

- ◆ "I need to be surrounded by inspirational objects that stimulate my creativity."
- ◆ "I can't write unless it's absolutely quiet."
- ◆ "I can't write unless I'm listening to music."
- ◆ "I have to be able to look out a window every now and then and see the world outside."
- ◆ "I prefer working with the blinds closed; that way I don't have any distractions."
- ◆ "I do my best work on the subway, going back and forth to my day job."
- ◆ "I write faster and more efficiently in my office—I guess I'm a creature of habit."
- ◆ "My 'writing space' is anywhere I plunk my laptop."

Virginia Woolf, the twentieth-century English author, wrote: "A woman must have ... a room of her own if she is to write fiction." I've met many Christian novelists of both sexes who proved Virginia wrong. If you're lucky enough to have an extra room you can commandeer as a writing space, grab it. But don't lament the fact that you have to share a guestroom, or work in the corner of your bedroom, or use an area carved out of a basement or attic.

Ad hoc writing spaces like these have accommodated the writing of thousands of published Christian novels. Square footage and privacy are only two of the criteria you should consider when you establish a comfortable writing environment:

◆ Adequate lighting is a must to limit eyestrain—a large computer monitor can help, too.

◆ Good ventilation and temperature control are important to help keep you awake and alert.

◆ Your writing space needs sufficient AC outlets to handle your computer and all the devices connected to it.

◆ A bulletin board or a marker board is handy for posting reminder notes and for organizing your story if you use the popular plotting technique of jotting down each scene on a three-inch by five-inch file card.

◆ Use any convenient table or desk, but buy an *ergonomic* chair, if you can afford one—back and neck strain caused by long hours working at a computer are common. An ergonomic chair has many different adjustments to "personalize" lower back support, raise arms to the right height, and the neck at a proper angle—all to reduce back and neck strain.

> **Chapter and Verse**
>
> **Ergonomics,** also called "human factors engineering," is the application of scientific information about humans to the design of objects for human use.

If you can, make your writing space permanent. You don't want to waste time setting up and taking down equipment. Perhaps even more important, a permanent writing space makes a statement to your family and friends: "I'm committed to writing Christian fiction. Here's where I plan to do it."

# Getting Away from It All

Nowhere is it written that you must write at home. The rapidly falling cost of laptop computers gives writers many other options—both permanent and part-time.

## Join a "Writer's Room"

Urban writers (translation: city-dwelling novelists who live in small apartments) are often writing-space challenged. A clever solution is a "writer's room"—a writer's space for rent in a facility that provides other amenities, including a kitchen, a lounge, Internet access, printers, possibly a reference library, and last but not least a built-in community of other writers.

The typical writer's space in a writer's room facility is a comfortable cubicle. These days, most renters bring their own laptops, but some facilities provide desktop computers.

Prices vary significantly in different parts of the country—from less than $100 per month to several hundred. Some writer's spaces also charge an initiation fee. Many offer both full-time and part-time memberships.

## Write in Coffee Bars

Writing in coffee bars is fast becoming a tradition among Christian writers. A coffee bar is a neutral environment, not especially noisy, with few natural distractions. The other long-term denizens are likely to be college students doing homework and studying for exams.

Several Christian novelists have told me that the atmosphere is conducive to writing and that if you choose the right table, you can even plug your laptop into a power socket. Writers who find the minimal background noise bothersome can connect noise-canceling headphones to their MP3 players and listen to gentle music while they work.

Some coffee bars don't mind if you don't buy anything. Others consider buying a cup of coffee now and then as the price of admission. In either case, the cost of a coffee-bar writing space is fairly modest: less than a few dollars a day. The most serious occupational hazard seems to be the danger of eating too many fattening snacks.

## Try a Writer's Retreat

To *really* get away from it all, go off on a secluded writer's retreat and be alone with your thoughts. You can find them on the Internet (search for "writer's retreat") and advertised in writing magazines. Most are secular, but welcome Christian novelists. You can choose retreats as short as a weekend or as long as a month or two. Some retreats provide a quiet place to work—often with the chance to chat with other writers after a day of writing. Others present the kind of workshops you'll find at a writers' conference.

**Literary Sins** _____

When you choose a retreat, make certain that it provides the resources you need to work on your novel. Many don't offer Internet access, a significant shortcoming if you plan to do research while on retreat.

A writer's retreat can be especially useful when you're planning your novel and have several plotting problems to resolve in your mind. Getting far, far away from your usual routine can give you the time, energy, and inspiration to "sort out" your storyline.

Prices vary significantly, because some retreats are little more than isolated cabins atop a mountain, while others are more resortlike in nature.

## Check Into a Motel or Hotel

A week at a motel—away from family and telephones—can be the writing equivalent of a runner's sprint to the finish line. I know several Christian novelists who check into a convenient motel as they near the end of their novels. They use the concentrated time alone to finish and fine-tune their manuscripts. The approach seems to work especially well for busy homemakers.

# Master Your Tools of the Trade

As a Christian novelist in the twenty-first century, it's absolutely essential that you own a good computer, a competent word processing program that's compatible with Microsoft Word (the file format most publishers require), have high-speed Internet access, and possess comprehensive computing and word processing skills. By "comprehensive," I mean that you are comfortable doing critical writing-relevant tasks on your computer. Here are a few non-negotiable computing skills:

- Create, edit, and reformat documents
- Type content into documents
- Use document reviewing features
- Print documents
- Send and receive documents via e-mail
- Set up folders and directories on your computer
- Copy documents to different folders and directories
- Copy documents to backup devices such as USB flash drives and USB hard-disk drives
- Use an e-mail client (such as Outlook) and a web browser (such as Internet Explorer or Safari)

## Does Anything on This List Sound Unfamiliar?

There's no way to bypass these requirements, although a few Christian novelists trapped in the 1980s try to. Computing skills have become as important to a writer as good grammar and spelling. Not having them will cut you off from many agents, most publishers, virtually all other Christian writers, and a universe of research and networking resources. If you lack confidence in your computing abilities, sign up for appropriate courses at your local community college.

## Virus Protection and Backup

The contents of your computer steadily increase in value as you develop a novel. Imagine the costs—measured both in emotional damage and lost time—if a hard disk failure, virus attack, or other computer disaster destroyed your work. The solution is to do what professional information technology managers do: anticipate threats and provide disaster recovery capabilities. For most of us, that means:

- Installing effective antivirus and antispyware software and keeping them up-to-date

- Scrupulously backing up our work on external storage devices—USB flash drives and hard-disk drives

You may also want to consider sending your precious word processing files to an online backup storage service (I've listed a few in Appendix A). Keeping copies of your files in another location ensures that a local catastrophe—say a house fire—doesn't destroy months (or years) of work.

Speaking of "local catastrophes" ... not long ago, I accidentally tipped a cup of coffee into my trusty laptop—my *primary* computer—and fried the motherboard. The computer took less than seven seconds to die! Fortunately, the hard-disk drive escaped the deluge and I was able to reclaim all of my files by installing the drive in a similar computer. My point is that surprisingly mundane accidents can threaten your work. Backup everything you do—frequently!

# Taking Advantage of Higher Technology

I have a simple philosophy about technology: I'll use anything that helps me write better or more productively. That little phrase "helps me" is the key to my approach. I'll *try* gizmos and gadgets that other writers recommend, but I only *keep* high-tech products that make a difference in my writing. Here are two somewhat unusual products that I use every day (see Appendix A for specifics). Perhaps you'll also find them of value.

## Voice-to-Text Software

*Voice-to-text* software, also called *voice-recognition* software, lets you dictate your novel directly into a word processing program. At least, that's what they're supposed to do. I'd tried several different voice-to-text programs over the years, and I'd been disappointed every time. Most of the programs had low recognition accuracy; they captured ludicrously garbled versions of what I actually said. If a program did an acceptable job of capturing my words, I became the problem: I found it difficult to dictate good words into the microphone.

I'd written off voice recognition as a useful tool for novelists, until an accidental slip on the ice during the winter of 2006 forced me to take a fresh look. My right arm was broken, I couldn't type single-handed, and the deadline for one of our cozy mysteries was less than four months away.

Reluctantly, I gave a new voice-to-text program a try. Dragon NaturallySpeaking "Preferred" proved more than accurate enough to do the job and my fast-approaching deadline gave me the motivation I needed to get ahead of the voice-recognition learning curve. It took me only a week to gain confidence, shake my discomfort of thinking aloud rather than on paper, and master the technique of dictating fiction.

> ### A Lamp Unto Your Feet
>
> I find that the single biggest problem with voice-recognition software are hard-to-spot errors that don't trigger my word processor's grammar or spelling checkers. For example, the program occasionally types "in" when I say "and," and "collar" when I say "dollar." The program continually learns, so repetitive errors tend to go away over time.

In what seemed no time at all, I was cheerfully inputting scenes and chapters via voice-recognition. I found it useful to keep my one available hand on the mouse as I spoke. That way, I could move the cursor quickly to any spot on the screen, then use my microphone to change words or speak new ones.

That's still a way I work today: I've developed my own blend of traditional typing and voice-to-text input. I find that using voice recognition software can significantly increase the speed of my writing. Simply put, speaking is faster than typing for me—some days a remarkable three times faster.

I use NaturallySpeaking now for much of my writing. It has an accuracy rate of better than 95 percent—if I help the software along in three ways:

1. Keep my voice well lubricated by drinking iced tea or another soft drink while I'm working.

2. Capture my voice with a high-quality USB microphone, not a cheap microphone that plugs into the standard microphone port.

3. Speak clearly, but not too slowly, making an effort to enunciate each word.

The complete package—software plus a USB microphone—costs about $200.

## Text-to-Voice Software

Software that "reads" your writing aloud can be just as useful as voice recognition software. I use a program called TextAloud to read each chapter of a novel that I finish. This is the best way I've found to spot clumsy language, grammatical errors, point-of-view problems, and generally sloppy writing.

Text-to-voice programs are much less expensive than voice recognition software—most cost less than $30, and some are actually available for free. Many software developers offer free trials. I went through several programs until I found one that sounded more or less like a real person reading my manuscript aloud. You usually get to choose among several different voices. I paid extra for Crystal, a pleasant female voice developed by AT&T. I enjoy sitting back in my chair, listening to Crystal read my latest writing.

Keep in mind that even the most sophisticated text-to-voice programs will have slips of the tongue when they speak unusual character names, complex place names, and other uncommon words. They also can be fooled by the kind of punctuation used in most novels. Nonetheless, listening to your computer read your book aloud is a startlingly effective means to hear your own authorial voice and identify writing problems you might otherwise miss.

## Software That Helps You Write

Hope springs eternal in the hearts of novelists. Maybe using a new computer program will help me plot a story that finally sells. Perhaps the latest creative-writing software can give me a leg up on other authors who crank out similar novels. The skinny on these programs is that some writers find them helpful—especially when they are learning the craft of writing fiction—but none of programs can replace your little gray cells when it comes to inventing a plot, creating intriguing characters, refining a storyline, or conceiving Christian messages.

My own experience with creative-writing software goes back to the early 1990s. The early programs I used back then asked lots of plotting questions, then organized the answers in a format that "regurgitated" a detailed story line. The results were useful to the extent that you answered the questions accurately and creatively. I quickly discovered that a tentative plotline was only the first step of writing a novel. The software didn't help me write dialogue, or describe characters, or come up with snappy magic paragraphs. In short, I was on my own when the writing began.

My advice to participants of writers' conferences who ask about creative-writing software is this: By all means, give it a try. See if it helps you write more effectively. But choose programs that come with money-back guarantees—or that let you try before you buy.

**It Is Written ...**

I don't want a machine telling me what my characters can and cannot do. My characters are people in my head, and sometimes they're even based on people in my life. I can't imagine any computer being able to predict what I'm going to do next, because I don't even know most of the time.

—Hannah Alexander, Christian novelist

# Help! I Don't Want to Write!

More than one Christian novelist has described sitting in front of a computer day after day writing a novel as a torment worthy of hell. I know the feeling well. I agree with Dorothy Parker, the witty writer and poet, who said, "I hate writing; I love having written."

Frankly, I'm always surprised to meet writers who tell me how easy it is to write fiction, how much they love turning out a new scene. For me, every sentence is hard, grueling work. Consequently, I've become adept at finding good excuses to stop writing—at least for a few minutes, if possible for a full day.

## Good Excuses Are the Worst Kind

If you want to be a published novelist, you must keep writing despite the good reasons not to and the diverse distractions that eat up your time. You can't *not* do things like research, or playing with your kids, or going shopping, or cooking dinner. But you also have to work in enough writing each day to keep your manuscript moving ahead.

The real danger is that accepting too many good excuses in a row will shift you far enough away from fiction writing that you never return to your novel. The discipline of writing *something* every day, no matter how little, no matter how busy you are, will keep you going. A high-risk milestone is 10 percent into a first novel—say, Page 35 of the manuscript. The snappy beginning is over, the motivated protagonist is beginning his or her long quest, the writing seems harder to do, and doubts creep in about the plot. The story seems dull. Who *cares* what the heroine wants? She's such a whiner, anyway!

Get used to it. You'll probably have the same feelings as you pass every major plot point (see Chapter 9). I do—with every novel. You have to recognize these potholes on your writing journey for what they are, and move past them. There are times when you won't believe you'll ever finish your novel. That's when the good excuses to stop writing look the best—but are the worst. Deal with them accordingly.

> **It Is Written ...**
>
> Writing is easy: All you do is sit staring at a blank sheet of paper until drops of blood form on your forehead.
>
> —Gene Fowler (1890–1960) American journalist, author, and screenwriter

## Eschew the "Time Sponges"

I can't remember the last time I typed "eschew," but it's the perfect word to use in a discussion about time-sponges. Eschew means keep away from, shun, abstain—all the right verbs to apply to other activities that:

◆ Have nothing to do with family, job, church, household, or civic responsibilities.

◆ Consume hard-won time from your busy schedule that you've managed to save explicitly for the purpose of writing your novel.

Time sponges are a lot like good excuses. They *seem* like sensible things for a writer to spend time doing. For example, blogging, writing long responses to your writing loops, writing and posting book reviews, and participating in "social networks" on the Internet all can be worth doing—unless you are pressed for time. Then, writing your novel is more important. Take a break from the time sponges until you finish your manuscript.

## Keep Your Story to Yourself

There are two kinds of novelists in the world: those who wisely refuse to talk about a work in progress, and those who are willing to try. If you are part of the second group, I advise you to fight the urge.

Attempting to share your story with other people—be they members of your writing group, family, or friends—usually is impossible until after you've created a good elevator speech (see Chapter 22). There are three reasons why:

1. You can *tell* a story, but you can rarely describe one briefly.

2. Your story isn't done until the printing press begins to run. Everything you write along the way is subject to change, so why talk about a story that's not ready for prime time?

3. When you discover that you can't describe your story, you may lose confidence in it—it may suddenly seem less interesting, less worthy of your time.

When people asked Janet and me about our first novel, we'd say, "We're writing a story about an English headhunter working in the United States. She runs into problems when a client commits resumé fraud." No names, no places, no story details—just enough information to get the listener to nod and say, "That's interesting."

## The Least You Need to Know

- Pray when you write fiction (you know why and how).

- Choosing the right place to write may help you write more effectively. Also consider getting away from it all to a writer's retreat or even a motel.

- Your computer and word processing software are your two most important tools of your trade; master them! Don't forget to back up your work diligently, and consider protecting your files against local disasters.

- Give creative-writing software a try—but look for programs that offer money-back guarantees or that let you try before you buy.

- Eschew the good excuses and time sponges that keep you away from writing fiction.

- Keep your story to yourself until it's done.

# Chapter 14

# Improve Your Craft at Christian Writers' Conferences

## In This Chapter

- ◆ The major national Christian writers' conferences
- ◆ What you'll gain from participating
- ◆ Getting the most from your conference
- ◆ Entering conference writing contests
- ◆ Getting your manuscript evaluated
- ◆ The pros and cons of secular writers' conferences

Ask a successful Christian novelist where he or she learned to write publishable fiction, and you're likely to hear: "I learned the basics of my craft at a Christian writers' conference." In fact, Christian writers' conferences excel in three important areas:

1. Offering workshops and seminars that teach you the nuts and bolts of writing fiction.

2. Allowing you to spend time with a group of like-minded Christian writers who will provide encouragement and inspiration—and help you overcome the many obstacles on the journey to completing a full-length novel.

3. Giving you a unique opportunity to pitch your completed manuscript to the agents and editors who attend writers' conferences to discover talented new writers.

Because a writers' conference can be useful to you both before and after you complete a manuscript, I've broken my discussion of conference-going into two chapters. This one will teach you how to take advantage of the educational opportunities. Chapter 22 zeroes in on pitching your finished manuscript to the agents and editors who attend major conferences.

# The Leading Christian Writers' Conferences

You have dozens of Christian writers' conferences to choose among. You'll find a complete list in the *Christian Writers' Market Guide* by Sally Stuart (see Appendix A). Most are local or regional conferences that will attract fewer than a hundred participants. A few are major national conferences that typically attract 350 to 450 participants each year (see Appendix A for details and websites ):

- ◆ **American Christian Fiction Writers Conference.** Usually held in September at a different venue each year, in a different region of the country.

- ◆ **Blue Ridge Mountain Christian Writers Conference.** Usually held in May at the Lifeway Ridgecrest Conference Center, near Asheville, North Carolina.

- ◆ **Glorieta Christian Writers' Conference.** Usually held in October at the LifeWay Glorieta Christian Conference Center, near Santa Fe, New Mexico.

- ◆ **Mt. Hermon Christian Writers Conference.** Usually held in late March or early April at the Mt. Hermon Christian Camps and Conference Center, near Santa Cruz, California.

- ◆ **Writing for the Soul Conference.** Usually held in February at the Broadmoor Hotel, in Colorado Springs, Colorado.

- ◆ **Write! Canada.** Canada's national Christian writers' conference. About half the size of its U.S. cousins; held in late spring in Guelph, Ontario.

Local conferences usually fill a single day or possibly a weekend. National conferences span three or four days. For example, Blue Ridge Mountain begins on a Sunday evening and ends on a Thursday at noon.

When you add in the cost of transportation, national conferences are not inexpensive—attending one can easily cost more than a thousand dollars, including room and meals. But they provide a different perspective than a local or regional event. You'll find more participants like yourself, a much larger selection of workshops and courses, and (probably) many more agents, editors, and published novelists.

> **A Lamp Unto Your Feet**
>
> If finances are a challenge, ask if the writers' conference you want to attend offers scholarships. Most of the national conferences have scholarship programs. Some conferences will allow a few participants to work during the conference to pay for their tuition.

# The Payoffs of Participation

For most unpublished novelists, the biggest payoff of attending a Christian writers' conference is learning critical fiction-writing skills. The workshops and courses are practical sessions taught mostly by working writers, agents, and editors. They understand the challenges you face—and the kinds of teaching you need—because many have been where you are on the learning curve a few years earlier.

The courses and workshops available at the larger conferences span all aspects of writing a novel—from research to self-editing. Many apply to any novel, some to popular genres (romance, suspense, women's fiction, and others; see Chapter 6). You'll probably find published novelists—including conference instructors—attending the hands-on workshops with you. They're there to refresh and hone their own writing skills.

## Recharging Your Batteries

Don't sell inspiration short. Writing a novel is a solitary endeavor, often filled with disappointment: unmet personal goals, painful comments at critique groups, baffling periods of writer's block, and unhappy self-evaluation of our manuscripts. Attending a Christian writers' conference can rekindle your enthusiasm for writing and restore your determination to finish your novel.

You'll meet writers like yourself who face the same difficulties you do. You'll hear speakers who've conquered these very challenges to writing publishable fiction—and must keep overcoming them with every new project they tackle. Both can provide the spark of encouragement you need to push ahead.

## Making New Friends and Networking

The thing I like most about attending a Christian writers' conference is spending a few days among a group of people who have the same interests and objectives as me. For three or four days, I'm immersed in a highly supportive environment, where I don't have to explain my "nutty" resolve to spend hours a day in front of a computer, writing proposals that may never be bought and book chapters that may never be published.

You're likely to make new friends at a writers' conference and also to join mutually supportive networks of novelists who can help you take the next step in your career. One thing to keep in mind is that many novelists are introverted by nature. We tend to sit quietly during meals, and stand by ourselves at receptions. You may have to leave your comfort zone to engage other writers. It's definitely worth doing.

# Plan Every Day Before You Arrive at the Conference

A writers' conference is like an à la carte menu at a restaurant: You build your own meal, item by item. You have to select the individual workshops, ongoing courses, and special sessions you will attend. Some first-time conference attendees try to participate in almost everything—and create back-breaking schedules that have them running hither and yon across the conference venue. Anyway, there are usually several different courses and workshops presented during each hour of the day—so you must pick and choose.

Yes, it's important to get your money's worth out of a writers' conference. But be sure to leave time for fellowship with other attendees, for the devotionals that Christian conferences schedule, and for personal time to reflect on useful concepts you've learned. When I chat with first-timers at the conferences I attend, I suggest that they select a logical series of workshops that will support their writing goals during the coming year.

What are your near-term challenges? Do you need better plotting skills? Then sign up for a sequence of courses on dramatic structure and story development. Or have you hit a stone wall in the quality of your dialogue? Then attend the relevant workshops on character development and dialogue writing.

As you've probably discovered, writing a novel requires you to juggle many tasks—to keep all of them in the air simultaneously. Each course or workshop will help you deal with one fictive "ball."

## Zero In on Instructors Who'll Teach You Best

With apologies to the agents, editors, and writing teachers who participate at Christian writers' conferences, I believe that published Christian novelists lead the most productive workshops and teach the most useful courses on the practical aspects of writing Christian fiction. The genre they write in is not important, unless you seek advice about a particular genre. For example, I often lead "generic" workshops on plotting and point of view (topics I cover in Chapters 9 and 10 of this book). The techniques I teach apply to all genres—they are not limited to the cozy romantic mysteries Janet and I write.

If you can, plan ahead and check out the teaching skills of instructors at the writers' conference you will attend. Published Christian novelists take on teaching chores with the best intentions; most of us want to help fledgling writers develop their skills. Unfortunately, life—and book deadlines—can get in the way. Several advertised instructors are likely to drop out in the days before a conference begins.

You'll find that some workshop leaders are better prepared than others, that some teachers of ongoing courses do a more thorough job of organizing their materials. A good way to learn the strengths and weaknesses of a particular instructor is via one of the Internet writing "loops" (e-mail lists) you belong to. Don't ask a direct question on the loop; the instructor may be a loop participant and take offense. Rather, find out who has attended the conference in recent years and strike up private e-mail conversations with those members.

**A Lamp Unto Your Feet**

If you browse around, you're likely to find your favorite Christian authors teaching fiction workshops at a writers' conferences. Note, however, that well-known writers often teach advanced courses that require prequalification or preregistration. Some of these offerings may be limited to published novelists. Check the sign-up requirements before you sign up for the conference.

## Check Out the Participants

Not surprisingly, the kinds of participants you interact with at a writers' conference can strongly impact what you take away from the conference. Some conferences attract a flood of beginning writers who seek to learn the basics of writing a novel. Others draw writers with almost-finished manuscripts who are preparing to pitch their work to agents and editors.

A beginning writer surrounded by experienced writers may become overwhelmed; a soon-to-be-published writer may feel out of place in a crowd of beginners. Mismatches limit a participant's ability to share experiences with his or her peers. Equally important, instructors and workshop leaders tend to shape their content to fit the "average" participant. A nonaverage attendee will probably not be happy with the curricula.

Finding other participants at your writing level can be more of a challenge at local writers' conferences. The larger national conferences usually have parallel "tracks" for beginning and experienced writers, and will attract a broad spectrum of writers. Here again, check with people who have attended your conference in the past. And don't be shy: ask the organizers of the conference about the participants before you plunk down your money.

## Make Sure the Right Editors Attend

You may not be ready to pitch a manuscript to an editor, but you can learn valuable things by listening to what he or she says. If you're still developing a manuscript, the kind of useful information an editor can provide includes the following:

◆ Length requirements for different genres

◆ Industry trends (such as which genres are hot, and which are not)

◆ Insights into the gatekeeping process (for example, the role of the publishing committee and marketing team in deciding to accept or reject a manuscript; see Chapter 5)

◆ What the editor looks for in a submitted manuscript (is authorial voice more important than a good story, or vice versa?)

**Wisdom and Knowledge**

You can pick up many valuable publishing insights from experienced novelists who keep track of industry goings-on. These are the people who teach most of the courses and workshops; they often have a less rigid appointment schedule than agents or editors, and may be easier to find and talk to.

Listen closely to any editor you talk to, but take into account that magazine editors are not book editors, and that nonfiction editors are not fiction editors—although some have experience in both areas. You'll learn the most from experienced fiction editors who currently work at major publishing companies. In these times of tight publishing company budgets, the most experienced fiction editors are more likely to attend major national Christian writers' conferences, rather than the smaller regional conferences.

## Speak to Agents, Too

The single most useful question I asked an agent before I was published is this: "What are the top five reasons you reject manuscripts?" The answer I got was:

1. "The manuscript doesn't fit a specific genre."

2. "The storyline didn't grab me."

3. "The manuscript is full of point-of-view errors."

4. "The dialogue is insipid."

5. "The writer has a weak authorial voice."

6. "I lost interest after the first page."

I know, I know—there are six reasons on the list. The agent became so enthusiastic that she threw in an extra fatal flaw.

Like you, I had read about the importance of doing these things right. But hearing the list from an agent made me take them more seriously. That's why I encourage you to buttonhole a friendly agent and ask the same question.

## Choose a Location That Suits You

You can find good Christian writers' conferences in every region of the country. This has become even more important as the price of transportation has increased. These days, the airfare to travel to a national conference can easily exceed the cost of attending the conference.

You can also choose urban or rustic settings—depending on your personal preference. I've discovered by talking with many participants that location can make a difference in how much people enjoy a writers' conference. First, there's a simple matter of comfort. If wide-open spaces make you antsy, don't choose a conference in the desert. Second, you may find more writers like yourself at a location you favor.

## Strike a Good Balance in Kinds of Writing

Only one of the major national Christian writers' conferences focuses solely on fiction: the conference sponsored by American Christian Fiction Writers, an organization of published and unpublished Christian novelists. Several local conferences also specialize in fiction writing.

Most conferences—national and local—encompass all manner of Christian writing, from poetry, to devotionals, to nonfiction magazines and books, to Christian curriculum, to novels.

Which should you attend? Actually, that's a tough question to answer.

On the one hand, a fiction-only conference will give you more fiction-relevant workshops and courses. It's likely to have beginning, intermediate, and advanced writing tracks, and will probably cover every significant Christian genre.

On the other hand, many well-known Christian novelists fine-tuned their craft at broad-based writers' conferences. You can learn many useful things in workshops devoted to other kinds of writing. To a great extent, good writing is good writing.

**A Lamp Unto Your Feet**

When you decide which courses and workshops to attend at a writers' conference, don't overlook noncraft offerings. Larger Christian conferences often have courses on such topics as time management, avoiding procrastination, and overcoming writer's block. If any of these issues are preventing you from finishing your novel, the techniques you'll learn could be life-changing.

For example, a well-taught workshop on the techniques of creative nonfiction will give you language skills that can be directly applied to a novel. And taking a course on writing poetry may improve your ability to turn a clever metaphor.

Having said that, you'll probably leave a writers' conference disappointed if it has too few fiction-related learning opportunities. This should never be a problem at one of the large national Christian writers' conferences—they all offer good selections of fiction workshops and courses. But if you're considering a local writers' conference, look closely at the teaching schedule. You may find only one fiction writer on the faculty, and one fiction workshop on the agenda.

## Don't Overlook the Facilities

Let me be charitable in phrasing this issue. Some Christian writers' conferences have "nicer" facilities—for teaching, for fellowship, for dining, and for sleeping—than others. The definition of *nicer*, of course, is highly subjective. But what you'll discover when you compare different conferences is that:

♦ Some are contained in a single hotel, while others require participants to travel throughout a multi-building conference facility.

♦ Some conferences require you to climb steep hills to walk from classrooms to dining halls to sleeping facilities.

- Some have participants sleep in facilities that resemble hotel rooms, others have simply equipped dormitories with paper-thin walls.

- Some serve gourmet food to participants, while others provide routine institutional cooking.

- Some have Internet access; some don't.

The quality of the food is certainly less important than the quality of the workshops at a Christian writers' conference—especially if you are on a tight budget. Nonetheless, three days of boring breakfasts can dampen the spirits. My point is that a Christian writers' conference represents a significant investment for an unpublished novelist. When you select a conference, look at all aspects of the experience that are important to you and choose accordingly.

## Talk to References

The national Christian writers' conferences have track records; thousands of people have attended them in recent years. It's easy to find past participants on Internet writing loops. Ask if they considered their investment money well spent. Get their opinions about the quality of workshops and instructors. Find out if they were able to apply what they learned effectively in their writing.

Many workshop instructors are also members of Internet writing loops. Ask for their thoughts. Explain where you are in your writing career; they'll be able to tell you if a particular writers' conference is right for you—and if not, which would be better.

# Writers' Workshop Contests

Most large writers' conferences have contests for different categories of writing, usually for a modest entry fee. There are several good reasons for entering:

- The contest may provide another opportunity to have your work evaluated— some contests provide feedback to losing entrants.

- The contest imposes an artificial deadline on you; it encourages you to finish a substantial piece of work by a certain date.

- A contest that has multiple categories may persuade you to try your hand at different genres—romance, suspense, or general fiction, for example.

◆ A winning entry—especially in the fiction category—will catch the attention of agents and editors at the conference.

◆ A win at a national writers' conference is a great "reference" in the query letters you write.

◆ Some conference contests pay cash awards or offer winners reduced fees at future conferences—someone's going to get a check, why not you?

# Manuscript Evaluations

Much of what I've said about contests applies to manuscript evaluations at writers' conferences. They can be worth their modest cost, if you take the feedback you receive with a large grain of salt. The single biggest problem is that the evaluator who reads your work may not be an expert in your genre. The evaluators are usually faculty members who have agreed to take on the extra chore of manuscript evaluation. Some may be editors and agents; most will be published writers. Conference organizers do their best to assign manuscripts to appropriate evaluators, but they don't always succeed. I say that with some confidence, because I've occasionally been asked to evaluate participant manuscripts in genres far from my own. Nonetheless, most evaluators will do their best to identify the generic weaknesses in your manuscript.

And therein lies a thornier problem. Some unpublished novelists who submit manuscripts at writers' conferences have daydreams of receiving glowing evaluations—pounds of praise for their writing and storylines, and recommendations that they immediately submit their work to agents. These writers may be disappointed, even disheartened, when reality strikes in the form of detailed critiques of their works' shortcomings.

It takes time to develop a thick skin; many writers never do. Some of the most successful Christian novelists I know ache when their books receive so-so reviews, or when readers send irate letters of complaint.

Remember, the chief purpose of a manuscript evaluation is to help you write publishable fiction. Don't be shocked if the critique you receive is full of criticism.

**Literary Sins**

A surprising number of contest entries and manuscripts submitted for evaluation are sloppy—full of typographical goofs, spelling errors, and grammar mistakes that inevitably cause judges and evaluators to reach for red pens. Take the time to proofread and edit your submission carefully; you never know if the person reading it can play a key role in advancing your career.

# The Joys of Secular Writers' Conferences

Janet and I credit a large secular writers' conference for giving us a jump-start in our careers as novelists. One particular workshop—on dramatic structure—helped us to understand storytelling. Another, on mystery writing, pointed me toward techniques for engaging the reader's imagination, including the magic paragraph (see Chapter 10). An excellent resource to learn about secular conferences is the online Shaw Guide to Writers' Conferences (http://writing.shawguides.com).

A few of the secular writers' conferences that Janet and I attended featured a different teaching paradigm. Rather than school-like courses, instructors invited participants to read their work aloud, then invited comments and suggestions from the other writers in the room. We enjoyed this approach—although you need to develop a thick skin to weather a barrage of criticism from a dozen different unpublished novelists. Keep in mind that the deeper the instructor (and often the class) delves into your work, the more you will learn.

However, there is a downside to secular conferences. The four major shortcomings for a Christian writer are:

1. Most participants will have different writing goals, which will limit fellowshipping and networking opportunities.

2. You won't meet many agents or editors who deal with or understand the Christian fiction marketplace.

3. Many of the other participants won't respect Christian fiction—although skyrocketing sales of Christian blockbusters have changed the opinion of many skeptical secular novelists.

4. Some of the participants may produce kinds of writing you find offensive—erotic romance, New-Age occult fiction, or stories where devout Christians are the villains, for example.

There's a fifth factor that may or may not rear its ugly head. The atmosphere at a secular writers' conference can be highly competitive—much more so than at a Christian conference. It's not uncommon for the participants in a workshop panel to spend much of their presenting time promoting their own books and trying to establish their superiority over other panelists.

**It Is Written ...** _____

> Usually, I'm teaching in the fiction track (at writers' conferences) and I stand before people who are going to pitch ideas, prepare proposals, pen novels that will compete with mine and may even cost me a contract. I don't care. From a business point of view, training your competition makes little sense, but writing for the Kingdom is different. It's not just business. Not in the long run. My "competition" is less rivalry than family, sharing the same beliefs and serving the same God. Why wouldn't I lend a hand by lecturing, conferring, and sharing?
>
> —Alton Gansky, Christian novelist

I know this happens, because I've participated in many such panels and have seen intense competitive zeal in action. A few years ago, I presented a workshop on plotting technique at a regional secular writers' conference. One of the other instructors sat through the class. Afterward, he asked why I was sharing "secrets" with 30 potential competitors. I know this is not the universal attitude at secular conferences—we learned invaluable skills at the conferences we attended—but there can be a major difference in tone. Christian conferences tend to be kinder, gentler, and highly supportive.

## The Least You Need to Know

♦ Christian writers' conferences are great places to learn the craft of writing fiction.

♦ You'll find conferences in every region of the country, but the large national conferences are likely to offer the most comprehensive selection of workshops and courses.

♦ Choose a writers' conference that meets all your needs—education plus amenities.

♦ Take the time to check out a writers' conference (and workshop leaders) with prior attendees.

♦ Entering conference contests and submitting manuscripts for evaluation give you a chance to have your work critiqued.

♦ Think about attending a secular writers' conference; many do an excellent job teaching basic fiction techniques.

# **15**

# **Getting the Most from Your Critique Group**

## **In This Chapter**

- ◆ Why critique groups are worth joining
- ◆ Secular versus Christian critique groups
- ◆ Pros and cons of critique groups
- ◆ Establishing some ground rules
- ◆ How to give, take, and benefit from effective criticism
- ◆ How to launch a new critique group

It's hard to find a published Christian writer who doesn't have nice things to say about critique groups. The bottom line is that critique groups have a phenomenal record of success transforming unpublished writers into published novelists. What's more, many authors remain members of critique groups long after they begin cranking out bestsellers. To prove the point, read the acknowledgment pages in the front of your favorite Christian novels.

More than twelve years ago, Janet and I joined a critique group for wannabe mystery writers. There were eight members. Within six years, five of the members sold first novels. Today four of the original eight are multi-published mystery novelists. If anyone asks me why the group succeeded, I answer: "Because we did our critique group right!"

This chapter will give you the know-how to identify a critique group that will help you polish your fiction skills, motivate you to finish your novel, and help you get published. I'll also give you tips for starting a Christian critique group if you can't find one in your community.

# The Trouble with "Aunt Matilda"

"Aunt Matilda" is my label for the knowledgeable relative most writers have—the person in the family who loves to read and is a self-proclaimed expert on Christian fiction. The trouble is, when Aunt Matilda reads your manuscript, she is likely to tell you what you want to hear rather than what you need to hear. Aunt Matilda is not objective. She *wants* to like what you write.

> ### Wisdom and Knowledge
>
> The Internet has made virtual critique groups possible and practical. Many novelists now have "crit partners" who live across the country (and some across oceans). They've met each other at writers' conferences, on writing group "loops" (e-mail lists), or through writers' organizations such as American Christian Fiction Writers. Interestingly, most of the rules for face-to-face critique groups apply to Internet groups.

And Aunt Matilda brings another shortcoming when she critiques your work: she thinks like a reader, not a writer. As the members of your critique group gain experience, they'll zero in on manuscript weaknesses that readers may not see or understand. A reader may sense a plot is flimsy; a writer will suggest specific fixes to strengthen the storyline. A reader may feel distant from the hero; a writer will point to the specific point-of-view error that created the problem.

Finally, Aunt Matilda has a single pair of eyes, while a critique group will evaluate your manuscript from multiple viewpoints. A variety of different opinions, different criticisms, different suggested corrections, and different takes on the same issues can be exceptionally helpful when you revise and refine your manuscript.

# A Secular or a Christian Critique Group?

This is not an easy question to answer. Although a Christian writer may feel more comfortable in a Christian critique group, a secular group may provide specific resources the writer needs to improve his or her writing.

The virtues of a Christian critique group include:

♦ More familiar with the work of successful Christian authors

♦ Better able to deal with Christian content and Christian themes

♦ More familiar with the most popular Christian genres—especially Christian women's fiction

♦ Less skeptical about the quality of Christian fiction

♦ More knowledge of language and topic limitations in Christian fiction

♦ More knowledge of Christian fiction resources—members are likely to have joined Christian writing organizations, such as American Christian Fiction Writers

♦ More knowledge of Christian agents, Christian publishers, and Christian writers' conferences

♦ Won't require members to read language and subject matter found in secular novels

At first glance, this list seems overwhelmingly in favor of Christian groups. It probably proves that most Christian writers should join Christian critique groups. But Christian groups also have shortcomings:

♦ Can take on the characteristics of a "small group" established for Bible study or ministry—the focus of the group may shift away from fiction writing

♦ Little familiarity with secular markets for Christian fiction

♦ May be "gentler" than a secular group and provide less intense criticism

♦ Will tolerate preachy writing and heavy-handed Christian messages more than a secular critique group

♦ May welcome members who are merely interested in writing fiction but are not actively developing a novel

♦ May include other kinds of Christian writers (poets, nonfiction writers, article writers, curriculum writers)

♦ Will have few or no male members (probably because the majority of Christian fiction writers are women)

♦ Members may have limited familiarity with fiction genres aimed at male readers

The limitations of a Christian critique group can be significant, depending on the kind of fiction you write and the expectations you have for your crit partners. For example, a man writing male-oriented Christian fiction may find a secular group more valuable—and more comfortable. So might a Christian author determined to write a crossover novel.

The mystery group Janet and I joined was secular, but many of the members identified themselves as Christian, although not as evangelicals. Which brings me to one other factor worth considering when you search for a critique group. If you join a secular critique group, you have the opportunity to be an authentic, nonthreatening Christian who can influence the other members. I'm not suggesting that you evangelize the nonbelievers in the room, or on the Internet; rather that your participation in the group—and the Christian-themed manuscripts you write and your critique partners read—will inevitably impact the other members, be they nonbelievers or nominal Christians.

# What Critique Groups Offer

Everyone knows that writing a full-length novel is a solitary—and often lonely—pursuit. Moreover, most writers recognize that it's difficult to get far enough away from their work to see the big picture. A critique group offers effective solutions to both of these problems, and more.

## A Test Audience

The members of the group serve as a "test audience" of knowledgeable readers who can provide creditable feedback about your writing.

Does your story work? Do your characters seem real? Are the hero and heroine likable? Are they sympathetic? Did the reader experience the emotions you intended? Is the pacing too fast or too slow? Do readers "get" the Christian messages you seek to deliver?

These days, you can't get this kind of feedback anywhere else. Years ago, agents and editors worked with promising writers to fine-tune manuscripts and eliminate rough edges. Today, an author—published or unpublished—is expected to deliver a publishable manuscript the first time around. Your critique group's advice can push your manuscript over the top.

## Fellowship and Motivation

Equally important, the members of your critique group are writers like you. They understand the challenges of writing a novel—the pains, the pleasures, the perils—they have "been there, done that, bought the T-shirt."

A good critique group will provide fellowship to compensate for the loneliness of writing—and also supply the essential motivation every writer needs. It's all too easy to give up, to stop writing a novel. At one time or another, every successful author I know has said to him- or herself: *The chances of writing and selling a successful novel are slim. Doesn't it make more sense to invest my time in a more productive activity? Shouldn't I do something that offers a greater potential payoff?*

Motivation is one of the most important benefits of a writers' group. You'll *make* the time to work on your manuscript because you know that your friends expect to see more pages. Simply put, you become accountable to your group for moving ahead with your novel.

 **Literary Sins**

Make sure that friendship doesn't encourage you to pull your punches when you critique a friend's manuscript. Friends don't let friends write bad fiction!

## A Chance to Fine-Tune Your "Manure Detector"

Ernest Hemingway said that every writer needs a "built-in, shock-proof, *manure* detector." Ernest actually used a pithier word, but his point is that it's important for every writer to recognize when his or her own writing is good or bad.

Members of critique groups discover that they learn more about good—and bad—writing by critiquing other member's novels than by listening to comments about their work. Critiquing a steady flow of manuscripts builds vital self-editing skills you can apply to your own writing.

## Shared Writing and Marketing Resources

The members of a critique group can share how-to writing books, writing guides, subscriptions to writing magazines and writing-oriented websites, even contacts made—and leads gathered—at writers' conferences.

A group library can save members a considerable sum of money, and also make it possible to replace aging resources more quickly. One face-to-face group I know owns a copy of *Literary Marketplace*, an improbable investment for a single writer.

## A Way to Meet New Friends

It's inevitable. Spend time with people who have similar interests, and lasting friendships will develop. This is a fine benefit of a critique group—as long as socializing during meetings—or over the Internet—doesn't overwhelm the group's real purpose.

# Writers Take Heed

All is not rosy in the world of writing critique groups. Some writers have had bad experiences. More than one has stopped writing fiction because of them. A less-than-effective critique group …

- May "whipsaw" writers with a barrage of conflicting suggestions.

- May leave major problems uncorrected in the spirit of not offending or upsetting its members.

- Can waste time that would have been better spent working on a manuscript.

- Can do too much socializing at the expense of critiquing.

- Can arouse unpleasant feelings of competitiveness and jealousy when some members land agents or sell their work before others.

- May tolerate some members taking more than they give—by monopolizing the conversation (both face-to-face and virtual), delivering weak critiques, and demanding that submission deadlines be rearranged to meet their schedules.

# Ground Rules for an Effective Critique Group

The purpose of a critique group is to help its members produce publishable manuscripts. A critique group is not a reading group or a social club. The unspoken contract among the partners states: I will help you improve your writing if you help me improve mine. Each of us will submit our work for criticism, and each of us will critique other members' work. This is much more than simply: You show me your writing and I'll show you mine. Members agree to be fair in their criticism and to accept criticism of their own work gracefully.

Commitment is a double-edged commodity in a critique group. As a writer, you demonstrate commitment by working on your manuscript at a steady pace. As a critiquer, you demonstrate commitment by doing a thorough job of evaluating your colleagues' work.

A critique group meeting should be viewed like a church service—an event that has a more-or-less fixed schedule that participants learn to accommodate. As a rule, membership starts to decline when a group makes frequent schedule modifications.

**Wisdom and Knowledge**

Members of a critique group should be …

♦ Serious writers of book-length fiction actively seeking to be published.

♦ Willing to give and accept criticism.

♦ Committed to participation and willing to attend meetings regularly.

More than enough critique groups have prospered—and failed—over the years to provide useful lessons learned about which approaches work and which don't. Following are some useful ground rules to help you identify a group that can help you learn to write better fiction.

## Members Should Have a Wide Range of Experience

Look for a critique group with a spectrum of writers at different points in their journey to publication. If a critique group has nothing but experienced, published writers, they may drift away, not have time to do thorough critiques, or find it difficult to understand why everyone doesn't write like they do. Conversely, a group full of wholly inexperienced writers is likely to flounder around, not know the requirements of publishable fiction, or not have the skill to diagnose problems and produce credible critiques.

## The Right Number of Members, the Right Kinds of Writers

You'll find lots of recommendations out there for the correct size of a face-to-face critique group. I've belonged to several over the years, and the best groups have had eight to ten members. Many more members than ten, and the group may generate too many manuscript excerpts to read comfortably every month. Many fewer members than eight may lead to a lack of "critical mass"—meetings feel empty and writers may receive too few critiques of their work to be useful.

Some critique groups invite all kinds of creative writers to join—from screenwriters to poets. I prefer a fiction critique group that limits itself to novelists, because I feel it's essential that members like to read—and intend to write—the kind of writing they must critique. Specialization can even go a level deeper. Many fiction critique groups focus on a specific genre; for example, romance or mysteries.

## Set a Realistic Writing Workload

Successful critique groups have members who both write and critique. The mystery group I talked about earlier tried to review three good-sized chapters at each monthly meeting. That meant, on average, that each member had to submit a chapter-length block of fiction—say 15 pages—every other month. On occasion, we would review four chapters; less frequently, two longer ones.

> ### A Lamp Unto Your Feet
>
> Keep your expectations realistic. It's unfortunate that some members of a critique group may never find an agent or be published, and that others will have to wait longer than they think is fair. One or two might go on to successful writing careers, while others will stall and go nowhere. A writing critique group won't make a noncreative person creative, or give a nonwriter the talent necessary to write a novel.

## Open Face-to-Face Meetings with a Prayer

Begin Christian critique group meetings with a prayer, then have members report on their writing progress, acceptances or rejections, experiences at writers' conferences, market intelligence, and other news of interest to the group.

## Take a "Businesslike" Approach During Meetings

Critique group meetings are not business meetings, but they should be run efficiently. For example, it's a good idea to limit each member's spoken critique of a manuscript to a fixed time—say 10 minutes. This will ensure that meetings end on time. One member should be chairperson at each meeting—you can alternate this role each month. His or her chief job is to keep the critiques on track and on time.

# The Key to Effective Criticism: Truth Spoken in Love

The best critiques are balanced—neither too harsh (which can shatter an inexperienced writer's shaky ego) nor too gentle (which may not encourage a writer to improve his or her work). Feedback on what works can be as important as feedback on what doesn't. It's not a question of making the writer feel good; the point is to help the group develop the skills to write good fiction.

## Be Specific, But Don't Become a Ghostwriter

By definition, *constructive* criticism offers a solution to a problem. Always pinpoint writing issues and offer specific improvement suggestions. Vague comments—*That scene doesn't read right* or *This chapter needs a better problem*—don't give the writer the actionable information he or she needs to make real improvements.

Some critique partners misinterpret the admonition to provide specific suggestions. This does not mean rewriting someone else's novel. A real danger is that well-intentioned, but excessive, editorial work will destroy the author's original authorial voice.

## Criticize Writing, Not Writers

Be alert not to say such things as: "I mentioned this same error last time … you don't listen to me!" Or, "How can you be so careless to make this kind of simple mistake?" Or, "*Everyone knows* that editors hate dialogue written this way." The problem with these statements is that they communicate implied criticism of the writer, and will likely make the writer respond defensively. Criticism should be aimed at the manuscript, not the person who wrote it.

## Remember, It's Not Your Novel

The writer will ultimately decide what suggestions and improvements to accept. Don't get upset if he or she ignores your great idea, or refuses to believe you identified the one change that will transform a mediocre novel into a bestseller.

Having said this, I encourage critique partners to pick their battles. Concentrate on the most important issues. Tell the writer when you think a change is essential, rather than merely optional. Rank—in your own mind—what is most important. Plan your critique to emphasize the must-revise items, then talk about the nice-to-make changes.

## Strike the Right Balance

Encouragement can be tricky. On the one hand, too little encouragement may lead to a discouraged writer: "There's nothing good about my work; it's full of problems. It's time for me to quit." On the other hand, effusive praise that's undeserved can dull the impact of criticism: "The reasons to like my work clearly overwhelm its few problems. It's time for me to start submitting the manuscript to agents and editors."

**Literary Sins**

I sometimes hear critique groups described as "writer support groups." A critique group is *not* a support group; its purpose is to help its members *learn* how to write publishable fiction. Encouragement must be part of the mix, but not the kind of encouragement that praises the unpraiseworthy.

Here again, the right balance is essential. When something works, say so; when something fails, explain why. Give feedback that encourages good writing. And commiserate with members when their hard work has not paid off.

What about the admonition to begin every critique by saying something positive about the writing? The problem is that most writers are smart enough to recognize the ploy—especially after participating in the group for a while. I heard the following comment at a face-to-face critique group I belonged to decades ago: "I really liked the way you described the rosebush in the backyard, but I couldn't warm up to your protagonist and I found the plot confusing." Not surprisingly, the writer began to laugh—and so did most of the participants.

## See the Forest, Not the Trees

Both small details and the big picture are important in a finished book. But during the manuscript development stage, it's probably more helpful to provide a "30,000 foot" view of what you read.

Don't waste time talking about minor details of grammar and construction during a critique group meeting; focus on story, structure, and contact. If you spot typos and other minor errors, note them on your copy of the manuscript and let the author deal with them after the meeting.

## Give Appropriate Feedback

Should feedback be written or oral? This, of course, applies to face-to-face critique groups. I think written is best, because it's impossible for a writer to simultaneously listen to and capture a barrage of feedback. Another problem with purely oral feedback is that the last person to speak is likely to say "I agree with everyone who spoke before me. I don't have anything new to add."

If you don't provide your feedback as a separate document, at least mark-up your copy of the writer's manuscript clearly. You don't need to use traditional proofreader symbols, but it's essential that the writer can understand your comments and suggestions at a glance.

## Some Members of the Group Should *Specialize*

After a few sessions of a newly organized critique group, one member will probably begin to concentrate on dialogue problems, and another on story shortcomings, and yet another on voice and style. Some specialization is inevitable; we each have areas of special strength as writers of fiction. A specialist is likely to provide the most useful insights to the writer. But the downside of members becoming too specialized is that each "expert" stops learning in other important areas.

## Hang Tough

Unless the members of a writing critique group deliver honest, comprehensive, and tough critiques, the participants are wasting their time. Don't let important problems slip by because you worried about hurting the writer's feelings, or because you've already identified a large number of issues in a manuscript.

## Tell 'Em Where You're Coming From

It's important for the members of a critique group to understand each other's genre preferences, biases, likes, dislikes, and life experience. For example, if you dislike cozy mysteries, I'd think twice before accepting your criticism about the weird location I chose for the story, the seeming incompetence of the police, or the fact that my heroine has no real reason for investigating the murder. These things are quite typical in the genre.

Conversely, I tend not to read Christian novels that have women wearing bonnets on their covers. If you write prairie romances or women's fiction set in Amish communities, you'd be advised to take my critiques with scoops of salt.

## Don't Apologize! Don't Explain! Don't Argue!

Respond to critiques graciously. Consider carefully, with an open mind, what members say about your manuscript. If several other writers express similar concerns about your work, consider their observations carefully. Even if they haven't diagnosed the supposed problem to your satisfaction—even if they've come up with six different suggested fixes—they may have located a weakness in your manuscript.

**A Lamp Unto Your Feet**

Don't overreact to criticism. When the critiquing is done, don't rush to your word processor and began to rewrite. Take some time to think about the criticisms you received. Separate must-do fixes from the nice-to-do suggestions. You decide whether you agree with them or not.

Resist the temptation to defend yourself or your work, or to argue about the rightness of details in your book. If someone spots an obvious mistake, don't explain or apologize. Every writer makes mistakes. That's why we rewrite our manuscripts again and again before we send them to agents or editors.

# Yes, Criticism Can Be Painful

Most of us daydream that our writing group will heap praises on our words and pronounce them worthy of awards. Most of the time, though, you will come away from your turn in the barrel with a long list of items to fix—and a somewhat battered sense of self-esteem. No one likes to hear that his or her "baby" is flawed.

Well, your manuscript really isn't your baby. The criticism you heard was directed at a collection of words on paper—not you. Writing a weak second act, or confusing dialogue, doesn't mean you're a bad person, or even a bad writer.

Keep reminding yourself that you didn't join your critique group for personal affirmation, but for help in writing a publishable manuscript. The more errors your critique group identifies, the more publishable your novel will be when you submit it to an agent or editor.

# Starting a Christian Critique Group from Scratch

On the one hand, you may live in a part of the world where there isn't an established Christian critique group. On the other hand, you may not like the apparent "disconnectedness" of an online group. The obvious solution is to launch your own critique group. Keep in mind that you, as founder of a new critique group, will do most of the work during the first few meetings. This can involve a significant commitment of time and energy. Moreover, you will probably have to host the group initially in your home.

The fundamental challenge of launching a new critique group is finding a group of Christian novelists to participate. Ideally, you'd like a group of writers at different points in their writing journey, including one or two published novelists. Here are a couple of proven ways to find potential members:

- Put out the word on Internet writing loops.

- Send a news release announcing the first meeting of your new group to your local newspaper's "events page" editor.

- Post a notice at your local Christian bookstore.

- Send announcements to churches in your community with a note asking that the new critique group be mentioned in each church's bulletin or newsletter.

You should prepare for the first meeting by predefining the group's ground rules. Use the suggestions in this chapter to put together a set of informal bylaws that will guide the group's activities and ways of doing business. The faster the new group starts critiquing manuscripts, the more useful it will be to every member.

## The Least You Need to Know

- A writers' critique group—face-to-face or Internet-based—can provide essential feedback a novelist will get nowhere else.

- The majority of Christian novelists will probably feel most comfortable in a Christian critique group, but secular groups can be effective, too.

- The purpose of a critique group is to help its members produce publishable manuscripts; don't waste time in a group that focuses on reading or socializing.

- When you criticize a manuscript, be balanced—tell the writer what worked as well is what didn't work.

- Don't take criticism personally. Writing a weak second act, or confusing dialogue, doesn't mean you're a bad person, or even a bad writer.

- If you can't find a critique group in your area or don't like the idea of being part of an online group, start your own!

# Chapter 16

# The Challenge of Fitting a Novel into Your Life

## In This Chapter

◆ To a Christian novelist, writing is one of many priorities

◆ It takes fewer productive hours than you think to write a full-size Christian novel

◆ How to turn unproductive time into writing time

◆ Proven time-management techniques for recovering wasted time

◆ Write smarter to finish your novel sooner

I'll begin with the obvious. If you want to write a novel, you have to find the time to write many thousands of well-chosen words. Where does this extra time come from? How do you fit a novel into your already hectic life?

I'll give you the detailed answers to these questions in this chapter. Here are the short answers: The bad news is there's no such thing as "extra" time. The good news is that we all waste bits of time that can be recovered. The chief secret of fitting a novel into your life is to make the best use of previously wasted time.

# The Challenge of Being a Christian Novelist

Writing a novel represents an enormous investment in time and energy. This is especially true of a first novel, because besides turning out a publishable novel you must also master the techniques of writing fiction.

If you were a nonbelieving writer, you could decide to chuck all the bothersome duties in your life and devote every waking hour to writing fiction. Live in a garret, think of yourself as an artist, and struggle mightily for your art. In the course of time, your single-minded focus on fiction might lead to a finished manuscript—although you'd be the only person in the room to rejoice over your accomplishment.

As a Christian, you probably recognize that kind of one-sided behavior as a form of idolatry. We've each been called to write, but not at the expense of the many other priorities in our lives. We can't ignore our responsibilities to our families, our households, our employers, our church, and of course to God.

Giving up your prayer time, or regular worship, or Bible study to write *Christian* fiction doesn't make logical sense. "What good will it be for a man if he gains the whole world, yet forfeits his soul?" (Matthew 16:26 NIV) Similarly, shattering your marriage, disappointing your kids, upsetting your household, and losing your day job are hardly good trades for writing a Christian novel.

**A Lamp Unto Your Feet**

Take heart! It can be done. Moreover, you can do it. As the oft-quoted epigram says, God doesn't always call the equipped, but He always equips the called.

What we have here is a genuine dilemma. On the one hand, unless you have sufficient time to write, you'll never fulfill your call to be a Christian writer. On the other hand, you must keep living your non-writing life, or risk enormous personal loss. Some first-time Christian novelists throw up their hands in surrender and never finish their manuscripts. Wiser authors resolve the dilemma by properly balancing both aspects of their lives.

# The Power of an Hour

A typical Christian trade paperback novel is 80,000 to 90,000 words long. Merely typing that many words would take an experienced keyboarder about 20 hours (assuming an average typing speed 75 words per minute). Actually writing 90,000 words takes much longer—upwards of 200 hours (assuming a novelist will write at an average rate of seven or eight good words per minute).

I'll do the math for you: 200 hours is equivalent to five weeks of eight-hour days. That's a month of 9-to-5 work. That doesn't sound like much time, but in fact, there are writers who can crank out a novel more quickly than that. (Ray Bradbury reportedly wrote the first draft of *Fahrenheit 451*, admittedly a shorter book, in less than 50 hours.)

Most of us can't write that quickly—because we take time to think, rewrite as we write, do research, sip coffee, stare at the computer screen, read our e-mail, participate in writers' loops, play computer solitaire, and generally do everything *except* output words at a steady pace. And so, writing a novel becomes a 2,000-hour project that can span several years.

But imagine the results if we could increase our productivity and write at a faster rate. Keyboarding six or seven good words per minute means that one hour later you or I will have written about 400 words. Do that one hour each day—every day—and you will produce a full-length first draft in only 225 days, less than eight months. I find these numbers encouraging, rather than discouraging. They demonstrate that writing a Christian novel is not an impossible dream, even when finding time to write poses a significant challenge. One hour here, another hour there, we'll get the job done—if they are productive hours spent writing effectively.

## Squeezing Out One Measly Hour Per Day

This heading is meant to be ironic. Many first-time novelists I've met at writers' conferences see a free hour each day as an out-of-reach luxury. Most of them have been women with jobs and families—and endless demands on their limited time. And yet, as I said, if you want to write you have to find time to write. The best way to do that is to *make* more of the time you have available. Employ several different time-management strategies to eliminate wasted time and make the best use of every other minute in your busy day.

In the beginning, you'll fumble, make mistakes, decide that some (maybe most) of the strategies won't work for you. But one or two will work—and give you a few hours of precious writing time. As you become more experienced at balancing the different aspects of your life, you'll find (as I did) that you can squeeze out enough measly hours to finish your first novel.

## Establish a Personal Calendar

For starters, keep track of everything you have to do. Schedule your activities so that they dovetail together without wasting time. For example, it's usually more efficient to spend an entire morning shopping and running errands than doing one or two tasks each day. Your goal is to transform the rush of daily living into a more gentle flow of essential pursuits that you can manage.

Next, make unbreakable appointments with yourself to write Christian fiction every day. I'm sure this sounds strange, but scheduling personal activities is a proven time-management strategy that pays big dividends. There are three benefits of setting aside time to write:

**Literary Sins**

Once you've created your calendar, be protective of your schedule. Keep to it; avoid giving in to last-minute requests for impromptu meetings. If you don't, you'll probably give up your hard-won writing time.

1. You won't schedule other activities in the same timeslots.

2. You establish a pattern of daily writing that will soon become a comfortable habit.

3. Writing now has a definite place in your daily life.

You can use the calendar in your computer, your personal digital assistant (PDA), or a Day Planner to carve up your available hours. Try to plan your activities weekly instead of daily. This makes it easier, for example, to consolidate multiple trips to a distant corner of town. Every minute you don't waste traveling hither and yon gives you another minute to spend at your computer.

## Write a Little Every Day

Try to set at least some time aside every day for your writing. Every successful author I know agrees with the notion that you have to wrap your brain around a novel when you write it. This means keeping your manuscript on your mental "front burners," where it will receive both conscious and unconscious thought.

You can't do this if you disconnect from your manuscript for weeks (or even days) at a time. The best way to keep connected is to write something new each day. A paragraph or two, a couple of hundred words, is enough. You don't have to write great words—you may even decide to throw them away the next time you turn on your computer—but the simple act of writing them down keeps your novel alive in your mind.

## Your Family Must Pitch In

Female novelists with families invariably acknowledge that their husbands and children have to collaborate with them—not in actual writing, but in ways that free up writing time. Perhaps your kids can do more chores, or begin to care for their personal needs like laundry, or find alternative ways of getting to after-school events. Perhaps your husband can do some of the shopping, part of the housecleaning, or take on a portion of the laundry.

This kind of "collaboration" may not come easy. Family members often find it hard to understand a novelist's call. They may see your efforts to write Christian fiction as a waste of time, or as a prideful quest for fame. At worst, they're likely to feel jealous of the time you spend writing.

There's no magic solution to this kind of problem. You have to explain your goals repeatedly—and the compromises everyone will have to make to help you reach them.

## Turn Unproductive Time into Writing Time

This is a "hurry up, then wait" world. We all have periods of unproductive time. You can often transform these periods into writing time. My mobile telephone has a voice recorder feature I can use to capture spoken thoughts. I also carry a small notepad I can use to jot down ideas. I can be "writing" in odd places during otherwise wasted times. For example, when I started to plan a 20,000-word Christian romance novella I wrote recently:

- I "cast" my story while standing on line at the airport. I observed the other people waiting to check their luggage and chose my heroine, my hero, and two other key characters. I used my phone's voice recorder to capture my summaries of their descriptions.

- I solved a central plotting issue while waiting to board the aircraft. Other passengers snoozed or read newspapers; I wrote down ideas in my notebook.

- I wrote the lead paragraph as my plane flew to St. Louis. I thought about cranking up my laptop computer, but the seating was too tight to use a computer comfortably, so I stuck with my trusty notebook.

## Set Up a Permanent Writing Area in Your Home

What does a quiet corner have to do with saving time? Quite a lot, actually. Writers who work at a kitchen table—a popular writing venue—have to waste time setting up and taking down their equipment and materials. A permanent writing area (you don't need more than a small computer table stuck in an empty corner) lets you sit down and start writing anytime you have an extra moment.

I've been writing long enough to justify my own home office. I leave my computer turned on all day so I can write whenever I get the chance. I've been known to knock out a few words while waiting for my microwave oven to heat lunch.

## Buy Extra Time

Yes, you can buy time. You can hire people to clean your house, mow your lawn, do your laundry, watch your kids, and run routine errands. You can transform money into ready-to-eat meals for dinner and use the time you've bought to work on your novel. These services are not inexpensive—not every first-time writer has the resources to afford them—but buying time can be a sound investment in your writing career.

 **It Is Written ...**

The question of how we balance writing with our other daily responsibilities ranks right up there in the top ten most frequently discussed subjects among writers. ... Like most other things about life and writing, this kind of "management" varies from writer to writer. Some things that help facilitate this constant juggling act, however, are common to us all. You've probably heard this ad nauseam, but the only workable solution comes down to choosing your priorities—and making certain those choices are aligned with God's will.

—B. J. Hoff, Christian novelist

## Lower Your Expectations

When other people take on your responsibilities—spouse, kids, even hired hands—they probably won't do as good a job as you could do. You probably recognize and accept that. Why not cut yourself the same slack? Your house will survive even though you vacuum less frequently, or dust the furniture less often, or let the grass get a bit taller before you mow it. This is a great example of another effective time-management strategy—readjusting current priorities to fit writing into your busy life. Settling for less-than-perfect surroundings is a small sacrifice that can yield a few hours a week of additional writing time.

## Learn to Say No!

Because writing is important to you, it also has to be a priority in your life, a claim to a reasonable amount of your time. That means that writing will occasionally "win" the competition for your attention and other equally important activities will lose.

Recognize up front that you'll never do it all, that you can't keep up business as usual in all of your volunteer work, all of your church activities, all of your social or service clubs, all of your hobbies, all of your support to friends and neighbors, all of your household duties, and all of the "little things" you do for your spouse and family.

You certainly don't have to become a recluse (you'll probably become a less productive writer if you do), but you have to learn to say, "No, I'm too busy to tackle that right now." Some people will feel let down, but most will understand.

## Bye-Bye, TV

It won't surprise you that most time-management gurus advise busy people to watch less TV, participate in fewer online loops, read their e-mail less often, text-message less, and cut back on telephone chitchat with friends and family. Many people spend three or more hours a day on these activities. Doing them "less" doesn't mean eliminating them from your life; instead, you should measure their importance against your goal of writing a publishable Christian novel.

Is watching an episode of *American Idol* worth *not* writing 300 more words? That's what viewing the show will cost you. On an evening when you're feeling especially tired, your answer may be *yes*. On another evening when you're bursting with creativity, your answer should be *no*. (But then, I'm not an *Idol* fan.)

Similarly, halving the length of nonessential telephone calls, and accessing your e-mail account twice a day rather than four or five times, can free up valuable time for writing.

 **It Is Written ...**

Writing takes a tremendous amount of time, energy, and commitment. If you're serious about writing as a career, you will probably have to give up some other things you enjoy. But oh, to be able to say, "I am a writer" makes it all worthwhile.

—Deborah Raney, Christian novelist

## Don't Sweat Every Decision

Another frequently taught time-management strategy is to simplify decision-making. You can waste hours analyzing your many choices when you buy a pair of shoes, plan a short vacation, or select fertilizer for your lawn. It's fun to go shopping, but the time you spend browsing is extra time you could be writing. Make fewer comparisons and don't concern yourself with finding "the perfect" product. Unless you're making a major purchase—a home or a car—extra searching rarely repays the time and energy you invest.

## What About Collaboration?

Are two novelists faster than one? Perhaps you can reduce the time it takes to write your novel by finding a collaborator. Well, Janet and I have proven that two authors working together don't automatically cut writing time in half. We each spend full time on every scene, so we actually double the "person hours" involved in writing our cozy mysteries.

None of the other collaborating couples we've met has reported significant time savings during the writing phase (although two people can save some time by sharing research and proofreading duties). The real benefit of collaboration is that it doubles the brain power applied to creating a novel.

## Motivate Yourself

Because writing fiction is hard work, novelists often look for good excuses *not* to write, as I discussed in Chapter 13. A busy day offers myriad legitimate reasons to do other useful things—and not feel guilty about your lack of writing productivity. Establishing a calendar, taking advantage of time-management strategies, will give you the time to write, but not necessarily the personal drive to stay glued in your chair.

Multi-published authors have deadlines to goad them forward, and agents and editors to remind them that time is fleeting. As a first-time novelist, you must motivate yourself. The drive to finish your manuscript—to find unused bits of time and make good use of them—has to come from inside you. Strive to take advantage of every opportunity to get to work on your novel.

# Write Smarter

To paraphrase the apostle Paul, when I was a first-time novelist, I wrote like a first-time novelist, I reasoned like a first-time novelist. When I became a published novelist, I put first-time writing ways behind me.

During those early days, words seemed to drip, drip, drip out of my mind and onto the computer screen. Every aspect of my writing process seemed painfully slow. But now that I have more experience—and have gained more confidence—I write much faster. I can even understand how some long-time novelists manage to write at a steady pace of 5,000 words per day.

## Write in Small Bites

A useful writing-related time-management trick is to divide your novel into small chunks of writing—short chapters with even shorter scenes—that you can write in brief periods of time.

I've always written longish scenes (2,500 words or so). But for my 20,000-word romance novella, I experimented with short, 500- to 600-word scenes. I found them simpler to write, because two blank pages are much less intimidating than ten. I also discovered that finishing a complete scene in one sitting gave me a mental boost—a feeling of accomplishment that made me eager to begin the next scene.

I've been told by two different editors that readers (also under time pressures, these days) prefer short scenes that enable them to read a book in tidy nibbles. Both cited the *Mitford* novels by Jan Karon as excellent examples of this technique.

Not every novel can be split comfortably into short scenes. You may need long passages of dialogue, action, and description to tell your story. But it's definitely an approach to consider when your plot cooperates.

## Stick to *Your* Kind of Fiction

As I discussed in Chapter 6, there are many different kinds of Christian fiction, many genres with their own preferred authorial voices and catalogs of conventions. I'll be hugely surprised if you're able to write publishable manuscripts in more than a handful of them. Each of us seems programmed for specific fiction genres. It may be that novelists instinctively learn to write in the genres we like to read. That would explain why Janet and I write cozy mysteries. Or perhaps our "natural" authorial voices are best suited for specific genres. Whatever the explanation, some genres come easier to us than others. "Easier" almost always translates into faster writing.

### Wisdom and Knowledge

I've known first-time novelists who chose to write against their genre—a practice much like rowing against the current. It makes little sense to spend additional weeks (or months) finishing your first manuscript unless your doing-what-comes-naturally genres have limited sales potential.

## Do Less Rewriting as You Go

I just wrote this sentence:

> Every how-to-write-a-novel book you've read has undoubtedly advised you to write a complete first draft before you begin to make changes or rewrite your work.

But now that I've taken a second look at it, I'm not so sure that I like what I see:

◆ How can I possibly know which how-to-write-a-novel books you've read?

◆ Isn't it wrong for me to assume that every how-to writing book out there provides that advice?

◆ That klutzy adverb—undoubtedly—doesn't do much for the sentence.

These are all good reasons for me to rewrite the sentence. After all, I'd hate to have you (or my editor) think I'm a sloppy writer. But there are equally good reasons for me to ignore the problems and keep writing.

When a writer starts rewriting in the middle of a paragraph, he or she changes hats and becomes a copy editor. The change is subtle, and most of us can bounce back and forth without much effort. But donning the editor's hat interrupts the creative factory that's hard at work generating a stream of words.

The point here is that trying to edit as you write is a surefire way of slowing down your writing. Some highly successful writers love to polish each sentence before they move on to the next. They can do it because they're full-time novelists, with plenty of time to spend worrying over a single word. Most of us need to write more quickly.

And so, many how-to-write-a-novel books advise novelists to finish a first draft before we make changes or rewrite our work.

Alas, I don't have the willpower to postpone rewriting until I've written a complete manuscript. I can generally make it through five or six pages without looking back—but then the irresistible urge to fix things takes over. I've managed to turn out 2,500 words on a good writing day, but I'll probably never reach the fabled 5,000.

## The Least You Need to Know

◆ As a Christian novelist, you need to find time to write fiction while you honor the other responsibilities in your life.

◆ Time-management strategies will help you eliminate wasted time and make the best use of every minute in your busy day.

◆ Turn dead time into writing time by always carrying a notebook or a voice recorder with you.

◆ Motivate yourself to write fiction whenever you get the opportunity.

◆ Learn to write smarter: stick to the genres you write best, carve up your story into small chunks, and do less rewriting as you go.

# Chapter 17

# Dealing with Distinctively Christian Writing Issues

## In This Chapter

- ◆ Are you called to write Christian fiction?
- ◆ Inspiration is an awesome power
- ◆ Learning to live with God's timing
- ◆ Telling stories about real people and true events
- ◆ Don't let the business side of writing make you uncomfortable

A Christian who writes fiction has more to think about than a nonbeliever. I've talked about different aspects of this challenge earlier in the book. In this chapter, I'll tackle several distinctively Christian concerns that might have an impact on your writing.

# Understanding Your Call to Be a Christian Novelist

I have a question for you: Are you *called* to write Christian fiction?

I suspect your answer is *yes*. Most of the Christian novelists I ask tell me that they are. And most go on to say that they do their best to write out of obedience to their calling.

But how can any of us be sure that we're *really, truly* called to be Christian novelists?

Consider the many non-Christians who feel compelled to write fiction. Few of them would label their feelings a "calling" from God. So why are we so confident? Did God really tell us to be writers? Or did our "inner voices" urge us to write Christian fiction so that we can see our names on book covers?

These are not idle questions. They cut to the heart of how each of us should approach our work as Christian novelists.

## A Tale of Two Writers

One Christian novelist I know—let's call him Bob—gave up a lucrative, prestigious career to be a fulltime writer. He felt that was essential, given his call to write fiction. He's written several successful books and has achieved financial independence as a Christian writer.

Another Christian author—I'll call him *me*—kept his day job and wrote the novels he felt called to write in his spare time. He's co-written several novels and has recently branched out to write solo fiction.

Is one response "better" than the other? More to the point, should I have chucked everything and devoted every waking hour to my new vocation? Is complete dedication a requirement when one answers a call to write Christian fiction?

**It Is Written ...**

Is novel writing a full-time or part-time job for me? Full-time, but I am not one to advise that this is something to jump into. Many a famous, and productive, writer has also held a day job. Anthony Trollope managed to become one of the best and most prolific of writers while working as a civil servant. ... A day job keeps toast on the table and allows you to concentrate on what you really want to write. It also keeps you grounded and close to people. You might find some good material there.

—James Scott Bell, Christian novelist

## Questions and More Questions

The notion that God called us to write Christian fiction can raise thorny questions. Here are a few more that I've heard over the years from first-time novelists:

◆ I can't find an agent; doesn't that mean I misinterpreted God's call to write fiction?

◆ I can't find the time to finish my book—should I feel guilty that I let God down?

◆ God called me to write my novel two years ago—when will he call a Christian publisher to publish it?

◆ God placed a story on my heart, but I didn't like it—what do I do now?

◆ My book didn't sell very well—why would God call me to write an unsuccessful novel?

◆ When is God going to explain to my husband that He's called me to write Christian fiction?

What makes these questions difficult to answer is that external forces seem to be standing in the way of God's plan. How can people honor God's call yet seem to fail?

Terry Burns, a Christian novelist and literary agent, offers an unusual (and useful) perspective on being called as a Christian writer:

For a Christian writer, the most important questions are these: Has God called me to write? Or do I want to write and offer my words to Him?

We initiate offerings to God. They will be accepted and be pleasing to God, but they will clearly be gifts from us to Him.

God initiates if we're genuinely called to write. If He does, writing becomes an assigned task—an obligation—and we must be acutely aware that God always finishes what He starts.

Determining whether we've been called to write is difficult. Finding out has to start with prayer. We must begin with something along the lines of 'Show me what you would have me do, Lord.' Then we must prepare our hearts and minds to receive the answer. Of course we must not be impatient, for such communication happens in His time, not ours.

# Applying Our Spiritual Gifts

*Every* Christian has been called to love and obey God. That's the one calling that every Christian writer shares and must honor. I've concluded that only a few Christian authors are called by God to write specific novels. The rest of us feel called to apply our gifts in ways that will honor God and advance His kingdom.

Christians are taught that God gives different gifts to different people—always with the expectation that those gifts will be used for His purpose. The ability to write Christian fiction is a multidimensional gift that encompasses many of the specific gifts mentioned in Scripture. Through our novels we …

◆ Minister to readers (the gift of pastoral care).

◆ Teach our readers how God works in the world.

◆ Exhort our readers (inspire and motivate them to do God's work).

◆ Entertain our readers, which without too much pulling and tugging can be seen as a kind of hospitality.

◆ Utter words of wisdom that reach specific readers who will benefit from them.

◆ Utter words of knowledge that explain God's actions.

◆ Heal and comfort readers who find solace when they read Christian fiction.

Not everyone who receives the gift of pastoral care is called to become the pastor of a church, and not everyone gifted with the skills to author Christian fiction is called to write a specific novel. But called or not, the Christian novels we write will impact readers' lives. Called or not, writing Christian fiction lets us grow in our relationship with God. And, called or not, we should use our writing gifts to glorify God and fulfill his purposes.

 **It Is Written …** _____

When I first started writing, I didn't know if God was going to allow my novels to be published, but the entire experience has taught me more about entirely, completely, totally depending upon Him, and submitting to Him aspects of my life that I never realized I was trying to keep control over. Now, I try to trust in His plans for me—I know that what I write is for Him to use for His own agenda. He knows how He wants to use me, so I just need to go with the flow.

—Camy Tang, Christian novelist

Being published is exciting, but not always necessary from God's perspective. Janet and I were strongly impacted by a Christian novel we read at our critique group. It remains unpublished, but we know that it changed our lives. I've heard of other novels that have done God's work, yet never made it all the way to bookstore shelves.

We're happy, of course, that several of our novels have been published—although we'll never fully understand what they've accomplished. We'll be content if their only purpose is to entertain believers, because that's a good purpose. Perhaps one day, the "still, small voice" will guide us in a different storytelling direction.

# Tapping the Power of Inspiration

Christians know a good deal about creative inspiration. We believe it's God-given— a divine influence that can't be fully explained or understood. We attribute our inspired moments to the work of the Holy Spirit. We're often bewildered at the results, and amazed at what inspiration has produced.

## A Force Outside Our Control

Christian novelists frequently talk about "the stories God placed on our hearts" (a lovely figure of speech that captures the wonders of inspiration). We recognize that inspiration is often not asked for, and out of our control.

We may have preferred different topics, different protagonists, different story out-comes, but … *Zap!* Literally uncontainable ideas popped into our heads. Like Amos, the Old Testament prophet, we're overwhelmed by the "Sovereign Lord" and must "prophesy." (Amos 3:8) We begin to write the novels God wants us to write.

But this kind of unbidden inspiration doesn't happen with every novel. And even when it does happen, the burst of creativity we feel is almost never sufficient to sustain a complete manuscript. We need *extra* inspiration along the way to build subplots, flesh out characters, write dialogue, establish settings—in short, to create a complete Christian novel. Furthermore, a novelist can't simply wait for creativity to strike. To be productive—to come up with 80,000 well-chosen words in a reasonable period of time—he or she needs to tap into the power of inspiration.

## The Secret Is … Writing

For a fiction writer, the "secret" of tapping into the power of creative inspiration is … *to write fiction.* God provides the inspiration, but we ultimately have to do the hard work. There's no way around the hoary old platitude that creativity is 1 percent inspiration and 99 percent perspiration. It's been said that the first thing to buy when you start a new novel is a jumbo-sized bottle of "butt glue." The first (and most difficult) challenge is to stay put in your chair and drive yourself to keep the words flowing.

# Accepting God's Timing

The Bible puts it this way: "There is a time for everything, and a season for every activity under heaven." (Ecclesiastes 3:1 NIV) "Everything" includes the publication date for your first Christian novel.

At the risk of sounding like a Sunday-morning sermon, let me remind you of something you already know: God's time is not necessarily our time. Consider how slowly things move in Scripture. What novelist wants to wait 80 years to be called (think Moses!) or spend 40 years wandering in a desert of rejections (think Israelites!)? But metaphorically, many Christian novelists wait and wander equivalently long times. Janet and I waited nearly nine years to move from "Hmmm … why don't we write a mystery novel?" to "Praise God! We sold our first manuscript." We used to think that was an incredibly long time, until we met Christian authors who waited even longer.

**Wisdom and Knowledge**

One of the key differences been new and experienced novelists is that the latter sit down at their computers secure in the confidence that inspiration *will come*. It may take time, the process may be painful and messy, but they know that the end result will be a block of good words on the screen.

On the other hand, we're astonished by the rapid pace at which good things happened when the timing was finally right. Everything seemed to drop into place like the tumblers in a lock—things we knew we couldn't orchestrate by ourselves.

Lots of novelists succeed more quickly—I hope you'll be among them—but as a Christian writer, you should recognize that you're ultimately following a timetable that you didn't create.

One of the more interesting explanations of God's timing I've heard came from a pastor I met at a writers' conference. I'd joined in the inevitable late-night discussion about how long everything takes in Christian publishing. The pastor pointed out that nothing that grows can be planted and harvested in the same season. "God could do it faster if He wanted to, but He takes time so *we* can adjust and get ready. Don't blame God when things go slowly. We can't handle things happening any faster."

Whether or not this is convincing to you probably depends on how long you've been striving to sell your first novel. In any case, trying to rush God's timing is a bad idea. Besides not working, it can have nasty consequences. The Old Testament offers several tales of people who tried to accelerate God's timing and failed (think Abraham and Sarah!). What was true in ancient Canaan seems to apply in the modern world of Christian fiction. I've "pushed" agents, editors, publishers, but have never succeeded—and always regretted the attempt.

**It Is Written ...**

I wait for the Lord, my soul waits, and in His Word I put my hope. My soul waits for the Lord more than watchmen wait for the morning, more than watchmen wait for the morning.

—Psalm 130:5-6 NIV

# Christian Fiction That Hits Too Close to Home

The French have a term for it: *roman à clef.* The literal translation is "novel with a key." It means a novel that hides events that really happened behind a façade of fictional details. Many Christian novels are romans à clef. Christian novelists often base their stories on real people who've done terrible things, and other people who've endured horrific experiences. Some novels retell tragic events in their authors' own lives. In most of these books, the horror and tragedy give way to redemption, as God "works for the good" in all things.

First-time novelists are especially likely to reach into their own experiences for story content because the first item of advice given to new authors is "write what you know."

I'm pulled aside at most of the writers' conferences I attend by participants who've read my biographical sketch. "Let me ask you a legal question," they say. "Can I get in trouble for telling the truth about a relative or a neighbor?" I start my answer with a line by Ernest Hemingway: "All good [novels] have one thing in common—they are truer than if they had really happened."

Despite what many novelists think, courts agree with Hemingway. That's why it is possible to *defame* living people (and also invade their privacy) by making them thinly disguised characters in a novel.

The typical upfront disclaimer in a novel states "This is a work of fiction. Names, characters, places and incidents are either the product of the author's imagination or are used fictitiously, and any resemblance to actual persons, living or dead, business establishments, events or locales is entirely coincidental." This general disclaimer is not sufficient to relieve the author (and the publisher) of legal liability. Simply put, you can lose in court and be told to pay significant damages to the real person who inspired the fictional character.

**Chapter and Verse**

**Defamation** is the communication of an untruth that harms a person's reputation. Libel is defamation committed in writing (as opposed to slander, defamation committed in speech). Because defamation requires untruth, the usual defense against a claim of libel is to prove that the challenged communication is true. Invasion of privacy is based on a different legal idea. A person's privacy can be invaded by a *true* communication that reveals offensive or sensational facts that are not of legitimate public concern. These can include health information, sexual details, past indiscretions, and even crimes committed long ago.

The solution is to disguise the relative or neighbor by changing virtually everything about the person: appearance, age, occupation, and the like. And while you're at it, change the setting, the circumstances, the historical era—anything that might cause readers to recognize the person in question.

Christian writers should think twice about revealing old truths. Even if your publisher's defamation attorney says you can tell the story without legal consequences, your decision to dredge up the past might lack *charity* (the word the King James Version uses to translate *agape*, the kind of love that Jesus urged us to have for our neighbors and even our enemies).

# The Christian Response to the Business Side of Writing

Jesus said it well: "No servant can serve two masters. Either he will hate the one and love the other, or he will be devoted to the one and despise the other. You cannot serve both God and Money." (Luke 16:13 NIV)

Does this mean that Christian writers should avoid the money aspects of Christian publishing? Many try. In fact, they feel decidedly uncomfortable when they …

**Wisdom and Knowledge**

You don't get paid what's fair—you get paid what you negotiate.

—A common business adage

- Negotiate publishing contracts and "argue" about the many different clauses.

- Contemplate the various contract provisions that seem to anticipate lawsuits and future legal wrangling.

- Talk about money—including royalty percentages, advance royalties, and financial terms and conditions.

The truth is there's really no way for a Christian novelist to dissociate him- or herself from these issues. An agent or attorney can take over many of the onerous details, but authors have to make final decisions. As I noted in Chapter 3, Christian publishing combines ministry *and* business.

Just as Christian publishers must exercise prudent business practices to survive in the risky fiction marketplace, Christian authors need to think of themselves as part-time businesspeople. Money needn't be your master, but you do have to keep an eye on it.

### It Is Written ...

An important key to writing success is to see yourself not only as an artist, but also as a businessperson. We won't succeed as writers unless we master the business side of writing. Now you may not think of yourself as a salesperson ... Indeed, the very term may be abhorrent to you, conjuring up images of pushy people peddling wares. But, the cold reality of being a writer is that you are a salesperson whether you like it or not. ... There is nothing wrong with selling. When you sell your writing, you convince an editor that your writing is valuable and that it will benefit the lives of those who read it.
—Mary Ann Diorio, Ph.D., Christian author and life coach

Chip MacGregor, a literary agent, Christian writer, and editor, urges Christian authors to "Read the fine print. I'm not kidding—READ THE FINE PRINT. If you don't understand what something is, ask.

"Seek help. I can guarantee you that your publisher has a team of lawyers and accountants supporting him. Don't think you know it all. Some things you might think unreasonable at first (like not allowing you to pick your own cover) are perfectly reasonable. If you don't have an agent, consider a contract review from an experienced person.

"Be careful about having [a family] lawyer look at your contract. Publishing law is very different from creating wills and drawing up home closings, so you need a specialist. I've seen lawyers try to completely rewrite a publishing contract—something the publisher won't do.

"A contract negotiation is just that—a negotiation. So feel free to ask for changes."

## The Least You Need to Know

- ◆ A few Christian novelists are called by God to write specific novels; the rest of us are called to apply our gifts in ways that will honor God and advance His kingdom.

- ◆ The "secret" of tapping into the power of creative inspiration when you write fiction is … *to sit down and write fiction.*

- ◆ Christian fiction writers succeed according to God's timing—we all follow timetables that we didn't create.

- ◆ Fiction that hits too close to home can create legal problems for you and your publisher.

- ◆ As a Christian novelist, you must see yourself as both an artist and a businessperson—you can't dissociate yourself from the "unpleasant aspects" of money and negotiations.

# Chapter 18

# The Dark Side of Writing Christian Fiction

## In This Chapter

- ◆ Taming jealousy
- ◆ Calming pride
- ◆ Overcoming fear of failure
- ◆ Facing unrealistic expectations of success
- ◆ Getting past wretched reviews

This may be a difficult chapter for you to read; it certainly was difficult for me to write. Few of us want to think that the exciting prospect of writing—and publishing—a Christian novel could have a dark side, but there are less-than-happy aspects you should be aware of. My goal isn't to frighten you, but rather to give you fair warning of the tribulations that many Christian writers have experienced during their novel-writing journey.

# Keeping Jealousy at Bay

Christian novelists are reluctant to talk about jealousy. For starters, it's embarrassing to admit being simultaneously envious and resentful of another writer's accomplishments. And then there are the religious implications. As one writer replied when I asked her about jealousy, "Jealousy is an un-Christian emotion—I simply don't see it among Christian novelists."

She's wrong, of course. Jealousy is a common plague among Christian writers that can …

- Cause endless pain to the novelist who becomes jealous, enough pain to slow down his or her writing.

- End friendships among Christian writers.

- Tear a Christian critique group apart.

- Trigger spiteful behavior (for example, jealousy has prompted the posting of bad reviews on Internet bookseller sites).

Jealousy has been defined as envy *plus* ill will. Envy merely "wants" what someone else has. Jealousy couples "want" with the hope that the other person loses what they've achieved. It's no wonder that a familiar metaphorical label for jealousy is the "green-eyed monster."

## A Popular Predicament

Many Christian writers acknowledge they suffer pangs of jealousy, including some successful novelists who've achieved significant prominence. This raises an obvious question: Why would writers who've "made it" ever feel jealous? The answer is simple: the rules of the fiction game—both Christian and secular—makes it certain that each of us will have countless opportunities to compare ourselves against fellow novelists.

Remember the novelist's pyramid I showed you in Chapter 5? Well, imagine a ladder standing against its side. Every writer is standing on a specific rung, somewhere on that ladder. Ahead of you—higher up on the ladder—are novelists who have agents, who have better agents than you do, who have written more words than you have, who are better writers than you are, who have more "product" circulating among editors, who have landed better publishers, who received better reviews, who have won more awards, who look better in back-cover photos than you do, who do a better job of marketing, who have sold more books, who earn more money, who will receive larger advances, whose books have been turned into movies … I think you get the point.

How can you not look gimlet-eyed at the accomplishments of writers who seem to be doing better than you? How can you not wish, even fleetingly, that you could change places with them on the ladder? How can you *not* be jealous of these other writers, at least once in a while?

It makes no difference if you're unpublished, published, or multi-published—you can always find some point of comparison, some writer who seems blessed with advantages you don't have, *for no discernable reason.* And guess what—while you're envying the novelists above you and thinking ill thoughts,

**Wisdom and Knowledge**

Curiously, some people make the argument that a smidgen of jealousy can help to fuel your creative process. Envy of another writer's success, they say, may keep you pounding your keyboard. And the heady mix of envy, anger, and pride—all potentially destructive emotions—may drive you to reach greater literary heights and produce better fiction.

other writers a few steps down the ladder are feeling jealous of you. They can't imagine what you've done to deserve the success you've achieved.

Christian writers, at least, should pay attention to the advice in Scripture: A heart at peace gives life to the body, but envy rots the bones. (Proverbs 14:30 NIV)

Like it or not, comparison is rampant in novel writing—and will always be. Agents, editors, reviewers, booksellers, and readers all hold yardsticks up against novels and their authors. We are measured dozens of different ways, from the quality of our writing to the power of our platforms. It's no surprise, then, that even Christian writers feel tempted to compare themselves against their colleagues. And once comparison begins, uncalled-for jealousy or unwarranted pride are sure to follow.

Ironically, the rush to comparison often causes us to overstate the similarities between us and other Christian novelists—and to understate important differences. You write about specific topics, in a particular genre, with a distinct voice, in an individual style. Remember this whenever you find yourself making comparisons. Why be jealous of a writer who's doing something you have no interest in doing?

## Dealing with Jealousy

Jealousy is a useless emotion. It makes you feel miserable but doesn't improve your writing or raise your chances of success. Quite the contrary, being jealous consumes energy that you can use more effectively to polish your novel.

Unfortunately, much of the advice about dealing with jealousy is incomplete; for example, "Be content with what God has given you" or "Remember that Christians are exhorted to expel evil thoughts from our minds by thinking uplifting thoughts." *Umm* ... right! But how do we pull off these little tricks?

A more practical suggestion for a Christian writer is to pray for the writer who has triggered your pangs of jealousy—even though you may prefer to munch on a hearty portion of broken glass. Asking God to heap more blessings upon a writer you envy helps to restore your awareness that his or her success is in accord with God's plan—a plan that may well include exciting news for you in the months and years ahead.

Another idea (I've never tried it, but one of my friends claims it works every time) is to follow this five-step process:

**It Is Written ...**

I have one thing to say about jealousy. Avoid it. At all costs. I'm talking personal jealousy, professional jealousy, someone else's jealousy, or your own. ... When I find myself feeling that green-eyed monster peer over my shoulder ... I go out of my way to make acquaintance with the person who is making me feel intimidated. I learn to care about them personally. And I pray for them.

—Hannah Alexander, Christian novelist

1. Acknowledge that jealousy is a routine aspect of our fallen natures—don't be surprised when it happens to you.

2. Immediately write a one-page letter denouncing your triumphant colleague that includes specific reasons why his or her contract/award/sales success was wholly undeserved—use as much vitriolic language as possible.

3. When you've fine-tuned the letter to produce maximum distress, print a hardcopy and read it carefully.

4. Run the hardcopy through your shredder and erase the file from your computer.

5. Congratulate the author with as much enthusiasm as you would expect when you announce an equivalent success.

# Pride Cometh When You Drink Your Own Bathwater

Sinful pride is another behavior that can afflict Christian novelists. I use the phrase "sinful pride" here because I don't want to suggest that all pride is destructive. Taking honest pride in our writing, like taking honest pride in our children, can be a good thing. It's one of the forces that compels us to write the best possible novels we can create. It impels us to develop new skills as Christian novelists. It gives us a proper perspective in the face of rejections and other discouragements.

What writer wouldn't feel proud when an agent agrees to represent his work, her manuscript wins an award, he receives a contract for a new novel, or she sees her first novel on a bookstore shelf? These are, after all, four of the most joyous moments of writing Christian fiction. You should enjoy and celebrate them. But *don't drink your own bathwater.*

 **It Is Written ...**

I'm reading a book on humility right now, so it's safe to say I know more about the subject than any of you.
—James Scott Bell, Christian novelist

## Don't Camouflage the Real You

"Don't drink your own bathwater" is a nifty expression I often hear inside the corporations I consult for as a marketing communicator. It means don't let sinful pride camouflage the *real you.* Don't start believing your own propaganda—or the nice things that other people will say about you when you take a step toward success.

Enough sips of bathwater will transform the "healthy pride" you feel into prideful behavior. And that's when the problems begin.

Pride is popularly known as "the first deadly sin"—first in rank because it's the most dangerous. The kind of pride that's sinful is a belief in one's own ability that's strong enough to impair one's recognition of the grace of God. Sinful pride opposes the virtue of humility (seeing ourselves as we actually are, and refusing to compare ourselves to other people).

If you look, you can find many flavors of prideful behavior alive and well in the Christian fiction community:

- Panelists at writers' conferences who spend big chunks of workshop time describing their accomplishments, and telling "and then I wrote" stories

- Writer websites that cater to vanity—featuring gushing testimonials, overblown biographies, and (occasionally) photographs that scarcely resemble the writer in person

- Verbal duels on writing loops fought by participants who absolutely, positively must have the last word

◆ Effusive praise and congratulations posted on writing loops by other participants at the request of a writer who fears that no one will offer praise if he or she doesn't arrange it

◆ Members of critique groups who defend against any and all suggestions, because they refuse to accept criticism of their "perfect-as-they-are" chapters

◆ Participants at writers' conferences who waste the time of agents and editors seeking "affirmations" of book ideas they will never transform into manuscripts

◆ Authors who believe that having written and published one novel makes them "experts" on a multitude of writing-related topics—and on the problems associated with Christian fiction and Christian publishing

◆ Novelists who blame everyone but themselves if their latest books don't do well in the marketplace—the publisher was too much in a hurry for me to deliver, my editor asked for silly changes, the art department came up with an awful cover, the marketing staff all but ignored the book, the sales force never cared about the novel

Happily, one item of potentially prideful behavior that's not on my list is the bestselling Christian author who struts, preens, and demands praise in the presence of less experienced writers. Perhaps such novelists exist, but I've never met any. In fact, in my experience, just the opposite seems true: successful Christian authors are among the most gracious folks I know. When you chat with them at writers' conferences and book signings, expect a smile and a friendly greeting.

> **It Is Written ...**
>
> Pride's opposite is humility, but don't think the most humble person is the one who hangs his head and goes around moaning about how untalented he is. He has taken the pendulum of pride in the opposite direction and is still self-centered. [Don't be] like the writer who said, "I've talked enough about my writing. Tell me—what did *you* think of my novel?"
>
> —Angela Hunt, Christian novelist

## The Vice of Fools

The English poet Alexander Pope described pride as "the never-failing Vice of Fools." Most people are foolish to some extent, so pride is a never-ending source of storylines for Christian novelists. You can build a successful career writing fiction about prideful people. Assuming, of course, you can eliminate the aspects of your own prideful behavior that can damage your professional interests. This is the problem of pride that I need to address here.

The apostle Paul urged, "Do nothing out of selfish ambition or vain conceit, but in humility consider others better than yourselves." (Philippians 2:3 NIV) Engaging in prideful behavior turns this upside-down. Writers bursting with unhealthy pride send obvious signals that they regard themselves as "better" than the rest of us. The agents, editors, and writers on the receiving end usually don't agree. That's why prideful behavior is ultimately off-putting—and can be career-destroying.

I know one prolific Christian novelist who seemed to go out of her way to insult an editorial assistant who was struggling to shepherd her book through the production process. She felt that a writer of her stature should work directly with a "real editor," not a "lowly assistant." Imagine her surprise when, months later, the assistant was promoted to a senior editorial position—and become someone who could advance (or impede) her career. As Solomon warned, "Pride goes before destruction, And a haughty spirit before a fall." (Proverbs 16.18 NIV)

## Puncturing Pride

Pride is one of those things that need to be continuously monitored and eliminated—not unlike the termites that might be eating away at your house. The three approaches that seem to be the most effective pride busters are:

1. Take pride in your work, not in yourself. If you write good fiction, it will earn praise. That's okay, as long you don't let the praise go to your head. When C. S. Lewis wrote about pride, he called it the "great sin." As he put it, "The more you delight in yourself and the less you delight in the praise, the worse you are becoming."

2. Don't compare yourself against other Christian novelists, the various professionals you meet in Christian publishing, or even with readers. If comparison doesn't trigger jealousy, it will likely lead to pride.

3. Don't drink your own bathwater. Discount the nice things people say about you and don't swallow the negatives. You'll be less likely to insult the soon-to-be-promoted editorial assistants in your life. There's great wisdom in the old saw, "Be nice to people on the way up because you're going to see them again on the way down."

# I'll Never Sell Another Book!

The description reads like part of a novel: a successful Christian novelist who questions his own writing skills, and is sure that when his next book appears, readers and editors will finally figure out he's a fraud, that he lacks the talent and creativity everyone assumed he had.

Unhappily, it's not fiction. Some multi-published Christian novelists struggle with painful fears of failure before every new book they write. Others wake up one morning to discover that disabling doubt has crept into their lives like the proverbial thief in the night—and paralyzed their writing.

I'm not talking about false humility. Fear of failure goes to the heart of the writing process. Proven authors lose confidence in their basic abilities to plan and write fiction. They gain the conviction that their futures are bleak, that everything good about writing Christian fiction lies in their pasts.

Fear of failure can be especially daunting for that handful of novelists who achieve early—and seemingly easy—success. Readers, critics, editors, and agents alike expect a previously triumphant author to produce new bestsellers, more award-winning novels.

### It Is Written ...

Crises of confidence are common to us all. For some, it's an almost debilitating issue and one of the primary reasons for the widespread depression among writers. Even some of the [most successful writers] find it next to impossible to keep the lid on their anxieties, often because they fall into the trap of comparing themselves with their peers—a deadly practice. Others consistently sabotage what little confidence they've managed to attain by allowing the least little failure or disappointment to throw them off balance, to the point that they spiral downward a degree at a time until they can no longer summon the stamina or the courage to go on.

—B. J. Hoff, Christian novelist

## It Takes Courage to Write Fiction

This is a good place to make an important point: we can't dismiss self-doubt as an "imaginary" problem for a novelist. Sir Walter Scott, the nineteenth-century Scottish novelist, got it right when he said: "In literature as in love, courage is half the battle." When you write fiction, you'll ...

- Confront frequent rejection.

- Receive disconcerting criticism from agents, editors, and critique group colleagues.

- Put yourself and your writing "out there"—and risk abrasive attacks on your work that may often feel personal.

- Reveal hidden aspects of your life and personality in your novels.

- Probably sell fewer books than you hope for.

All of these things can be scary to contemplate. They prove that being a novelist is not a vocation for wimps. Moreover, writing fiction is full of missteps. To paraphrase the old epigram about making mistakes, "If you haven't failed at some aspect of writing a novel, you haven't written anything."

To a great extent, novelists learn by trial and error. Writing, as they say, is re-writing. Failure is a good teacher—we're taught by our many mistakes—but the psychic tuition can be expensive.

Despite our best efforts to the contrary, we often see our novels as extensions of ourselves—as our babies. If they are ugly, we feel ugly. And so, we can easily imagine "everyday" writing doubts amplified over time in the minds of some novelists until they become debilitating fears of failure.

## "Stage Fright" for Writers

The good news about fear of failure is that most novelists who contend with crushing doubts manage to overcome them and keep writing. The problem seems to have much in common with stage fright. Anxiety often seeps away when the show begins, when the author starts taking small first steps that will eventually lead to a finished novel.

I consider myself fortunate that I haven't had to deal with this challenge. But many of my friends have. Their advice is to fight back—to refuse to believe the lies that fear tells, to focus initially on what you know you can do, rather than what self-doubt suggests you can't do.

They also urge doubt-laden writers to "lighten up." Fear of failure is a highly personal emotion. No one else is telling you that you can't succeed.

**A Lamp Unto Your Feet**

If you're suffering from self-doubt, it can help to write something new. Switch genres, author a magazine article, try your hand at a devotional. Writing progress in a different area can kick-start your stalled project.

Finally, they warn about the dangers of comparing your writing gift with those of other writers. The kind of comparison that breeds jealousy can also bore even deeper and convince you that you'll never, ever be able to match the skills of writers you envy.

# Don't Give Up Your Day Job ... Yet

What hopeful Christian novelist hasn't imagined his or her first novel generating a huge advance and becoming an immediate bestseller? You see yourself graciously accept a Christy Award a few months later, humbly thanking your agent and editor.

Visions of great success can be the chief ingredients in the "bottom glue" that keeps many of us seated in front of our computers when we'd rather be doing other things. And *some* Christian writer is going to write next year's blockbuster novel—why not you?

Daydreams can be fun, but don't let them morph into unrealistic expectations of how fast your fiction-writing career will blossom. The hard-but-true facts of writing Christian fiction are these:

◆ Most of the "overnight writing stars" you've heard about have been toiling at their craft for many years. They published 5, 10, possibly 15 novels until one caught fire with readers and became a "breakout" bestseller.

◆ Unless you're one of the handful of genuine quick successes I noted earlier in this chapter, your life won't change much at all when your first, second, or even third novel is published.

◆ Few Christian novelists earn enough from their writing to support themselves and their families reliably, year in and year out.

I've met several unpublished novelists at writers' conferences who want to chuck their current jobs and devote themselves to full-time writing. "I feel called to write Christian fiction," they say. "Shouldn't I take a leap of faith?" I've met other people who've lost their jobs and hope to switch to fiction-writing as a new career.

My counsel to both is the same: some writers have leapt into Christian fiction without a safety net and succeeded—but many others have failed. Writing any kind of fiction is an uncertain vocation; it's wise not to rely on it to support yourself and your family until you have solid evidence of long-term success.

# Wretched Reviews

Book reviewers seem to be among the most fallible of human beings. Janet and I have gathered significant evidence to prove this point: a collection of wretched reviews written by people who should have known better. Again and again, well-thought-of book reviewers misinterpreted our carefully crafted mysteries, overlooked the central ideas we meticulously incorporated within our stories, and misconstrued the Christian messages we cleverly delivered.

Scathing book reviews can have enormous impact. Few novelists remember the positive reviews their books received; most can't forget the negative. The kid's playground rhyme says, "sticks and stones may break my bones, but words will never hurt me." Don't believe it for a moment. The words in a harsh review can inflict all sorts of lasting pain to a novelist. And as much damage can be caused by an amateur reviewer who posts an abrasive review on an Internet bookseller site as by a professional critic who writes for a magazine or newspaper.

Every published writer I know can point to unfavorable—even nasty—reviews of their work. (I've attended writers' retreats where one of the break-the-ice games is a bad review contest. Happily, Janet and I have never won.) One of my friends found this achingly pithy comment in a bad review: "I cry for the trees that died for this novel to be printed."

Many scathing reviews are simply wrong. They're merely personal opinions presented as absolute truth. After all, several experienced professionals will read and evaluate a novel before it reaches a reviewer's hands. Why assume that a critic is a better judge of Christian fiction than your agent or editor?

 **It Is Written ...** _____

I'm stinging a little right now from a less than glowing review of my new book. Never mind that this reviewer did say a few nice things about my story. Never mind that another publication gave the same book a bunch-and-a-half of stars. Never mind that I just got a letter from a reader who said "[after reading your book] my heart is full of God's love, forgiveness, and redemption as I haven't experienced for a while." Never mind that I know in my heart that my worth is not tied up in what one reviewer thinks of my book. For now, all I can think about are those few pithy phrases that call my talents as a writer into question.

—Deborah Raney, Christian novelist

If you write fiction, reviews—both good and bad—come with the territory. One strategy to cope with bad reviews is to ignore *all* reviews of your books. Not reading reviews protects you from the (possibly) undeserved praise in good reviews and the (probably) unfair condemnation in bad reviews. Alas, this approach also eliminates potentially useful feedback that may identify areas of improvement for future novels. I suggest you consider—without taking to heart—every harsh comment about the books you write. Ask yourself if it implies a suggestion that will help you write better fiction. Then put it out of your mind.

## The Least You Need to Know

♦ Comparing yourself with other writers can cause jealousy, pride, and fear of failure—don't do it!

♦ Jealousy is an un-Christian feeling that many Christian writers experience— getting past jealousy is difficult, but essential.

♦ Prideful behavior is off-putting to the agents, editors, and other writers; it can harm your career.

♦ Unchecked fear of failure can paralyze your writing—if you are susceptible to the problem.

♦ Keep your day job until steady earnings from your Christian novels make you confident that being a full-time fiction writer will support you and your family.

♦ Don't believe the scathing reviews of your novels—or the good reviews that make you blush.

# Part  Get Your Christian Novel Published

If there's any more difficult chore than writing a novel, it may be getting your finished manuscript published by a "real" royalty-paying publisher. You'll hear near-miraculous tales of a first-time novelist finding an agent on the first try, or selling a novel with a single query. Well, that's not the way things work for most of us. The process of placing a novel with a publisher can take years of effort—and involves frustration, heartache, disappointment, and a true test of patience.

In this part, I'll tell how you improve your likelihood of success. The approaches I'll suggest aren't "secrets"; rather, they are commonsense strategies that have helped other Christian novelists become published.

# Chapter 19

# Increasing Your "Odds of Success"

## In This Chapter

- Understand the realities of Christian publishing
- The right way to think about your "competition"
- Do older Christian novelists face a disadvantage?
- The things an unpublished novelist should do to advance his or her career
- The things an unpublished novelist should never do

This chapter has a trick title. It's really not about the "odds of success" as a writer, because the notion of "odds" doesn't make much sense in Christian publishing. Novelists who talk this way make an elementary mistake. They view writing fiction as some sort of lottery, with editors randomly pulling successful manuscripts out of the slush pile. If a particular publisher receives 5,000 unsolicited manuscripts this year and plans to publish one new author, the so-called odds of success is 1 in 5,000.

The problem with this perspective is that it's built on two incorrect presumptions. First, that all unpublished Christian authors write equally good manuscripts. Second, that publishers see all first-time novelists as more or less inter-changeable. That's not the way people or publishing work. You have a 100 percent chance of selling your novel if you submit the right manuscript to the right publisher at the right time. Conversely, you have a zero percent chance of success if you offer a manuscript that an editor dislikes or can't use. It's almost silly to talk about "odds."

This chapter is really about things that make you—and your manuscript—of more or less interest to agents and editors. If you do the do's, don't do the don'ts, and ignore the irrelevant factors, the critical gatekeepers you need to impress will be more will-ing to evaluate your work—and perhaps even think more favorably about it. That's the only proven way to increase your "odds of success."

# Writing Christian Fiction Is Not for the Fainthearted

It is a fact that very few first-time writers sell novels. In all of publishing—Christian and secular—fewer than 200 new authors are published each year by major houses. But it's equally true that very few high school athletes go on to play with professional sports teams, very few kids who gaze at the stars go on to become astronomers, and very few aspiring politicians become senators. But in every case, *hundreds*, even *thou-sands* of people do—the people who have what it takes to play football and baseball, chart galaxies, and lead the country.

Writing a Christian novel takes courage, persistence, a supportive family—plus the skills to create publishable fiction. Surprisingly, few first-time authors assemble all of these key ingredients before they sit down to write. Consequently, *most* of the propos-als and manuscripts submitted to agents and publishers aren't good enough to get past the gatekeepers (see Chapter 20).

That's why it shouldn't make much difference to you how many writers are writing: your chief concern must be *your* ability to write Christian fiction that meets the pub-lishability criteria. If you write a cracking good novel, you can be confident that some publishing house *will* publish it.

The other side of the coin—the less happy side—is that a string of rejections typically means that your manuscript is not ready for prime time. This simple relationship between quality and rejection took me a long time to "get." It was easier for me to blame the "long odds" of publishing—to believe that the editor chose another manu-script because the author was a friend of a friend, and I wasn't.

I now understand that editors select books they believe readers will want to read. Good books; the kind I like to buy. I also will admit to myself that if I get a rejection (and I get dozens a year) it's almost always because I submitted a weak proposal, or because I sent a strong proposal to the wrong publishing company.

I now offer the single most painful sentence in this book: most of the rejections you'll receive will be your fault. Sorry—I couldn't come up with a way to soften a vital truth that too many first-time novelists ignore. I hope you won't throw this book across the room. (Or failing that, I hope you'll pick it up again and keep reading, once you've tossed it.)

# When You Think About Your Competition

All Christian writers have a common purpose—we want our fiction to advance the kingdom—but like it or not, we also compete with each other. There are a limited number of slots for Christian novels available each year (several hundred for proven novelists, less than one hundred for unpublished novelists). You're butting heads with every other first-time Christian author who …

- ◆ Writes similar books in your genre.
- ◆ Designs them for the group of readers you've chosen.
- ◆ Takes aim at the same target publishers.

And you may represent potential competition for an established author in your genre. What if you show up at his or her publisher with a better-written, more compelling novel? The editor might decide to switch horses. (This scary possibility keeps more than one multi-published author awake at night.)

Don't think of your direct competitors as your enemies, but do recognize that they are working hard to publish their novels. If they succeed—if they capture a precious Christian publishing slot—you might not sell your manuscript. Your best strategy in this situation is to forget about your competitors and write the best possible novel you can.

# Are Older Christian Novelists at a Disadvantage?

This question is asked a lot at Christian writers' conferences—not surprisingly, by older participants. The answer is: Not especially!

A recent study of 62 multi-published Christian novelists found that 30 of them were between 40 and 50 years old when they published their first novel, and 9 were older than 50 years. Publishers chiefly care about publishability—not about age, ethnicity, where an author lives, and other factors that don't impact a novel's quality.

Age doesn't seem to diminish writing ability:

- Raymond Chandler published his first Philip Marlowe mystery novel at age 51.
- Agatha Christie wrote into her 70s.
- James Michener wrote into his 80s.

Older writers have some disadvantages—health issues, other competing interests, possibly less energy—but they also have several key advantages:

- More hours available to write each day
- Fewer family responsibilities
- More life experiences to write about
- More resources to support their writing—from writing space at home, to money to afford writers' conferences

# Things an Unpublished Writer Should Do

If you do want to "increase the odds of success" (it really is a handy way to express the concept that you can do things to make your manuscript more attractive to agents and editors), here are several possibilities. I've talked about some of the key *do's* in other chapters, but they are important enough to mention again.

## Understand Your Market

Christian novelists who understand the market are more likely to write novels that fit publishers' needs. In turn, their novels are more likely to be purchased. It's that simple.

Because Christian publishing is a fast-changing industry, savvy writers pay attention to changes on publisher's websites, read industry publications (*Publishers Weekly*, for example), attend editor and agent panels and writers' conferences, and watch what kinds of novels are being sold to publishers (a good source of information are the "praise" messages on writing loops).

## Choose a Salable Genre

I've made this point before: you maximize your opportunities to sell a first-time novel when you write in a popular genre. You can prove this point simply by reading the success stories you see on writing loops.

The lion's share of sales by previously unpublished authors are in women's fiction, contemporary fiction, historical romance, suspense, and romantic suspense. By contrast, most of the occasional sales in the "minor" genres (science fiction, fantasy, Biblical, and westerns) are by previously published authors who have staked out a reputation with readers.

## Go with Limited Edginess

The few Christian publishers who are willing to publish edgy fiction typically reserve these slots for proven authors who have large readership bases. Set your edgy story aside until you have established yourself as a Christian novelist.

## Favor Third-Person Point of View

There are some Christian genres where first-person point of view dominates. The private-eye novel is an example. Although proven writers can use first-person almost everywhere, first-time writers should take notice that many editors still prefer third-person. If you have no pressing reason to use first-person POV, stick with third-person.

## Join an Effective Critique Group

As an unpublished author (possibly without an agent), you rely on your critique group for meaningful feedback about your writing. Choose a group with knowledge-able members who are committed to reviewing your work thoroughly and honestly. A group that focuses on fiction—rather than all genres of Christian writing—will probably give you more useful critiques, as will a group that contains a few published writers. (See Chapter 15 for more on choosing a critique group.)

Be wary of a critique group that's committed to "being nice," or to not hurting its members' feelings. Overly gentle criticism actually does participants a disservice. You need relevant suggestions and comments—the kind that sometimes hurt.

# Network

It's been said about advertising that only 50 percent actually works—but no advertiser knows in advance which half is worth doing. That's even truer of networking. *Most* of the networking you do will never repay the time and effort you invest—if you measure the dividends in terms of landing an agent or selling your novel to a publisher.

> **Wisdom and Knowledge**
>
> Networking can help you make friends with editors and agents—and these are relationships worth having. At the end of the day, however, networking will help get your proposal or manuscript read, but it won't sell a not-ready-to-be-published novel.

But when networking does pay off, the results can be spectacular. The right contact, at the right time, can open the right door—and lead to a sale. That makes networking worth doing. Equally important, networking can pay back your efforts in a different currency: you'll make new friends and gain useful knowledge about Christian publishing.

Networking has its own Golden Rule: Aid people in your network as you would have them help you. While you're at it, you should also follow the scriptural admonition to cast your bread upon the waters.

In other words, go out of your way to help other Christian writers when you can. And don't limit your network solely to writers you think can help your cause.

# Build a Platform

A platform that can help you sell books to readers can also help you sell your manuscript to an editor. If you're well known as a speaker or clergyman, if you have a large organization behind you, if you've written a bestselling nonfiction book, if you are a celebrity in your own right … wonderful! You'll have an easier job convincing an editor to run with your manuscript.

If you don't have a platform, think about building one. Speaking and blogging are two possibilities that are increasingly popular among unpublished novelists. A platform-building strategy can return big dividends—if you don't let the work involved get in the way of writing fiction.

# Get Endorsements

I know! It can be agonizing to ask a published author you met at a writers' conference for an endorsement, but overcome your reluctance. Asking does no damage; most writers will understand why you're doing it. Don't be surprised if the writer declines—endorsing a manuscript requires reading it first, and few published novelists have the time to read unpublished work.

But there's always a chance that a writer will say *yes*—and provide an endorsement that will help open agents' and editors' doors. A good "read" from a proven writer can turn a quick "No" into "Hmmm. Let me take a more careful look."

## Get Recommendations to Agents and Publishers

If you know a published novelist (perhaps a member of your critique group, or someone you met at a writers' conferences), ask if he or she will recommend your work to their agent or publisher. That's another way to transform an unsolicited proposal into a requested submission. Tread gently when you ask; many writers are reluctant to make recommendations for fear of "bothering" their agent and editor. You can also strain a friendship if the published writer doesn't like your work but doesn't feel able to tell you.

## Consider Having Your Manuscript Professionally Edited

A clean manuscript is more likely to survive the scrutiny of an eagle-eyed gatekeeper. You'll feel more comfortable when you submit an edited manuscript to an agent or editor. You'll also give the agent or editor fewer reasons to reject your work.

If you're comfortable with your own editing skills, you can certainly do the job yourself. (Successful novelists have done so for hundreds of years.) But think carefully before you rely on your own skills, because so many other Christian fiction writers are turning their manuscripts over to freelance editors that the manuscript quality bar has been raised. In recent years, agents and editors have come to expect error-free queries, proposals, and manuscripts. Even if you are a good self-editor, a "pair of eyes" can often catch mistakes that you might miss—or suggest improvements.

## Fine-Tune Your First Impression

Think of the agents and published writers you've met at writers' conferences and book signings. Recall the first impressions they left with you—both positive and negative. The pendulum swings the other way, too. Agents and editors can't help judging, and remembering, factors other than your writing skill when they meet you at any writers' conference.

Many writers are introverts. I certainly am. Years ago, I'd get tongue-tied meeting new people. I took public speaking courses that built my confidence and taught me techniques for thinking on my feet. They worked so well that today I teach managers and engineers how to deliver oral presentations. More to the point, I'm much more comfortable—and chatty—when I meet a new editor.

## Improve Your Computing Skills if Necessary

Your computer, and your word processing software, are essential tools of your trade (see Chapter 13). Any fiction writer who can't produce a well-formatted document, print it, and (perhaps) e-mail it to an agent or editor is at a severe competitive disadvantage. He or she may have written the Great American Christian Novel, but no one is likely to read it.

At a time when many agents and editors don't think twice about asking a writer to "use the Track Changes feature to indicate your edits," or "give me your complete proposal as a single Microsoft Word document," or "please output your manuscript as a PDF file," limited computer skills can endanger a sale.

> **Literary Sins**
>
> Don't rely on other people's computing skills; develop your own. And don't turn the job over to a "typing service." You need to be fully in charge of your own manuscript—including the ability to make fast edits whenever you get a new idea.

I'm not sure how widespread a problem this is. The last time I met a Christian novelist who took pride in writing a novel longhand on a yellow legal pad was at a major writers' conference in 2003. Nonetheless, I bring the subject up in this chapter because a good computer and appropriate software have become the price of admission to a fiction-writing career. There are no alternatives.

## Produce Lots of Product

One novel is not enough. If you're serious about writing Christian fiction, you should "keep swinging" and have several projects in the hopper. This does not signal a lack of loyalty to your primary fiction manuscript—the novel you've pinned your hopes and dreams on. Instead, it *unpins* those hopes and dreams from a single manuscript that may (I'm sorry to say) not succeed. Be as loyal as you'd like to your first manuscript, but have another novel in your back pocket to offer when an agent or editor says, "You know, I love your writing, but this particular story leaves me cold. Can you show me something else?"

## Make Sound Investments to Advance Your Career

This is another touchy issue; I'll do my best to address it carefully. First-time novelists who have the resources to invest in their writing careers without thinking about the cost may enjoy an advantage in today's tight marketplace. They can polish their craft more quickly, network more effectively, meet agents and editors more easily, and react more rapidly to market changes.

I know that many Christian novelists live on tight budgets, that cutting-edge computers, the latest software, fancy home writing spaces, writers' conferences, writer's retreats, and the like are out-of-reach luxuries. While having these things doesn't ensure success; not having them forces a writer to work even harder—and invest every available dollar more carefully.

## Finish Your Novel!

I admit that I'm tempted to tell you to close this book and get back to writing your novel. But I won't, because I want to make several other important points in this chapter.

Practically speaking, you have to finish your first novel, because hardly anyone will give an unpublished writer a contract on the basis of a proposal. Even if this wasn't true, you'd be foolish not to finish your first novel before you try to sell it.

Let me tell you a story: Janet and I are dedicated outliners; we try to figure out every aspect of the story before we start writing. Surprises are impossible … or so we thought. When we'd completed roughly 60 percent of the manuscript of our fourth book, we ran into a surprise so significant that it forced a major change of our storyline. We had to rewrite major chunks of the book to solve the problem. (I won't go into the details, because I hope you'll read *Dead as a Scone*.)

 **It Is Written …** _____

> Keep turning plot ideas "over in your head." Most new writers I encounter have a single project in hand. I tell them to get to work on their next project. If their present manuscript is still being written, I say "Finish it, and as you do be developing your next book, and getting ideas for the ones after that." Keep an idea file, where you jot down one or two line concepts that you might want to develop later. Go over this file from time to time and nurture the most promising ideas. In this way, you'll never run out of things to write about.
>
> —James Scott Bell, Christian novelist

Because this was our fourth novel, we had reasonable confidence in our ability to write publishable fiction. We weathered the initial shock, caught our breath, took the problem in stride, and dealt with it—all during a rather hectic five days. We were soon back on schedule. Had this been our first novel—sold on the basis of a plot summary—I feel certain that we'd have panicked, and probably would have decided to abandon the book.

My point is that you need to have the experience of writing a complete novel under your belt before you take on the added responsibility of promising to deliver a manuscript before you've actually written it.

# Things an Unpublished Writer Should Not Do

The suggestions in this section switch viewpoint. They're ways to "reduce the odds" that you'll never finish your first novel, or that your manuscript will be rejected.

## Don't Wish Rather Than Write

When it comes to writing a novel, wishing *doesn't* make it so. Only the hard work of writing does. "Wishing" comes in many shapes and sizes—including several that resemble sensible preparation. Going to too many writers' conferences (because they are so much fun) is a form of wishing. So is reading an endless array of how-to books. Taking a string of writing classes may be wishing, unless the homework forces you to work on your novel.

Writing a first novel can feel as daunting as climbing a mountain. Seen from the bottom, the trek up seems impossible. Many hopeful novelists never get farther than the foothills. But take one step at a time—each can be as short as a single paragraph—and you'll eventually reach the summit. Encouraging words: the mountain is not as high as it seems from the bottom. Once you get into a pattern of steady writing, it becomes easier and easier to add another thousand words each time you sit down at your computer.

## Don't Whine

Anyone who reads an Internet writers' loop regularly knows that some first-time novelists like to whine. They complain about bad writing days, troublesome computers, their general unhappiness, recent rejections, the "callousness" of agents and editors, the uncertainties of Christian publishing, "unfair" award judges, and (sometimes) other Christian writers.

 **Literary Sins**

You never know who's "listening" to an Internet loop, or where your post might be forwarded. A whiny complaint may accidentally annoy (or insult) the very agent or editor you plan to impress.

Whining is not a good idea. To begin with, many other writers on the loop are tempted to say "Suck it up!" because we've all faced similar trials. "What ..." we ask, "is so special about the whiner's experience receiving a rejection?" Whining in private—a lengthy complaint to an editor who encouraged you at a writers' conference, but subsequently rejected your proposal—is also a foolish thing to do. Editors move from publisher to publisher; they also talk to other editors. No unpublished writer will benefit from a reputation as a whiner.

## Don't Waste Golden Arrows

Don't ask for a "golden arrow" unless you intend to use it. (I use the term "golden arrow" to describe any invitation from an agent or editor to send a query, proposal, or manuscript. You collect golden arrows when, for example, you talk to agents and editors at a writers' conference. I'll tell you more about golden arrows in Chapter 22.) If you chat with an agent or editor at a writers' conference and get permission to submit a query or a proposal, follow through quickly.

The good news is that most editors and agents will forget the writers they invited to make submissions. You can probably ask again next year. The bad news is that you've wasted an opportunity that doesn't come along every day. Who knows if the editor will have any open publishing slots for a first-time novelist next year?

Keep in mind that you can ask for advice about your work-in-progress without offering to submit a query or proposal. Be honest about the status of your novel. If you're working on the second chapter, don't imply that you're "almost finished."

## Don't Be Inflexible

Never say that you'll never change the direction of your writing. Never lock yourself in to a specific genre, or topic, or style of writing. We have a good friend who's now writing for a Christian publisher she'd "never, ever write for," in a genre that "she loathed and detested with every fiber of her being," about topics that "she couldn't care less about." She now says, tongue-in-cheek, "It's a good thing I'm a Christian, because Christianity taught me how to be repentant."

A sound piece of advice I offer every Christian novelist (including first-timers) is keep your options open. It's hard to know where God will lead us—and, as is often pointed out, God has a sense of humor.

## Don't Settle for an Ineffective (or Shady) Agent

A publishing proverb that is (unfortunately) true is that no literary agent is better than a bad literary agent. A bad agent may give you bad advice, which can prompt you to go in the wrong direction, writing-wise. A bad agent often lacks respect among editors; they'll accept the agent's submissions, but assume that his or her clients are marginal at best. They start reading your work with a preconceived negative bias you may never overcome.

"Shady" agents are even worse, because they'll waste your most precious resource: time. The warning signs are:

◆ A fee to read your manuscript

◆ Extravagant promises of success

◆ Conditional acceptance as a client if you agree to use a specific editor or "book doctor" who's linked to the agency

**A Lamp Unto Your Feet**

First-time novelists become most vulnerable to agent scams after receiving a few rejection letters from legitimate agents. Don't "settle" for a less-than-reputable agent because you fear that you'll never land a good one.

Ethical literary agents don't charge reading fees, tell you the truth about fiction markets, and are happy to see any good editor fine-tune your manuscript.

Christian publishing seems to have fewer bad (and shady) agents than mainstream publishing. Two rules of thumb: you can usually trust the agents you meet at Christian writers' conferences and you can *generally* feel confident about the agents listed in the leading Christian writers' market guides.

## The Least You Need to Know

◆ You have a 100-percent chance of selling your novel if you submit the right manuscript, to the right publisher, at the right time.

◆ Listen to your rejection letters—they may be telling you your manuscript is not quite ready to be published.

◆ A head of gray hair doesn't impact your ability to sell a Christian novel.

◆ Don't think of other Christian writers as your competitors—focus your energy on developing the best novel you can write.

◆ Network, build a platform, and fine-tune your first impression.

◆ Don't be inflexible, don't whine, and don't waste your golden arrows.

# Gatekeepers and the Publishing Process

## In This Chapter

- ◆ The role of gatekeepers
- ◆ The publishing process: from proposal to finished novel
- ◆ The relationship between author and editor
- ◆ What editors and agents wish writers knew
- ◆ Don't take rejection personally!

Getting published can be a long, arduous process. Many novelists spend *years* pitching—and fine-tuning—their manuscripts until they finally manage to land publishers. Along the way, as the rejection letters pile up, it becomes easy and convenient to blame the principal gatekeepers I introduced to you in Chapter 5: agents, editors, and editorial committees. *They* don't know what they want. *They* care more about earning money than publishing good Christian fiction. *They* don't appreciate good writing when they see it.

In this chapter, I'll tell you why this isn't true—and how your success as a Christian novelist depends on the gatekeepers doing an effective job. Then we'll look beyond gatekeeping to the process inside a publishing company that transforms your accepted manuscript into a finished novel.

# Why Christian Publishing Needs Gatekeepers

Let me be brutally honest. *Most* of the manuscripts sent by unpublished authors to agents and editors are not ready for publication. Janet and I shipped dozens of "not-soup-yet" proposals and manuscripts to agents and editors during our early days as wannabe novelists. We weren't alone; our writing friends and critique-group partners also filled slush piles with premature submissions. It's no wonder that agents say less than one in a hundred "over the transom" submissions are good enough to deserve a positive response.

Looking back, we regret submitting unpublishable work—but that's what inexperienced authors do. I hope you'll resist the urge to do what we did, but I'll understand (and forgive) your eagerness if you feel compelled to send your early efforts out into the world. It's often said that you can't consider yourself a "real" writer until you amass a collection of rejection slips.

Gatekeeping is a necessity throughout Christian publishing to identify publishable manuscripts, keep unpublishable manuscripts from clogging up the system, and provide a modicum of feedback to struggling writers. As every novelist knows, rejection is a major byproduct of gatekeeping.

## Gatekeepers and Rejection

From a writer's perspective, gatekeepers seem to spend most of their time rejecting perfectly acceptable manuscripts. If you think that's true, why don't you join the fun and do some heavy-duty rejecting yourself?

The other day, I enjoyed an entertaining experience. I spent an hour in a large room where I saw *hundreds* of novels rejected. In fact, I rejected about a dozen novels myself—mostly on the basis of whether I liked the opening paragraph and what I thought about a short summary of the story. I can truly say that I felt no remorse, nor did I worry whether my rejections caused any pain for the authors.

The large room was conveniently provided by … Barnes & Noble. In other words, I made my "rejections" in a bookstore, where I considered twelve published novels and purchased only one. My point is that you and I "reject" novels by the dozen every time we browse through a bookstore's shelves.

Like it or not, most decisions made by gate-keepers are subjective. I've chatted with enough editors and agents "off the record" to realize that they exercise their judgment when they pick and choose among submissions. They fight for manuscripts they like and reject manuscripts they don't like—although few rejection letters tell that simple a story.

Given the financial risks of publishing, gate-keepers must fall in love with a manuscript to stick their necks out and push it forward. Accepting a manuscript for publication, after all, reflects the gatekeepers' confidence that tens of thousands of readers will willingly purchase the novel.

**Wisdom and Knowledge**

Every reader "rejects" published novels by the carload, often for the flimsiest of reasons: I don't like stories about [fill in the blank]. I don't like [fill in the blank] genre. The opening paragraph didn't grab me. The blurb on the back of the book struck me as silly. Agents and editors are really exercising the same kind of freedom to make highly subjective choices when they reject manuscripts.

I often make the point in my writers' conference workshops that I generate far more rejection letters now that I'm a multi-published novelist. I usually receive at least one per month. That's because I subscribe to Babe Ruth's philosophy of proposal submission. The Babe was noted for hitting balls out of the stadium. In 1927, he hit a record 60 home runs. Yet during that same baseball season, Babe Ruth achieved a second record. He had the most *strikeouts* of any American League player, a total of 89.

The point is that the Babe kept swinging. He said, "Never let the fear of striking out get in your way." Those are good words for every Christian novelist to remember. Rejections are part of the writing game. Each one you get proves that you took a swing at a potential book contract, and each rejection represents the chance to learn something new about your writing.

## The Gatekeeping Process

Each of the four primary gatekeepers has a distinct role:

1. **Agent**—performs an initial review of publishability; decides which publishers are likely to want to publish the specific genre and topic.

2. **Acquisitions editor**—gauges whether the initial proposal outlines a novel that will fit well in the publisher's line and is likely to be enjoyed by readers; then evaluates the full manuscript; and finally becomes the manuscript's chief advocate inside the company. This is an important point that I want to emphasize: the acquisitions editor—the first gatekeeper you must pass inside the publishing company—changes roles and becomes an active campaigner for your novel. He or she "sells" your work to the other internal gatekeepers.

3. **Publications board**—estimates the financial risk of publishing the novel along with the potential financial benefits; determines whether the novel will compete with similar books published by the company.

4. **Marketing team**—determines the marketing needs of the published novel and whether or not it is likely to succeed among the readers the publisher serves.

A novel must pass through every gatekeeping hurdle before you receive a contract. Many authors—including us—have had the unhappy experience of getting past agent and editor only to have the publications board or the marketing team say no.

The following list summarizes the various steps of the generic publishing process that leads from the submission of a manuscript to its acceptance. Different publishers will vary the process and may have fewer or more stages, but manuscripts typically pass through a minimum of four gatekeepers and five approval gates.

1. Author submits proposal to agent.

2. Agent likes the proposal; asks for full manuscript. This is the first "approval gate" your proposal must make it through.

3. Agent decides to represent author; they sign an agency agreement.

4. Author creates an improved proposal. Agent fine-tunes the proposal, then queries appropriate publishers. Acquisitions editor responds positively to agent's query. This is the second approval gate.

5. Agent sends full manuscript to interested acquisitions editor.

6. Acquisitions editor likes the manuscript; tells agent of interest and moves it forward. Your project has just passed through the third approval gate.

7. Acquisitions editor presents the manuscript to publications board and marketing team.

8. Publications board and marketing team accept the manuscript. Your novel has made it past the fourth approval gate.

9. Acquisitions editor initiates the creation of a publishing contract with author.

10. Author, agent, and acquisitions editor take part in negotiations.

11. Editor works with legal staff to create final publishing contract.

12. Author signs final publishing contract.

# Every Aspect of Gatekeeping Takes Time

One of the more frustrating aspects of the gatekeeping process is the cumulative time it takes for proposals and manuscripts to inch past the gatekeepers. I've heard many unpublished novelists—both Christian and mainstream—complain, "At this pace, my first novel will be published posthumously." Although I hate to be the bearer of sad news, here are typical gatekeeping "delays":

- 2+ months for an agent to read and respond to query from a nonclient

- 1–2 weeks for agent and author to discuss and conclude an agency agreement

- 1–2+ months for editor to respond to an initial proposal

- 2–4+ months for editor to read a full manuscript

- 1–3 months for a publication board to review—and approve—the purchase of a manuscript

- 1+ month to prepare publishing agreement

- 1–2 weeks for author, agent, and editor to negotiate the publishing agreement

Janet and I have had a novel that flew through the approval process—mostly because the timings dovetailed perfectly. For example, the editor was able to take our proposal to the publication board meeting held days after she decided to move the proposal ahead. But another of our novels took upwards of a year to work its way through the system, because scheduled meetings were cancelled and other projects had higher priority than our proposal.

For an unpublished writer, many gatekeeping evaluations lead to dead ends: agents who decline to represent a manuscript or editors who decide they liked the proposal more than the complete manuscript. These days, it can take five years or more of determined effort to sell a first novel. You'll hear stories of blessed writers who sold their first draft at their first writer's conference—but don't count on doing the same thing. It's much more likely you'll experience a long and slow journey, like the rest of us did.

The bottom line: becoming a Christian novelist will almost certainly test your patience, and your commitment to writing fiction.

# The Editing and Production Process

Once you've sold your manuscript to a publisher, the editing and production process begins. Unless the publisher has a pressing reason to rush your novel into print, the process will take at least six months, and could last as long as two years. (Publishing agreements typically give the publisher a maximum of 18 to 36 months to produce a finished novel.)

It takes several kinds of editorial focus to move your manuscript from initial submission to a finished novel. At smaller publishing houses, a single person may wear different editorial hats; at larger companies, three or four specialized editors will shepherd a novel during the various editorial and production steps. As with most other aspects of fiction, the definitions are subject to arguments. Here are the editorial labels I like to apply.

## Acquisitions Editor

The acquisitions editor acquires manuscripts. This includes identifying publishable manuscripts, recommending them for publication, and initiating publishing agreements with authors. An acquisitions editor may also work with an author to improve a proposal or manuscript before it goes to other gatekeepers.

A closely related role is finding new authors for the company's "stable" of writers. Because novelists work so hard to impress editors, we often forget that publishers need authors as much as authors need publishers. We provide the product they sell, which explains why so many acquisitions editors attend leading writers' conferences.

## Development Editor

The development editor—sometimes called the line editor, the substantive editor, or the content editor—will look at your manuscript from two viewpoints:

1. The macro perspective, including such factors as story, dialogue, authorial voice, point of view, characterization, Christian worldview, and adherence to the publisher's guidelines

2. The micro perspective, which zeros in on grammatical errors, minor inconsistencies, continuity errors, and factual mistakes

Development editing is the single most important phase of the editing process—and often the most time-consuming, because it may entail significant rewriting. It's not unusual, for example, for a development editor to ask an author to add, delete, or move chapters, introduce new characters, rethink existing characters, strengthen the Christian message, and redo openings and endings.

## Production Editor

A production editor—also called a project editor—manages the various steps of book production. That process can begin in earnest when development editing is complete. It includes copyediting, typesetting, proofreading, book design, cover design, and printing.

Few novel manuscripts are actually "typeset" these days. Rather, desktop publishing programs such as *QuarkXPress* are used to make camera-ready pages that are sent to the book printer.

## Copy Editor

The copy editor corrects grammatical, spelling, capitalization, and word-choice errors and makes certain that dates, times, numbers, possessives, punctuation, and words that have different acceptable spellings and/or forms are presented in ways that follow the publishing company's style guide.

A good copy editor is typically the last line of defense against errors appearing in your novel. We've been lucky enough to have had copy editors who spotted inconsistencies and continuity errors that everyone else missed.

## Proofreader

The proofreader reads galleys and camera-ready pages before they go the printer. This is typically the last editorial quality-control check and is aimed chiefly at finding missing lines, transposed type blocks, and incorrect typography (wrong type font, size, or weight).

> **It Is Written ...**
> Proofread carefully to see if you any words out.
> —Anonymous

Development editors and copy editors can't help proofreading when they edit a manuscript. Well, proofreaders may also do some last-minute "sanity checking" of the camera-ready pages they read—but don't count on them finding minor errors that you and the other editors missed.

The following list picks up where the previous one left off, summarizing the generic editing and production process that transforms a manuscript into a novel. As with the first half of the publishing process, different Christian publishers will have their own ways of doing things.

13. Line editor reviews the manuscript, then requests revisions from the author. Art staff develops concept for cover.

14. Author revises manuscript.

15. Development editor reviews author's changes; if okay the novel is moved to a copy editor. Cover art is developed; book is designed.

16. Copy editor reviews the manuscript for grammatical errors. A cover "mock up" is designed.

17. Final cover designed; *galley proofs* are made.

18. Galley proofs are proofread.

19. Production editor sends galley proofs to author.

20. Author reviews galley proofs.

21. Production editor reviews author's galley revisions.

22. Production editor makes last-minute changes to galleys. *Camera-ready* novel is sent to book printer. Marketing begins; sales personnel take orders; ARCs (advanced reading copies) sent to book reviewers.

23. Book is printed. Promotion begins; media kits sent out; book signings scheduled.

24. Books shipped to warehouses.

25. Book is distributed.

### Chapter and Verse

Galley proofs (or **galleys**) got their name from the slender trays that once held movable type. A true galley proof is a column of type impressed on a long sheet of paper; it enables a proofreader to check the block of type for typographical errors. Today's galleys are output by desktop publishing programs and are likely to look like the pages of a book. The modern process of printing a book typically begins by photographing desktop-published pages and using the captured images to produce printing plates. Thus, **camera-ready** pages have been through every aspect of editing; they are ready to deliver to the book printer.

## Editorial Miscellany

At a small Christian publisher, the *editorial director* will manage the publishing side of the house. At a large publisher, he or she may administer an imprint (a line of books). At the other end of the chain of command, *editorial assistant*s act as the interface between editors and authors and frequently have the task of giving submissions from unpublished authors a first read.

These days, the editors at Christian publishers are just as skilled and knowledgeable as those at secular houses—and in many cases have additional training in theology and ministry. Some have actually attended seminary or equivalent. Where most Christian editors differ from their secular colleagues is viewpoint. Christian editors, like Christian authors, are likely to perceive Christian fiction as a ministry.

It's increasingly common for specialist editors—acquisition editors, development editors, copy editors, and proofreaders—to be freelancers who work outside a publishing house and live in different parts of the country. A *general editor* inside the publisher will coordinate the hand-offs among the specialists as a manuscript moves forward through editing toward production.

Some Christian publishers send manuscripts to outside reviewers, to gauge reader interest and, sometimes, to evaluate Christian content and message. Their remarks and suggestions may be folded into editorial comments, or you may receive them separately.

# The Dance Between Author and Editor

If you ever need a fine example of a relationship that features mixed emotions, look no further than the "dance" between author and editor. While the pair spend most of their time together on the same side of the fence, they sometimes may glare at each other from across a wide divide.

In theory, both author and editor are after the same thing—a "perfect" novel that readers will enjoy and recommend to their friends. Both editor and author have vested interests in mending imperfections, expunging inconsistencies, eliminating careless errors, and correcting factual errors. In practice, though, the subjectivity I talked about earlier can raise its ugly head. When this happens, an editor and an author may bump heads.

Editors have read enough sloppy writing during their careers to conclude that many—if not most—novelists need editing help. You'll occasionally hear editors say that writers are too close to their work to be objective, and too egotistical to admit it when there are flaws in their writing. Experienced editors can provide chapter and verse about novelists who fought against essential corrections in grammar and style, to eliminate content on the no-no list (see Chapter 11), or to repair inconsistencies in the storyline.

Novelists, of course, have other tales to tell—usually about editors who overstepped their responsibilities and imposed their visions and personal preferences on a manuscript. One of our friends ran into a development editor who rewrote a major chunk of her mystery novel and even changed the ending. There are editors out there who ask for frivolous fixes, spot problems that don't exist, demand needless rewrites, and then insist that their judgment is correct.

### A Lamp Unto Your Feet

Janet and I have been exceptionally lucky with our editors—so far. If you are less fortunate, heed the advice that a seasoned writer gave us. Don't get into a fistfight with your editor. Novelists rarely win them. If you really disagree with what an editor asks, if there's no way you can accommodate his or her requests without ruining your manuscript, get your agent to do battle for you. That's one of an agent's principal jobs.

# What Gatekeepers Wish Novelists Knew

I asked several Christian gatekeepers what they'd like you to know about the work they do. Here's what they told me to tell you.

## Don't Take Rejection Personally

Your manuscript is *not* your baby. Your work can be rejected for myriad reasons that have nothing to do with its quality:

- ◆ Your proposal doesn't fit the publisher's strategy for the future.
- ◆ Your novel would compete with a similar book currently in production.
- ◆ The genre or the topic is wrong for the house's target reader.
- ◆ A book perceived as similar did not do well with readers.
- ◆ The publisher reduced the number of fiction "slots" this year and all of them are full.
- ◆ The acquisitions editor didn't love it enough to buy it.

Publishing is a hard-nosed business, and editors think as much about "product" as they do "literature." They have to, given the financial risks involved with publishing a new novel—and the even greater risks of publishing a new novelist.

## Edit Carefully Before Submitting

I've said this earlier in this book: clean up your proposal and manuscript before you submit them. If careless errors kill the fictional dream for an agent or editor, you deserve the rejection letter you'll receive.

There's really no excuse for sloppy writing and bush-league mistakes in grammar, spelling, or punctuation. Any of these things makes you look less than professional and casts doubt on your abilities as an author. If you are editorially challenged (many writers are), consider hiring a freelance copy editor to review your proposal and manuscript.

Keep in mind that using the spelling and grammar checkers built into your word processor is *not* the equivalent of carefully editing your manuscript. These features are handy, but no substitute for a careful read. For example, the spell checker will find nothing wrong with "there" when you meant to type "their," or "to" when "too" is correct.

**It Is Written …** _____

I find I make messes all over the pages of my manuscript. I type "to" when what I really want is "too." How about the old *your-you're* foul up? And of course, the ever popular *its-it's* boo-boo. … It's not my editor's job to take them out. It's mine. Simply put, when we submit a manuscript, it should be clean. Whether published or not, our job as writers is to present the most sparkling piece of work we can, pristine and polished, so our editors can do their real job, locating weaknesses and elongating strengths. It's not only what we have to say that separates a good writer from a mediocre writer, but how we say it—all the way down to the small messes.

—Lisa Samson, Christian novelist

## Don't Fret About Manuscript Format

Neatness counts—but despite what you read on many writers' loops, there are no magic formats that agents and editors insist on before they'll read your manuscript. What really counts is an easy-to-read page layout:

- Minimum one-inch margins all around

- Double-spaced

- Standard readable typeface (12-point Times New Roman or 12-point Courier New)

- No desktop-publishing "frills" (such as designer typefaces, dropped initial capital letters, or right justification)

When your manuscript is finally accepted, the publisher will have its own author guidelines regarding format. Any fancy formatting in your manuscript will probably just have to be stripped out. Simple and straightforward is best. Much the same is true when you format a proposal to "market" your novel to an agent or editor. (I'll talk about proposal format in Chapter 21.)

## Learn How Christian Publishing Works

This book is a start, but you can find lots more information on the Internet, in magazines, and at writers' conferences (see Appendix A for a sampling). The more knowledge you have, the more likely you are to prepare a successful proposal. Many gatekeepers recommend that you read *Publishers Weekly* magazine to keep abreast of changing industry trends.

## Gatekeeping Is Rarely a Full-Time Job

Agents, editors, and the members of publishing boards spend most of their time on other activities. Your manuscript is at the center of your universe, but it's not top priority to an agent preparing for a writers' conference or negotiating a contract, or to an editor struggling to meet a book production deadline or getting ready for a marketing team meeting. That's a major reason why the gatekeeping process takes as long as it does.

## Multiple Submissions Have Become the Norm

The days of exclusive submissions are all but over. Given the long time it takes to get your proposal or manuscript evaluated, agents and editors expect you to submit your work simultaneously to more than one agency or publisher. A possible exception is this: if you receive an *especially* golden arrow—say an expression of immediate interest at a writers' conference—hold back multiple submissions for a reasonable period of time. One month is a fair delay.

## Keep Swinging!

This means more than merely submitting one proposal—or one manuscript—over and over again. You need lots of "product," as many as four different novels. If the thought of writing four novels "on spec" makes you cringe, consider this: having multiple projects prevents an over-focus on a single manuscript, reduces the pain of rejection, enhances your writing skills, builds your confidence as a writer, and reduces writing burnout.

## The Least You Need to Know

- ◆ Christian publishing needs gatekeeping because the majority of submitted fiction manuscripts are not ready for publication.

- ◆ The label "editing" applies to many different essential activities that transform a manuscript into a published novel.

- ◆ Both author and editor have the same goal—a novel that readers will enjoy and recommend to their friends.

- ◆ Keep rejections and formatting in perspective.

# Chapter 21

# The Well-Crafted Christian Fiction Proposal

## In This Chapter

- ◆ The basics of submitting an effective proposal
- ◆ Why a proposal isn't enough to sell your first novel
- ◆ Using a manuscript submission service
- ◆ The elements of a winning proposal
- ◆ Writing an effective (and successful) story synopsis
- ◆ Marketing your book

You can find lots of advice in books, in magazines, and on the Internet about writing a fiction proposal. If you come across any that tells you, "An effective fiction proposal *must have* …" you can safely ignore it. The phrase "must have" doesn't make much sense, because there's no such thing as standard content or standard format for a fiction proposal. One size does *not* fit all. Each agent, every publisher, will set his or her own rules. You'll have to adjust content to fit every submission you make. That's why it's essential to track down specific submission guidelines on agent and publisher websites. (A few agents and publishers still make them available via snail mail.)

In this chapter, I'll talk about the different "chunks" of information you may be asked to provide. Some guidelines will call for all of them, some for only a few. My focus will be on getting each chunk right. That's what I mean by "well-crafted."

# Proposal ABCs

Your proposal has one overarching purpose: to encourage an agent or editor to become sufficiently interested in your novel that he or she will invest the considerable time it takes to read the entire manuscript.

Equally important, your proposal introduces *you* to an agent or editor. A well-crafted proposal speaks volumes about your professionalism as a novelist and commitment to writing high-quality Christian fiction. Look at things from the perspective of the other side of the transaction: would you take the risk of building a long-term relationship with a novelist who submitted a sloppy, ill-conceived proposal?

## The Bare Essentials

What's the minimum submission that could get an agent or editor interested in your novel? The simplest possible "proposal" is one or two chapters from your novel. Nonfiction writers often submit sample chapters from different parts of a book; novelists always provide beginning chapters. The reason, of course, is that *everyone*—agents, editors, critics, and customers in bookstores—begins to evaluate a novel by reading its opening paragraphs. As a Christian literary agent told me, "If an author can pull me into a fictional dream and the story on page 1, I begin thinking of the author as a new client."

## Two Schools of Thought

How does a proposal work? How does it persuade an agent or editor to ask for your complete manuscript? Surprisingly, there are two schools of thought on the subject:

1. Your proposal should dazzle the reader with fabulously written words that make the reader want to read more.

2. Your proposal should not give the reader any reason to toss your proposal away.

The latter "strategy" deserves some explanation. Consider the poor agent or editor who has the unenviable job of reading the torrent of fiction proposals that arrive every day. After a while, he or she will develop ways to speed up the process. One logical approach is to reject any proposal that has one or two problems on page 1.

These could be amateurish grammatical and spelling mistakes, an uncompelling lead paragraph, or perhaps a point-of-view error that shatters the fictional dream.

The rationale for a quick rejection is simple: errors on the first page will probably be reproduced on the second, third, and fourth—so why read sloppy work any further?

**Literary Sins**

Never, ever submit a half-baked proposal. An opportunity to send a solicited proposal to an agent or editor is a true golden arrow. Recognize its value and treat it accordingly.

## Choose the Right Agents and Editors

You get to choose who receives your fiction proposal. Choose carefully, or else expect to receive more rejections than you deserve. It's tempting to "paper the world" with sample chapters, to send a proposal to any literary agency or publisher who'll read an unsolicited manuscript, but it makes little sense to do so. Virtually the first thing an agent or editor does is decide whether or not this is an appropriate proposal to read. If yours doesn't fit, it will be rejected out of hand—and you run the risk of annoying someone you may want to deal with later.

*Literary Market Place* (available at most libraries) and annual writers' guides are great starting points to identify valid targets for your proposal. The Internet is often even better; an online search will surface a wealth of information about agents and publishers. And you can always visit your local bookstore and see who publishes novels similar to yours.

## Neatness and Quality Count

Don't rush to develop your proposal; take time to do a proper job and proofread carefully. (It shouldn't be necessary to say this, but a remarkably large number of proposals include off-putting mistakes.) If you are a grammatically challenged writer, think about hiring a freelance editor to fine-tune your proposal.

## Fun with Formatting

Christian writers must be a highly superstitious bunch. That's the only way I can explain all those formatting questions asked on writers' loops, at writers' conferences, in writing magazines, and on author chat boards. You'll find even more discussion about proposal formatting than manuscript formatting (which I talked about in Chapter 20). First-time novelists seem to share the belief that submitting a proposal in the wrong typeface (Courier New rather than Times New Roman, or vice versa) will bring instant rejection. Ditto for "incorrect" margins, "inappropriate" line spacing, or page numbers in the "wrong" places.

Many of the answers these questions receive are triumphs of form over substance. They perpetuate the myth that minor formatting variations will impact the success of a proposal. Trust me! It's the content that counts, not the typeface (provided you stick to a standard font). Agents and editors don't walk around with type guides and rulers. They don't waste much time worrying about formatting details, as long as your proposal is easy to read. Yes, many agents and publishers will tell you how to format a proposal or a manuscript for submission. This typically ensures easy readability.

**A Lamp Unto Your Feet**

When you submit your solicited proposal, affix a sticker on the front of the envelope that says, "Requested Submission." It may prevent an accidental detour through an agency or publisher slush pile.

Minor formatting variations will not cause alarm bells to ring, unless the editor decides to buy your manuscript. That's when proper formatting becomes significant. Your manuscript will have to fit into a well-defined production process that may involve a pre-designed editorial template. The bottom line: when you sell your manuscript, your editor may ask you to reformat the document to meet strict specifications.

## Look Like a Professional

Your proposal sends signals about you. Make sure it announces that you're a *real* novelist—a *professional* writer an agent can confidently represent, an author that an editor can rely on. If you don't want your submission to scream *Amateur!* take the following recommendations to heart:

- *Don't* use colored ink or unusual typefaces.

- *Don't* format pages in fully justified type (flush edge on the right side of the type column).

- *Don't* insert clip art or photographs on the cover page of your proposal.

- *Don't* use elaborate binders, fancy cover stock, or presentation paper.

- *Don't* put © symbols or elaborate copyright statements on every page. Agents and editors are not going to steal your writing. In any case, you can't copyright an idea.

- *Don't* automatically include a stamped, self-addressed envelope, unless the guidelines for a hardcopy submission call for one.

Standard typefaces, simple page layouts, and plain white copy paper work fine for proposals. None of the gizmos and doodads will impress an agent or editor. Quite the contrary, the fancy add-ons will make them skeptical about your writing.

## Electronic vs. Hardcopy

An increasing number of agents and editors prefer electronic submissions. They ask you to submit your proposal as a word processing document, typically in Microsoft Word file format, attached to an e-mail message. (This shouldn't be a problem if you use WordPerfect or StarOffice Writer instead of Microsoft Word; both allow you to output files as Word documents.)

Electronic submissions are faster—and less expensive—for everyone involved. However, don't use graphics, fancy typefaces, or elaborate e-mail "signatures." All of them can trigger anti-spam software and route your proposal into a cyberspace black hole.

 **Literary Sins** _____

It goes without saying, but I'll say it anyway: take care *not* to submit files that contain viruses or other dangerous computer code. This is the fastest way I know to lose the goodwill of an agent or editor.

# Can a Proposal Sell My First Novel?

One of the most common questions asked by first-time novelists is, "Can I sell my first novel before it's actually finished on the basis of a proposal?" Generally speaking, you can't. Few agents will represent a first novel without a finished manuscript, and fewer publishers will buy one. It's simply too risky, because despite their writers' best intentions, *many, many* first novels are never completed. And those that are may not be publishable. Consequently, sensible agents and editors require first-timers to prove they can write a publishable novel by actually doing it.

There are exceptions to this rule: examples of first-time novelists struck by lucky lightning, who've been able to sell not-yet-completed manuscripts with brief proposals. It happens, but don't count on it happening to you.

Once a novelist has proven him- or herself by delivering a publishable first novel, the key question in an editor's mind becomes: Am I convinced that our readers will want to buy this author's next book? That question doesn't require a full manuscript to answer. A good story synopsis (perhaps with a sample chapter or two to make the synopsis easier to understand) is sufficient to land a contract. This may not seem fair to first-time writers, but it's the way things are.

# Do Those Manuscript Submission Services Really Work?

Most leading Christian publishers won't accept unsolicited proposals, but almost all take advantage of one or both Christian manuscript submission services: The Writer's Edge and Christian Manuscript Submission Service (formerly ECPA First Edition).

These services charge a fee—approximately $100—to make an electronic query and brief proposal available to publishers. Your submission remains online for six months. (See Appendix A for their websites.)

Do submission services work? This is one of the most frequently asked questions of editors at Christian writers' conferences. The answer I hear most often is, "They can work."

Some leading publishers have bought manuscripts via submission services, including first novels from writers who are now well known. Other companies have never spotted an offering to their liking. This isn't surprising, because relatively few online submissions are likely to meet the "publishability" requirements I told you about in Part 2 of this book.

My recommendation: if you can afford the fee—and if you are convinced you have a publishable manuscript to offer—a submission service may be worth a try.

# Be Persistent!

Sending out a stream of proposals can feel like an exercise in futility. At least, that's the way Janet and I felt when we were trying to find a home for our first novel. It can take upwards of five years to develop and sell your first novel. There's not much you can do to change this reality (especially if God has a hand in the timing) other than to pray that you are one of the few first-time novelists who learn to write publishable fiction more quickly than average.

But you can be persistent. You can use the downtime when you're waiting for a response to improve your novel and develop additional fiction projects. You can keep searching for other appropriate agents and publishers. And you can refine the elements of your proposal to make them more effective. Every improvement you make will increase the possibility of a solid "hit."

# Your Proposal Is a Plan

A comprehensive fiction proposal will include all of the elements described in the following sections. Each major element—query letter, "one-sheet," biographical sketch, and others—should be on a separate page.

Why are there so many elements? I suspect my answer will surprise you. Your book proposal is a special kind of business plan—an invitation to an agent or publisher to enter a long-term business relationship with you that's built around the novels you write. Your full-scale proposal provides information a literary agency or publisher needs to evaluate your broad capabilities as a business partner. And you thought you merely had to describe your book.

This is a time to write enthusiastically, robustly, and boldly. You are writing to persuade, to sell yourself and your novel. Be confident, but don't exaggerate your accomplishments and be sure to provide solid facts to substantiate any of the claims you make about yourself.

## Query Letter

Your query letter is the first thing an agent or editor reads—and sometimes the *only* thing. A good query letter will "grab" the reader's attention. Its purpose is to introduce your novel, detail its genre, length, and target audience, describe its appeal to readers, and explain why it stands out from the crowd of other novels. One clear and succinct page is more than enough to do the job. Countless books, blogs, and articles offer advice on writing "winning" query letters. Follow their guidance cautiously.

 **Wisdom and Knowledge**

A query—the "spear tip" of a fiction proposal—can be the first element of the proposal, or it can stand by itself. An agent or editor may ask you to send a query before you send your proposal. In that event, the recipient will use the query letter to decide whether or not to ask for a detailed proposal.

As one gatekeeper told me, "First-time authors often overstate the importance of a query letter. The first paragraph of a manuscript tells me much more than the query letter in front of it." Nonetheless, your query makes a first impression. Keep it brief, straightforward, enthusiastic, and … oh yes, did I mention brief? Keep in mind that many agents and editors dislike "innovative" gimmicks and urge you to write a straightforward letter that showcases your work. Don't forget to proofread your query. Like all readers, agents and editors get discouraged by spelling errors, punctuation mistakes, and poor grammar.

The classic query letter structure has four segments:

1. The hook—an opening paragraph that wins over the reader and builds interest in your novel. (The hook paragraph should also include genre, length, target audience, and relevant competitive comparisons.)

2. Story blurb—the kind of extra-short story synopsis you find on the back of a novel.

3. Biographical blurb—a sentence or two that sums up your writing credentials, plus any other details about you that may intrigue the reader.

4. Call to action—an invitation to ask for more information.

Let's look at each part in more detail.

## The Query Hook

Your hook has to capture a reader's interest, but that doesn't mean it should be bizarre or overly cute. Remember, agents and editors are searching for books that sell. They find fresh ideas highly interesting. They don't appreciate overblown marketing language or strained attempts at humor.

Here, for example, is the hook paragraph we used to sell our first Christian cozy mystery novel, *Little White Lies:*

> *Little White Lies* is the first of the Pippa Hunnechurch Mysteries—classic cozies about a savvy British "headhunter" who lives and works in Maryland. Pippa follows in the grand tradition of the amateur English sleuth. She has an eye for detail, an unquenchable need to seek out the truth, and an inviolable commitment to fair play. We designed Pippa to appeal to the legions of Christian women who read mystery novels and who, like Pippa, trudge to their offices and face a daily grind. *Little White Lies* is 85,000 words long.

Our hook strategy was to emphasize our heroine—our amateur sleuth—because cozy mysteries typically succeed or fail on the strength of the protagonist. We also wanted to communicate that our book had many of the elements of a classic British mystery, the sort written by Agatha Christie, without actually saying so.

## The Story Blurb

The story blurb in a query letter serves the same purpose as the blurb on the back of a novel: it provides just enough story detail to make the reader want more. Here's the blurb we used for *Little White Lies:*

> Pippa parted company with God seven years ago, but today she needs a miracle. Her challenge: An unforeseen economic downturn in Maryland that threatens to scuttle her one-woman executive recruiting business.

Pippa's luck seems to improve when she teams up with Marsha Moran, a highly successful headhunter. But when Marsha drowns in what everyone assumes is a freak accident, Pippa's joy turns to confusion.

After another death—this one clearly not accidental—Pippa finds herself searching for a clever murderer and trying to stay alive.

## The Biographical Blurb

The trick here is to reach into your past to find any relevant experience that might impress an agent or editor. Any kind of writing you've done is fair game; any links to the publishing industry are worth mentioning. Here's what we chose to mention:

> We're a husband and wife writing team with broad experience. Ron has written six nonfiction books. Janet has been the editorial director of a small press.

Don't be upset if you have no relevant publishing experience. Many published Christian novelists had none before they sold their first manuscript. Unless you're a merchandisable celebrity, the quality of your manuscript is more important than your previous writing credentials. In the end, your work has to speak for itself.

## The Call to Action

Many first-time novelists overlook this important part of a query. What do you want the agent or editor to do next? Once you've answered that question in your mind, use the answer to close your letter. For example:

> The Christian cozy mystery genre is still uncrowded. We believe that Pippa Hunnechurch represents just the sort of cozy protagonist who will become popular during the new millennia: strong-willed, loyal, independent, resolute as a Royal Oak.
>
> May we send you a detailed proposal, complete with sample chapters and a story summary? Or perhaps you'd like to see the entire manuscript? We're confident that you will like Pippa as much as we do.

## Proposal Cover Page and Table of Contents

A cover page is more than a convenience for readers. It provides a road map that makes it easier to find different proposal elements (which can be a challenge in a document that may reach 40 or even 50 pages long). Include the title of your novel, its genre and word count, your name, your physical address, and your e-mail address. I also like to add a simple table of contents that points to specific pages for the various elements.

### "One-Sheet"

A one-sheet is a single-page overview that captures the essence of your novel and serves as a calling card for your novel. I'll describe the contents of an effective one-sheet in Chapter 22. You build it around your "elevator speech"—a short sales pitch designed to be delivered in person (also described in Chapter 22).

A one-sheet is a key element of your proposal package, because it includes the first real description of your novel anyone sees. A good one-sheet lives on after your proposal has done its job. An agent will use it when contacting editors, an editor will use it to sell your novel inside the publishing house, and the marketing staff may use it to create promotional materials. Take the time to do it well.

### Biographical Sketch

A biographical sketch is more detailed than the biographical blurb in your query letter, but it covers the same ground. Describe your writing experience, prior publishing history, education, and relevant achievements. These days, publishers look as closely at authors as they do at manuscripts. Don't be modest. Include any writing-related awards you have earned. Include any details that will make you seem unique, or at least unusual. Editors are always searching for the octogenarian holy man who writes Christian chick lit.

## Those All-Important Sample Chapters

Given the wide variation in chapter length, it might make better sense for agents and editors to ask for a fixed number of pages (say 25 or 30) of your novel, rather than one, two, or three chapters. Some do, but many still think in terms of chapters.

Clearly, the idea is to request a sufficiently long sample of your writing to prove—or refute—your belief that you write publishable Christian fiction. "Two or three" chapters is really much more than necessary. Any literary agent, any acquisitions editor worth his or her salt, can evaluate your authorial voice, your writing skills, and your abilities to tell a compelling story and generate an exciting fictional dream after reading the first three pages. The rest gives them more to read, if they decide to delve more deeply into your manuscript.

When you prepare your sample chapters, keep two points in mind:

1. First-time novelists often overwrite the first few pages of their manuscripts. You've been told that agents and editors zero in on a book's opening, so you may return to it a hundred times—to poke, prod, and fine-tune. The danger is that the most important pages of your novel will "sound" fragmented and lack a consistent, confident voice. Overzealous rewriting can also damage the signals that readers interpret to form fictional dreams. If this happens, your opening pages will seem lifeless. Take care that you don't "fine-tune" your novel into oblivion.

2. The early drafts of many novels—written both by first-timers and veterans—tend to have "quiet" first chapters that introduce the protagonists and other key characters. I know this is true, because I've read the opening chapters of many unpublished novels, and because—sigh!—I manage to write a dull Chapter 1 every time I begin a new novel.

If an editor buys a manuscript with a quiet first chapter, the first editorial suggestion that he or she will make is, "Rewrite the opening and begin *in media res* (in the middle of things)." But that doesn't happen often, because few editors will continue to read sample chapters beyond a dull opening.

Well-written prose describing events that moved slowly was all the rage in the eighteenth and nineteenth centuries. No longer. Today's readers, editors, and agents like (and buy!) fast-paced stories that start off with bursts of excitement. Your opening chapter should introduce your protagonist, make his or her overarching problem clear, and begin to set up the story.

> ### A Lamp Unto Your Feet
>
> Don't waste Chapter 1 by presenting background information you can deliver to readers later. Begin with action or dialogue. Get the reader wrapped up in the story and caring about your protagonist immediately. Don't defend long descriptions of your heroine's country estate in Kent or tell me that your critique group thinks a lengthy history of how your hero worked his way through law school is exciting stuff. Instead, repeat after me: "I promise to write an exciting opening for my novel so that I will be able to sell it."

# The Dreaded Story Synopsis

Your story synopsis can be the single most difficult piece of writing connected with your novel—much tougher to finish than the novel itself. You may also consider your synopsis the worst piece of writing you've done this year; most published novelists hate everything about the synopses they write.

A typical guidelines request for synopsis will read: "Develop a three-to-five page synopsis of your story, including its resolution. The goal of your synopsis is to convince an acquisitions editor that you have crafted a complete and compelling story."

Unless guidelines state otherwise, it's okay to produce a single-spaced synopsis, so three-to-five pages is equivalent to six to ten manuscript pages. Still, shoehorning 350 pages of story into a few dozen paragraphs is an intimidating challenge for most of us.

Use your "elevator speech" (see Chapter 22 for suggestions on how to create one) as the core of your story synopsis, then expand the details. I admit this is easier said than done, but I've found that the trick is to ask yourself—and answer—a series of simple questions. You'll soon have the content you need to flesh out the elevator speech:

◆ What are your protagonist's chief strengths? What are his or her chief weaknesses?

◆ What is the most significant challenge your protagonist faces?

◆ What is at stake for the protagonist? What happens if he or she fails?

◆ Why can't your protagonist merely "go home"? Why does he or she have to move forward through the storyline?

◆ Who is helping your protagonist on his or her quest? What is unusual about these secondary characters?

◆ What does the villain want to achieve? What is driving your villain to oppose the protagonist?

◆ What good points does your villain have?

◆ What is the unifying theme of your story?

◆ How does the theme play out in the storyline? What events are related to the theme?

◆ What will the reader take away from your novel?

◆ What Bible verse captures the essence of the Christian message you're trying to deliver?

# Market Analysis: Who'll Read Your Book?

Both agent and editor expect you to know the target audience for your novel. Simply put, who is willing to plunk down as much as 15 dollars to buy a copy of your book? Vague, generic statements—"readers who enjoy cozy Christian mysteries set in craft shops will like my novel"—are okay for a query letter, but not for this element of your proposal. You need to identify specific audience groups. For example, middle-aged women in small towns, or young, recently married women who are struggling with the challenges of setting up a household.

Agents and editors will also assume that you've identified similar novels published within the past five years and can articulate why your book is a better read. They'd like to believe that you've read the various novels that might compete with your manuscript, but this will rarely be true. You've probably read a few of them—after all, if you didn't enjoy reading the genre, you probably wouldn't write in it.

**A Lamp Unto Your Feet** _____

You can do a remarkably thorough market analysis online. Start by searching available Christian novels in your genre, and note which current books have the same settings or are about the same topics. Once you've assembled your initial list, you can expand your search to find other, recently out-of-print books that are similar to yours. A brief list—perhaps five or six— is sufficient for your proposal.

# Your Personal Marketing Plan

Few novelists enjoy marketing their books, but the fact is that novelists who actively promote and market their fiction sell more books and ultimately advance their careers. The reason is that publishers rarely invest huge sums to market first novels. The typical, modest marketing budget pays for:

◆ A marketing plan

◆ Production of advance review copies (ARCs) that go to book reviewers, large booksellers, and other "thought leaders"

◆ A partial page in the publisher's catalog

◆ Displays at large Christian bookseller conferences, along with book-signing sessions

◆ A news release or a media kit

◆ Limited promotional activities—for example, a sponsored radio interview

Where's the "book tour" that invites you to book events and signings across the country? What happened to the elaborate media campaign that puts you on dozens of TV shows? Sorry! They are generally reserved for bestselling authors whose future sales can justify the considerable expense.

In these more frugal times, publishers expect authors to carry some of the marketing load. And so, proposal guidelines from both agents and publishers may ask you to "Describe your ability, if any, to sell books at speaking engagements, seminars, conferences, and other events. Tell us if you have (or plan to create) a website, a blog, or newsletters for readers. Tell us also if you will be able to get a well-known writer to endorse your book, and whether you plan to create promotional "giveaways" (e.g. bookmarks), arrange your own book signings, or attend writers' conferences. Please think out of the box when you come up with marketing ideas."

I'll tell you more in Chapter 24 about specific kinds of marketing activities you should consider when your first novel is published.

# Where Is Your Proposal Today?

Because most authors submit proposals and manuscripts to whomever will read them, agents will ask for a history of every proposal and manuscript they evaluate. They need to know the when's and who's of your previous submissions to gauge whether there are untapped markets for your work. And both agents and editors will want to know if someone else currently considering your proposal has expressed interest. Neither wants to waste time evaluating a proposal that's about to be accepted by someone else.

## The Least You Need to Know

- One size proposal doesn't fit every agent and publisher; different agencies and houses establish different submission guidelines.

- First-time novelists need to finish their manuscripts before they send out queries or proposals.

- Christian manuscript submission services have worked for some novelists; if you can afford the fee, they may be worth a try.

- A query letter can stand by itself or be the first element of a fiction proposal.

- Take care not to overwrite the beginning pages of your sample chapters, and submit sample chapters that are exciting and begin *in media res*.

- Use your "elevator speech" as the heart of your story synopsis.

# Chapter 22

# Pitching Your Novel at Christian Writers' Conferences

## In This Chapter

- Plan to meet agents and editors at writers' conferences
- Getting "golden arrows"—invitations to send proposals for your novel
- Creating an effective elevator speech for your novel
- How to pitch your novel
- The one-sheet: a "business card" for your novel

Your manuscript is finished. Now what?

For many Christian novelists, the answer is: "Get thee to a writers' conference." It can be the perfect place to fill your quiver with golden arrows: invitations from agents and editors to send proposals.

In Chapter 14, I explained how you can learn the craft of fiction writing at writers' conferences. This chapter tells the rest of the story: how attending a writers' conference can help you market your finished manuscript.

Many writers have made contacts at writers' conferences that have directly led to the sales of their books. This happens scores of times each year; it can happen to you, too, if you follow proven techniques for "pitching" your novel.

# Why Agents and Editors Attend

Many unpublished novelists are astonished to learn that leading agents and editors take time out of their busy schedules to participate in Christian writers' conferences for the express purpose of finding publishable novels. Editors need good manuscripts to fill the holes in this year's publishing schedule; agents need new manuscripts to represent. Consequently, a writers' conference can be a win-win situation for the authors, agents, and editors who attend.

**It Is Written …**

Attend at least one writers' conference every year. They … come in all sizes and times of year. I've sold at least 90 percent of my work through contacts made at writers' conferences.

—Gayle Roper, Christian novelist

A writers' conference actually changes the rules of the manuscript marketing game. Editors who normally refuse to consider unagented manuscripts will talk to you about your unagented manuscript—and may agree to read your proposal. Agents who don't usually read proposals from unpublished writers will chat with you about your work—and may invite you to submit a proposal for review.

Some writers who've previously sent review copies of their manuscripts to a writers' conference bring extra copies with them in the hope that agents and editors will take them home to read. Forget it! Agents and editors have the same size suitcases as you do; they don't have the space to carry hefty manuscripts. If you receive a golden arrow (more about that in a moment), it will typically be a request to send a *proposal* to the respective agent or editor after the conference is over. (Review Chapter 21 for the essentials of an effective fiction proposal.) If your proposal generates interest, you will probably be invited to send the full manuscript for consideration.

Even if you talk with agents and editors who occasionally read unsolicited work, an invitation to submit a proposal is far better than cold-submitting a manuscript or proposal that will surely land at the bottom of a "slush pile," underneath scores of other unsolicited submissions.

## You Need the *Right* Agents and Editors

When you have finished your manuscript, the time has come to chat with the *right* agents and editors. It makes no sense to discuss speculative fiction with an editor who specializes in Christian historical romances. And you won't get much insight about which publishers are buying women's fiction from a magazine editor who's an expert on how-to articles.

Similarly, some literary agents specialize in nonfiction, some focus on fiction, and others handle both. Among those who will represent fiction manuscripts, some have genres they prefer to market, and others genres they refuse to handle.

You should opt for a writers' conference that gives you an opportunity to meet with agents and editors who specialize in the specific kind of manuscript you wrote. Conference websites usually name the editors and agents who plan to attend and tell you their areas of expertise.

 **A Lamp Unto Your Feet**

These days, a number of leading editors and agents participate on Christian writing blogs. You can often discover their skills and interests by doing an online search of their names.

## Follow Through Promptly

You may wonder why I call the opportunity to submit a proposal to an agent or editor a "golden arrow." Well, I think of the invitation as *golden*, because it's valuable; and I see it as an *arrow*, because it carries your work directly to a key gatekeeper who has expressed interest.

Surprisingly, a large percentage of writers who get golden arrows throw them away. Many of the agents and editors I know have told me that *more than half* of the authors they invite to submit proposals at writers' conferences never follow through. Some of these writers were merely seeking encouragement. They didn't have ready-to-submit novels—or even nearly complete manuscripts. Others probably rethought the readiness of their manuscripts after coming home from the conference. They decided to rewrite some more before submitting.

My point is that the editors and agents who attend a writers' conference are likely to be happily surprised when a publishable manuscript or proposal lands on their desks a few days after the event is over.

Don't delay! Send your proposal as soon as you're back home. Include a brief cover letter that reminds the agent or editor that your proposal was requested during a specific writers' conference. Write "Requested Submission" on the front of the envelope or in the subject line of your e-mail.

Sometimes, life gets in the way of submitting your proposal. An illness, job-related responsibilities, or a family problem can upset your best intentions. Drop the editor or agent a note—via snail mail or e-mail—explaining that your submission will be delayed. Provide a specific date when you will follow through—and meet your new deadline.

# The Fine Art of Pitching

When you chat with an agent or editor, you have the chance to *pitch* your book. Pitching is the fine art of selling in person. It's a skill that every novelist needs to develop—even the shyest and most introverted.

All of us compete with many other writers. Their writing may be no better than ours, their storylines no more compelling. And yet, they may sell their manuscripts because they managed to intrigue an agent or editor during a face-to-face meeting at a writers' conference.

# You Can Have (a) Perfect Pitch

A good pitch to the right agent or editor—those interested in your kind of novel—can earn you a golden arrow by accomplishing five things. Your pitch will ...

### A Lamp Unto Your Feet

What if you pitch to both an agent and an editor at a writers' conference, and both ask to see your proposal? Should you send to both simultaneously? My advice is yes, send out twin proposals. If the editor expresses interest, tell the agent—it will make you a more attractive potential client.

1. Describe the storyline of your novel in a compelling manner and build interest in your work.

2. Explain what makes your novel special—and why readers will enjoy reading it.

3. Demonstrate that you really understand your story, which indicates that you can write fiction and that your plot probably hangs together well.

4. Communicate that you feel excited, enthusiastic, and confident about your novel—feelings that are highly contagious.

5. Distance you from less-prepared authors at the conference and help start a "buzz" about your novel.

As you can see, pitching your novel at a writers' conference conveys as much information about you as about your novel. Agents and editors know that it's impossible to separate the two; the way you pitch your novel speaks volumes about the quality of your work.

## Every Novel Needs an Elevator Speech

Many people who have difficulty pitching face-to-face are merely uncomfortable inventing something to say on the fly. That's why I urge every novelist to develop—and *learn*—an elevator speech for his or her book. An elevator speech is a short sales pitch—short enough to be delivered during a proverbial elevator ride with an agent or editor—that builds interest in your novel. It conveys the essentials of the storyline and lets the person hearing it quickly decide whether or not to ask for more information.

A person who talks rapidly can speak about 140 words per minute. If we assume the elevator is in a tall building and the ride will take about 90 seconds, your quick pitch should be no more than 200 words long. That's roughly two thirds of a page of double-spaced Times New Roman type—approximately twice as many words as the typical blurb on a novel's back cover.

## That's Impossible!

I can hear the question forming in your mind: How can anyone possibly shrink the story of a full-length novel to a measly 200 words? My answer is: Get used to it! Most editors and agents believe that novelists who can't sum their stories in a few paragraphs don't fully understand their novels. You know what? They're absolutely right.

It's not easy to develop a good elevator speech, but it's not impossible either. I like to use a simple three-part model: begin with a hook that builds interest, continue with a story summary, and end with a memorable statement.

Here's the elevator speech that Janet and I wrote to pitch our first novel, *Little White Lies*:

> Have you ever told a "little white lie" on your resumé? Even a small exaggeration can have deadly consequences—as Pippa Hunnechurch finds out.

Pippa is an executive recruiter who scoffs at the idea that God cares about her future. When an economic slowdown threatens to destroy her one-woman firm, Pippa *knows* she's on her own.

Pippa's luck seems to improve when she nails down a plum recruiting assignment and teams up with Marsha Morgan—a successful headhunter who finds the perfect candidate for the job.

Pippa's joy ends when Marsha drowns in what looks like a freak accident. As Pippa struggles on, she finds herself caught in a web of deceit, spun out of "harmless exaggerations" in the resumés of Marsha most successful candidates.

Another death—this one clearly *not* an accident—creates an impossible dilemma for Pippa: If she cooperates with the police, she'll ruin her own reputation and destroy the careers of four celebrated executives whose only crime was to embellish their credentials. If she remains silent, she'll become the target of a ruthless murderer.

Pippa's battle to save her business, her reputation, and her life leads her through a journey of discovery—about herself, about God, and the destructive power of *little white lies.*

We found that the opening question intrigued editors and agents, most of whom have written their own resumés. The story summary captures the atmosphere of the mystery and does a reasonably good job of condensing the plot. We think the final sentence is sufficiently memorable to sum up our novel and wrap up the pitch.

## Learn, Don't Memorize

I noted earlier that you should "learn" the elevator speech you write. That's important, because some writers try to memorize what they plan to say to editors. That's not a good idea, because you don't want your pitch to seem canned, or for you to come across as a mindless automaton.

A good elevator speech will sound natural, with the words tripping effortlessly off your tongue. Learning the pitch means that you have internalized all of the essential details. You won't speak it word for word, but you will cover most of the content.

You're halfway down the road to learning your pitch when you write and rewrite it. You can finish the job by reading your words over and over again.

## Speak Confidently

Writers, especially unpublished novelists, tend to put agents and editors on pedestals. This can surprise agents and editors; they deal every day with published writers who often assume that they're standing on even higher pedestals. Trust me on this: there's no need to be nervous in the presence of a Christian agent or editor. They are a friendly and charming bunch, eager to help new writers.

So don't rush through your pitch. (You don't have to speak 140 words per minute.) Pretend that you're talking to a good friend. Speak self-assuredly and enthusiastically about your book. Smile a lot and project the excitement you feel.

Similarly, don't be aggressive or overly assertive. An agent or editor will note that kind of behavior with concern: a pushy *wannabe* at a writers' conference is likely to become an annoying client and a troublesome author later.

If you finish your pitch session early, thank the agent or editor and leave. He or she will appreciate a few minutes of free time until the next appointment.

**Literary Sins**

A novelist should never come across as "needy" at a pitch session. Agents and editors are business people; they came to the conference to find publishable novels, not to make "desperate" authors happy. Practice your pitch so that your attitude and body language project your confidence in yourself and your project.

## Be Prepared for Follow-Up Questions

After you've delivered your pitch, the editor or agent may simply say, "Not for me." But if you did your homework before the conference, and have pitched to the right agent or editor, you'll probably be asked a few follow-up questions about your novel. Be prepared to answer questions like these:

- What's your genre?
- What's your central theme?
- What similar novels have been written?
- What makes your story different?
- Why will readers enjoy your novel?

The first two questions probe your understanding of your novel. You should know the answers before you start writing. Janet and I thought of *Little White Lies* as a Christian cozy mystery. Our central theme was that even minor lies can have major consequences.

The next three questions zero in on the competitive analysis you've done. These are the kinds of questions an editor will have to answer inside the publishing company. You'll have to do some research before the conference—possibly by looking for similar novels at an online bookseller. Answering "I don't know" will probably turn off the agent or editor who asked the questions.

In the case of *Little White Lies*, our unique feature was the use of a "headhunter"— a corporate recruiter—as our protagonist. Pippa's unusual profession let us tell equally unusual stories. We explained to agents and editors that because Pippa worked with many different kinds of businesses, we could write different novels with a lively assortment of settings and plotlines. We ended up selling three Pippa Hunnechurch novels.

# Creating a One-Sheet for Your Novel

A "one-sheet" is a great marketing tool that savvy novelists have borrowed from Hollywood screenplay writers. It's a single-page overview of your novel that you can give to anyone who asks about it at a writers' conference. Think of your one-sheet as a business card for your novel—a "reminder" that you hand out whenever you're given the opportunity. Agents and editors who don't want to be weighed down with a full manuscript will often accept a one-sheet.

Your one-sheet presents a written version of your elevator speech and adds a few items of additional information:

- Complete title and byline
- Genre and length
- Logline
- Contact information

The most important new item is the "logline," another Hollywood innovation. This is a one-sentence summary of the storyline that captures the highest of the high points.

You'll recall that your elevator speech will span two thirds of a page; the other items fill the remaining third. Here's how our one-sheet for *Little White Lies* began:

*Little White Lies* by Ron & Janet Benrey

Christian Cozy Mystery—85,000 words

Pippa Hunnechurch parted company with God seven years ago—today she needs a miracle to save her fledging executive recruiting business and escape the clutches of a ruthless killer.

Let me close this chapter with an observation. I know that many first-time novelists find it difficult to pitch their manuscripts. Janet and I certainly did. Shrinking our novel to a few phrases felt awkward, until we realized that the marketing team at the publisher that purchased *Little White Lies* would do the same thing to sell our novel to reviewers, bookstores, and readers. Your initial sales pitch is the first of many, but it's the single most important. Nothing happens until you interest an agent or editor in your first novel.

## The Least You Need to Know

◆ A writers' conference is a great place to meet agents and editors and possibly generate interest in your novel.

◆ Don't waste the golden arrows you're given; if you're invited to submit a proposal, do so promptly.

◆ A good elevator speech conveys the essentials of the storyline in fewer than 200 words.

◆ Don't memorize your pitch; deliver it naturally, as if you're speaking to a good friend.

◆ Create a one-sheet to serve as a "business card" for your novel.

# Chapter 23

# Self-Publishing for Christian Novelists

## In This Chapter

- How self-publishing works
- The pros and cons of self-publishing
- Figuring the cost of self-publishing
- When self-publishing makes sense
- Self-publishing in action: three real scenarios

After the tenth or twelfth rejection letter—after a few years of waiting for The Call from an agent or editor that announces the good news of a sale—a Christian writer is bound to start thinking of self-publishing his or her novel. The idea in a nutshell is that you pay a company that specializes in self-publishing books to produce your novel, and also to help you promote it.

Despite the negatives you may have heard, self-publishing a novel is a valid option for some Christian novelists. I'll examine the upsides and the downsides in this chapter, and tell you a few success stories.

# Self-Publishing 101

A traditional publishing company assumes the financial risk of publishing a novel, including paying the author an advance royalty and funding the initial costs of publication: editing, book design, cover design, desktop publishing, and printing. In exchange for making these significant investments, the traditional publisher keeps most of the profits generated when the novel is sold—the writer receives a royalty payment (typically about 7 to 9 percent of the cover price).

### Wisdom and Knowledge

There are two common ways to calculate author royalty payments: 1) as a percentage of the cover price of a book (popular among mainstream publishers), and 2) as a percentage of the "net to publisher," the actual amount the publisher receives after the bookstore and distribution channel take their cut (popular among Christian publishers). The author's share in the second approach will be expressed as a higher percentage in a contract—say 12 to 14 percent of net to publisher—but this generates roughly the same dollar payments as a smaller percentage of cover price.

This arrangement lasts as long as the novel remains in print. When the publisher decides that the novel no longer has a market, the publisher declares the book out of print. The rights to publish the book revert to the author. (These rights were leased to the publisher in the publishing contract that was originally agreed to between the author and publisher.)

Self-publishing shifts the front-end costs—and long-term financial risk—to the author. The author retains control of the publishing rights and should make most of the money that a publisher would earn from the sale of each book.

There's a lot to do when you publish a book—a long list of activities from editing the manuscript, to setting type, to designing a cover, to registering the copyright, to getting an International Standard Book Number—or ISBN number—that uniquely identifies the book in commerce. However, it can be inefficient to do everything yourself. For example, the American company that provides ISBN numbers in this country sells them in blocks of 10. And there can be a dozen or more individual vendors and service providers involved in the production of a book. Consequently, most self-published authors turn book production chores over to companies that specialize in producing self-published books. The two leading Christian self-publishing companies are Winepress Publishing and Xulon Press (see Appendix A). The fees these companies charge will reduce the author's earnings; even so, the proceeds per book sold will be significantly greater than the typical author's royalties paid by a traditional publisher.

# The Pros of Self-Publishing

You see an increasing number of self-published Christian novels each year, because self-publishing offers several attractive advantages.

## A Published Book ... *Now!*

Self-publishing guarantees that you get to see your novel published during your lifetime, something that may not happen if you follow the traditional publishing route. Given the harsh realities of Christian publishing—the intense competition for a diminishing number of fiction-publishing slots—self-publishing may be the only realistic option for some novelists.

## In Charge of the Details

The author of a self-published novel can get fully involved in the production process—if he or she wants to be—and can steer book design, cover design and illustration, sales copy, marketing, promotion, distribution, and even the book's title (a decision that traditional publishing companies often take away from authors).

## Rapid Turnaround

Self-publishing offers much faster turnaround than traditional publishing. It's not unusual to experience a two-year delay between the day an author submits his or her manuscript and the day the novel is actually published. Self-publishing companies typically ship your finished novels in six months—and can work faster if necessary.

## You Control the Marketing

As a self-publisher, you control marketing and promotion—not a risk-averse publisher who may be more concerned about ensuring the sales of a novel from a big-name author who received a mega-advance. First-time novelists rarely get large marketing budgets; first-time novels suffer the consequences and rarely achieve significant sales.

## No Worries About Staff Changes

Self-publishing eliminates most of the vagaries that impact Christian publishing today. You don't have to concern yourself about editors leaving, a change in publishing strategy, or your publisher being acquired by a secular conglomerate that is largely focused on bottom-line profitability. You're the boss when you self-publish.

## No Traditional Contract to Negotiate

You won't have to fend off onerous terms in a traditional publishing agreement between author and publisher, because you effectively sit on both sides of the table.

## Impress Traditional Publishers

If everything goes right, a self-published novel can prove your marketability to a traditional publisher. There's nothing more impressive to an editor than hearty sales numbers. More than one self-publisher (including a novelist I'll talk about later) has leveraged the success of a self-published book into a contract with a traditional publisher.

## Build a Platform

Some authors have used a self-published novel to build a platform. Having a real book in print—self-published or not—can set the stage for speaking engagements and ministry opportunities that, in turn, can build a following of readers.

## Earn More Money

The author makes more money from the sale of each copy of a self-published book than a traditionally published novel. But you won't receive the full cover price for every book you sell, unless you sell your novels directly to readers at speaking engagements or other venues.

> **Wisdom and Knowledge** _____
>
> Novels sold in bookstores that move through the customary distribution channels are subject to all of the usual discounts along the way. For example, bookstores expect to buy the books they sell for 40 to 50 percent below the cover price. Factor in other distribution costs and shipping costs, and the "net to author" for a self-published book can be less than 40 percent of the cover price.

# The Cons of Self-Publishing

Before you succumb to the benefits of self-publishing, also consider the negatives. There can be significant disadvantages to publishing your own novel; every author should weigh them carefully.

## A Novel Without a Market

The single biggest worry when you self-publish a novel is that the agents and editors who rejected your proposal were right to do so. As authors, we all want to think that we've written the next Christian blockbuster—but most unpublished novels are anything but. The unhappy truth is that many self-published novels are books without a market. Christian readers have no interest in reading them, so they don't sell more than a few copies a year.

## The Risk of Lower Quality

There's no inherent reason why self-published novels can't meet all of the quality standards of traditionally published novels. Alas, many don't. Their writing is often less crisp, their stories less compelling, and their characterization less interesting. The obvious reason is that most self-published novels go through a much less rigorous development process.

All those gatekeepers in traditional publishing serve a valuable purpose: they impel authors to strive for excellence in every aspect of the novels they write. Self-publishing is different. The author remains in control, because he or she is paying the freight.

It's not that a self-published author is willing to settle for less quality in a finished novel. The problem is that he or she doesn't have the same motivating pressures. Authors published by traditional publishing houses know that they must do better with each new novel they write. Both editors and readers expect their craft to improve with experience. They need to run faster just to stay in place. They must continuously find ways to write better novels.

## Sell, Sell, Sell

The author of a self-published book has to wear many hats, including chief marketing executive. Paying for book promotion and marketing can entail a large additional investment, so most self-published novelists do it themselves—which is why so many self-published novelists point to marketing as the most time-consuming aspect of the exercise. An author who takes on the marketing responsibility must do it effectively, or else run the risk of owning a warehouse full (or a garage full) of unsold books.

Unfortunately, marketing requires a different set of skills than writing a novel. Some novelists are good marketeers, but many aren't. These days, even royalty-paid novelists have to do some marketing (see Chapter 24), but their efforts supplement the work being done by a publisher. Self-publishers are largely on their own.

## That's Not a *Real* Novel

Life isn't fair. The author of the self-published novel may have worked just as hard as the author of a novel published by a royalty-paying house—but many influential people don't see it that way. Many book reviewers, magazine editors, contest organizers, bookstore buyers, and organizations of professional writers don't consider a self-published novel to be the equivalent of a traditionally published novel. Worse yet, some view self-publishing to be a modern-day synonym for *vanity publishing*.

**Chapter and Verse**

The classic definition of a **vanity publisher** is a publishing house that makes its money from an author rather than by selling books to readers. Although one could argue that self-publishers meet this definition, the important difference is that a reputable self-publisher produces books of comparable quality to those issued by a traditional publisher. This includes editing, book design, and cover design that meets professional standards.

Curiously, most readers couldn't care less who published the novels they read, but those other book-industry naysayers make it difficult to get self-published novels reviewed, publicized, judged, sold in bookstores, or recognized as legitimate literary efforts.

Christian self-publishing companies have taken steps to reduce the severity of the problem. Self-published novels can have the same high production values as traditionally published novels. Simply put, they don't look like books from a vanity press. Equally important, the companies have taken on many of the roles of traditional publishers. They have their own promotion and marketing staffs that are adept at publicizing self-published books—and getting them reviewed.

## What Does Self-Publishing Cost?

There are many variables that make it almost impossible to figure the cost without a detailed consideration of your particular novel and the optional services you can choose. But here are some quick, back-of-the-envelope estimates.

The least expensive self-publishing option these days is *Print on Demand* (POD) publishing, because you don't have to make a large front-end investment in printing books.

You can use POD to test the market for your novel and see if it makes sense to invest in a large print run. Preparing a 50,000-word manuscript for publishing costs $3,000 to $4,000, for copy editing, proofreading, cover development, book production, and access to distribution channels that serve Christian and mainstream stores worldwide. Publicity and marketing services cost extra. A larger novel—say, 85,000 words—would cost upwards of $5,000. This represents a significant investment, but nowhere near as great as self-publishing a book cost a few years ago.

**Chapter and Verse**

**Print on Demand** (POD) publishing takes advantage of electronic printing technology to print a small number of copies of a book as they are needed, as few as two or three at a time. The economical print runs for traditionally printed books are measured in thousands of copies, which represents a significant up-front investment.

Interestingly, you can recover most of the initial costs by selling only 400 to 500 novels directly to readers—assuming a cover price of about $15. A novelist who lives in or near a large city can probably count on selling that many books locally, through a fairly modest marketing and promotion effort.

# When Does Self-Publishing Make Sense?

Deciding to self-publish a novel is a highly personal decision. Only you can determine whether the obvious advantages outweigh the potential disadvantages. The approach is not appropriate for every Christian novelist, but there are times when it makes good sense to self-publish your novel.

One of the most sensible times is when you have a platform and can sell your novels directly to readers. If that's your situation, then why not maximize your profits from book sales? Self-publish and you'll pocket the cover price of the book, instead of a much, much smaller royalty payment.

**Literary Sins**

Keep in mind that self-publishing does entail a front-end investment, and that you are taking on all of the financial risk. If you choose to self-publish, be certain to count the costs and be sure you have the time—and inclination—to market your novels.

Another sensible occasion is when you write a Christian novel that has a distinctly narrow readership base—say it's aimed at a particular ethnic community, or involves a topic that many readers are likely to avoid.

A third possibility is a novel in a genre that's currently unpopular among royalty-paying publishers. Christian westerns, for example, still have a significant readership, even though it's become too small to attract most publishing houses. If you have a way to reach these loyal fans, perhaps through websites, perhaps through direct-mail marketing, you may be able to sell a healthy number of books.

# Three Self-Publishing Scenarios

Here are the stories of three self-published novels. Their authors provide valuable insights into the process, benefits, and disadvantages of self-publishing.

## Something That Lasts

Jim Jordan, a Texas trial attorney, describes his novel, *Something That Lasts*, as a story of faith, family, and forgiveness. Jim worked on his manuscript for six years. "When it was finished," he says, "I didn't want to wait another six years to sell it and see it published."

Jim commissioned a literature professor at a local university to oversee line and copy editing, so minimal editing was necessary when he turned the manuscript over to Winepress Publishing. Because Jim had many local media contacts, he decided to do his own promotion and marketing.

Once published, *Something That Lasts* achieved good sales in the Dallas/Fort Worth Metroplex. And then, the novel was selected by Crossings Book Club—only the second time they'd chosen a self-published book. Soon after, Integrity Publishers, a royalty-paying, traditional Christian publishing house recently acquired by Thomas Nelson, purchased the rights to publish the book.

Jim considers speed the biggest virtue of self-publishing, but he acknowledges several downsides. "A self-published novel can be hard to get reviewed, hard to get into bookstores, and hard to get written about in newspapers and magazines. I see self-publishing as best for writers who have a platform and can sell their own books."

## Reaping the Whirlwind

Rosey Dow had been published by royalty-paying Christian publishers, but when she wrote *Reaping the Whirlwind*, a novel about the famous 1925 Scopes "monkey trial" in Dayton, Tennessee, she wanted the book published in time for the trial's 75-year anniversary. Because no traditional publisher could work that quickly, she decided to self-publish. Winepress produced the book in about six months; it's still in print today.

*Reaping the Whirlwind* won the prestigious Christy Award in 2001, the first self-published novel to be so honored.

Rosey feels that the biggest downside of self-publishing for authors is financial risk, although that has decreased because of the POD publishing option. Another important issue is marketing. "I spent lots of time contacting people, mailing postcards, and selling books," Rosey says. "I haven't fully recouped my investment, but I consider my money well spent because I won the Christy. I would definitely do it again."

She also points out that self-publishing a Christian novel is riskier than publishing nonfiction. "It's best if the story is attached to a well-known issue or event that will increase the book's marketability. You need a good hook to sell fiction."

## Raindance

Joy DeKok's Christian novel, *Raindance*, tells a fairly edgy story in which a Christian woman has an abortion and another woman is infertile. Because of the subject matter, two traditional Christian publishers who liked the quality of her writing advised her to look into self-publishing. She did.

"I found self-publishing a great experience," she reports, "because of the opportunity to be involved in all aspects of the book, including cover design." She adds, "The hardest part of self-publishing is marketing. You don't have a choice, you must become a marketer and learn both online and direct marketing. It's really useful if you also have a speaking platform."

Is there a downside to self-publishing? Joy acknowledges that she sometimes receives "a mixed reaction" from writers who are published by traditional publishers. "Some don't respect self-published books," she says, "because they confuse self-publishing with vanity publishing." Nonetheless, Joy self-published two children's picture books and plans to self-publish another novel and a nonfiction book.

## The Least You Need to Know

◆ Despite the negatives you may have heard, self-publishing a novel is a valid option for some Christian novelists.

◆ Before you commit to self-publishing, understand *all* the potential downsides.

◆ Self-publishing can be expensive—but not as expensive as it once was, because of the POD option.

◆ As a self-publisher, you take on the full financial risk of producing your novel; you may not recoup your full investment.

◆ Self-publishing requires that you work hard to promote and market your novel; be sure that you have the time and inclination.

◆ Self-publishing makes the most sense for authors who have platforms and can sell their novel directly to readers.

# Chapter 24

# Afterward: Your Responsibilities as a Published Christian Author

## In This Chapter

◆ The role you play in marketing your book and building a readership base

◆ Responding to letters from your readers

◆ Your responsibilities to other writers

◆ The unexpected (and astonishing) fellowship of Christian writers

◆ The right ways to support less-experienced Christian writers

◆ Supporting the growth of Christian publishing

Congratulations! You've written a Christian novel, sold it to a publisher, and enjoyed the indescribable feeling of holding an advance copy of a published novel with your name on the cover.

Now what?

Well, along with your hot-off-the-press novel, you've been given a whole new set of responsibilities. In this final chapter, I've arranged them in three groups: responsibilities to yourself, responsibilities to your readers, and responsibilities to other Christian writers.

Oh … one other thing. I've cut way back on how-to advice in this chapter. You need to know fewer specifics now that you've been published, so I can talk to you like the colleague you've become.

# Responsibilities to Yourself

A first Christian novel is the essential first step in building your fiction-writing career, but it's not enough to solidify your status as an established writer of Christian fiction. You do that by helping to establishing a base of loyal readers and by expanding your Christian fiction skills.

## Novels Don't "Fly Off" Shelves

Writing novels is one thing. Getting tens of thousands of people to read them is a whole other matter. When you were busy writing your first novel, you probably assumed that readers would appear more or less automatically when your book was available for sale, that your novel would fly off bookseller shelves and into readers' eager hands. Unhappily, the "publish it and they will read it" approach hardly ever works. Like any other product, books must be sold to customers. This is the reason that newly published authors receive a never-ending stream of advice to become deeply involved in the marketing of their novels.

I know that the thought of doing marketing distresses many novelists. We tend to be an introverted bunch and selling books seems such an extroverted activity. After all, marketers ask people to spend money.

That's one way to look at marketing. Another way is to recognize that you've worked hard to create a book that tells a compelling story and delivers a solid Christian message. Marketing ensures that people get to read your book, that they have an opportunity to enjoy the story and receive the message.

## Isn't Marketing My Publisher's Job?

Newly published authors often ask this question—usually a few seconds before they complain that their publishers aren't doing enough to market their first novels.

It's certainly true that more money spent marketing a new title will probably increase its sales. The question publishers most often ask is *how much* should they invest to promote this book considering that the author doesn't have a track record of previous sales. The conventional wisdom held by the marketing teams inside publishing companies is that marketing budgets should reflect the initial sales estimates—then make them come true.

If the publisher concludes that your first novel will sell only 10,000 copies, the marketing team is likely to recommend a correspondingly small budget for marketing and promotion. Why? Because the in-house marketers are far more concerned about recouping the large advances the publisher paid to one or two big-name writers. Those are the novels that will get the big marketing budgets, because the publisher can't let them *not* succeed.

Yep! It does seem strange that the books that need the least marketing investment often receive the most. Strange, but logical. Once again, the publisher is following a course of action designed to reduce financial risk. You can treat this as one more example that life can be unfair. Or you can be realistic about the economics of publishing and take the view that three "interested parties" care about selling your book: booksellers, the publisher, and *you*. All three have marketing roles to play, because all will succeed when lots of your books are sold to readers. Your chief role in the marketing trio is to help build—and grow—a sizeable readership base.

## Your Ulterior Motive for Marketing

Actually … when it comes to building the readership base for your first novel, you're a much more "interested party" than your publisher. A publishing house has other titles to fall back on if your first novel tanks. You don't.

Publishers see a first novel as a kind of experiment—a chance for readers to read your fiction and respond to it. A favorable response in the marketplace encourages your publisher to publish more of your novels. An indifferent response … well, that leaves publishers uncertain about buying more manuscripts when your initial contract is fulfilled. (If you delivered an impressive manuscript for your first novel, your initial publishing agreement may have involved two or three novels. However, you want to sell even more in the future.)

To become an in-demand writer, you need to establish a pattern of sales growth that, ideally, has every new novel you publish selling more copies than those that came before. Demonstrating continuous sales growth from book to book is the best—most reliable—way to build a career in fiction.

## Ways to Build a Readership Base

Here are some of the base-building techniques that Janet and I have considered over the years. We've done many of them, with varying degrees of success:

- Launch a personal website that focuses on you, but that also includes content of value to visitors and provides a reason to browse through your pages (merely bragging about yourself and your book is not enough).

- Participate in "affinity" web loops (e-mail lists) that are read by readers interested in the various "MacGuffin topics" you've built into your novel—hobbies, geographic locations, mental and physical illness, cats, dogs, gardening, whatever. (I defined "MacGuffin" in Chapter 6; it's the thing or things that the characters in your novel care about as they move through the story.)

- Start up websites that focus on your novels and the MacGuffin topics they involve.

- Start blogging.

- Create an e-newsletter that emulates the look and feel of your website.

- Build an e-mailing list of potential readers by adding a guestbook feature on your website and extracting e-mail addresses from e-mail correspondence.

**A Lamp Unto Your Feet**

These are early days; don't worry about writing a "breakthrough novel" or a "blockbuster." Slow and steady is your best strategy for winning the race.

- Write articles for e-zines, published magazines, and other websites, for the purpose of getting your name (and your novels) out there.

- Answer loop queries—become known as a cooperative expert in your field (don't mention your book in every message; let your e-mail signature do that unobjectionably).

- Sponsor contests on your websites, offering copies of your book as prizes (these represent legitimate occasions to promote your website on writing loops).

- Ask for interviews on websites that interview authors.

- "Chat" wherever and whenever you can.

- Get your novels reviewed widely by contacting reviewers personally and sending out review copies.

- Join "author marketing groups"—groups of authors who write in the same genre and work cooperatively to market their novels.

My list of activities to build a readership base seems overwhelming, even though it's hopelessly incomplete. Marketing is a whole other world—a bottomless pit of additional work that will rapidly become the equivalent of a full-time job, if you let it. Finding enough time for marketing can be a daunting challenge if you already have a day job, or are busy writing your second or third novel.

As with most business-related activities, you have a choice: you can do marketing work yourself, or you can pay other people to do it for you. Not surprisingly, good marketing support doesn't come cheap. I know several first-time writers who invested all of their advance royalties into promotion and marketing.

Of course, the investments can be significant even when you do the work yourself. For example, launching a personal website costs money: to pay for a hosting service, to buy specialized webpage software, and for classes to learn how to build a site.

## The Bottom Line

Plan to make *some* marketing investments in your writing. Time, money, or both—you get to choose. These investments won't come cheap; they may even cause pain. Try to work in partnership with your publisher on marketing (ask what they plan to do; expend your precious resources in ways that will complement their efforts.

**Literary Sins** _____

Stay clear of expensive marketing that may not pay back its initial cost. Many novelists become annoyed when a publisher won't buy expensive ads to announce their new novel. In fact, it rarely makes sense to spend big bucks advertising a first novel. Advertising works best when an ad announces an upcoming book from a known author.

## Ongoing Learning to Improve your Craft

The best way to learn to write better is to write more and read more. If you have the talent to write fiction—at this point we can assume that you do—every new scene you write will stretch your capabilities and enhance your skills. Almost without thinking about it, you'll find yourself doing new and different things in your writing.

Set aside time to read other novels in your genre. Wear your author's hat when you read them, and you'll spot useful techniques—solutions to common problems—that you can adapt to your novels. Similarly, keep reading those industry publications. Now that you're published, you need to stay even more alert to the changes at Christian publishers.

Attending writers' conferences can also be useful. Most major writers' conferences, for example, offer advanced tracks for published writers (a few require *two* published novels to participate). And don't forget theology courses at your church and the ubiquitous Bible studies: the more you know about Christianity, the better Christian writer you'll be.

## The Last Comment I'll Make About Genre

I've written a lot about genre in this book. Let me make one final point: switching genres after your first novel is equivalent to beginning all over again. You lose the "goodwill" that you've established with a group of readers who may be anxious to read your future novels.

While you have some flexibility—many Christian authors write in complementary genres; for example, contemporary women's fiction and romance—publishing two, three, or four books in one genre will establish your identity among potential readers and help to build a readership base. The process is analogous to opening a specialty shop that sells a specific product line. In time, customers come to know what you have to sell. They grow accustomed to "shopping" at your store, and also tell their friends about you.

Sticking with one genre is a good idea. Think carefully before you switch.

# Your Responsibilities to Your Readers

Your primary responsibility to your readers is to write the best novels you can. But this isn't your only responsibility. The readers of Christian fiction demand even more from you. They often write letters and e-mails to Christian authors—and they expect to receive answers.

The letters and e-mails you'll receive will fall into several categories:

◆ Fan mail—typically full of praise

◆ Constructive criticism—pointing out, for example, that your book contains an actual mistake in content, grammar, or (gasp!) Christian theology

◆ Sincere complaints about language or content (for example, some Christian publishers will allow "golly!" even though some readers find the word an offensive taking of the Lord's name in vain)

- Goofy complaints that criticize nonexistent content errors or offer vague statements of disapproval: "This is the worst Christian novel I've ever read because the heroine does stupid things."

- Heartfelt letters that explain the impact your novel has had in readers' lives

- Exceedingly personal letters in which readers pour out their hearts and reveal private details of their lives

While there are no general rules for answering letters from readers, most published authors go through a kind of maturing process. At first, they attempt to respond to every letter with a personally written response. Over time, they realize that this is impossible to do (unless like most big-name authors they're able to afford a secretary to handle the additional workload of reading and answering correspondence).

Moving from personal notes to form letters can be a painful journey of discovery, because as a group, Christian writers are a compassionate bunch of folks. Each of us has been taught to have a servant's heart, so it's difficult to ignore a call for friendship—or a cry for help—from a distant reader.

The majority of the Christian novelists I know strive to find an appropriate balance between personal and impersonal. They respond to most reader letters with a generic "form letter" reply. They sometimes provide individually drafted replies to especially interesting notes from fans or highly personal letters, but they are careful not to:

- Offer the kind of advice a minister or a professional counselor would provide.

- Begin ongoing dialogues, or running correspondences, with troubled readers.

- Become a confidant for "needy" readers.

A "better than form letter" compromise that several of my friends use is a generic letter that has room for a brief note and a signature on the bottom. Even a few quick scribbles—the cite of a Bible verse, or the kind of short thank-you appropriate at a book signing—will personalize your response and satisfy most readers.

But—and this is a big but—whatever approach you choose, be sure to reply to every letter or e-mail you receive, even if your answer is only a form response. When a reader makes the effort to write to an author, they expect an answer. They hope for a detailed response, but most will be satisfied with a brief reply that proves the author actually read their correspondence.

# Responsibilities to Other Writers

One of the joys of Christian fiction is that Christian novelists rarely see each other as direct competitors—even though there are times when some of us do compete against each other. You compete directly with the handful of novelists who write similar books in your genre. Writers selling into other genres (or who write different kinds of novels) are not your direct competitors and have little impact on your sales—other than their ability to increase readership of Christian fiction, and thus benefit every Christian writer.

# The Fellowship of Christian Writers

I chose the word *fellowship* carefully. It's not an exaggeration to say that I feel part of a remarkable fellowship with other Christian novelists. Nor does Angela Hunt exaggerate when she writes about a "bond of love" among Christian authors (see sidebar). I can't explain where this fellowship, this bond of love, comes from, but I know that it's based on more than our shared interests as writers, or even our enthusiasm for Christian fiction.

**It Is Written ...**

We must work to keep the unity in the bond of love, for other writers are our co-laborers, whether they write in our genre or not, whether they sell along-side us or not. We ... are pulling the same yoke, straining for the same purpose: to honor God with our livelihood.

—Angela Hunt, Christian novelist

A visible aspect of the fellowship is the support that Christian authors gladly provide to other Christian authors:

- We take time from writing our own books to answer questions and provide essential information for other works-in-progress.

- We help each other cope with the details of writing technology (it's astonishing how many questions on Christian writing loops are about word processing).

- We cheer for good news (winning a contest, finding an agent, or landing a contract, for example).

- We write endorsements in the hope they'll increase the sales of other writers' novels.

- We offer financial support in times of crisis.

- We encourage other novelists during the inevitable "down" times.

- Most important of all, we pray for each other.

You may have noticed that I did not make any distinction between "published writer" and "unpublished writer." That's another remarkable thing about the world of Christian fiction. There are relatively few occasions when being unpublished excludes a Christian writer from "full participation" in an organization, a writing loop, or other beneficial opportunities.

# Supporting Upcoming Writers

Prepare for a change in tone. At the risk of undoing those warm feelings of fellowship, I have to point out that this is an area that requires published writers to set boundaries—another aspect of the professional writing life that demands balance. Writers at the start of their journey in Christian fiction need information, guidance, skills, and encouragement. Writers farther down the road have a responsibility to provide these things, to the extent that they can without impacting their own careers. This is why so many successful Christian authors lead workshops at Christian writers' conferences, teach writing courses, mentor unpublished writers, and provide writing advice on their websites.

But do published writers also have a responsibility to read chapters written by unpublished writers and provided editorial advice? This can be a tough call. As I said, first-time novelists need guidance and encouragement. They might well benefit from the observations and suggestions of an experienced author. Sadly, as many published novelists have discovered to their dismay, an "over the transom" request to read unpublished writing usually comes with a daydream. The first-time writer expects the author to shout, "Huzzah! I've found the next Janet Oke." He or she is really looking for affirmation, not for advice.

A few writers I know will accept a manuscript to read. The great majority won't, and they usually explain why on their websites or in "sorry, no" letters. The common excuses:

◆ Sorry, but I'm swamped with writing work and can't break away to read anyone's manuscript—I'm sure you understand.

◆ You'd be unhappy with the results if I did read your chapters—I'm a terrible editor and an even worse evaluator of manuscripts.

◆ I have no clout with agents or editors; in fact, I'm not at all sure what publishers are looking for these days, so I'd be unable to give you any useful guidance.

Everyone knows—including the unpublished writer—that these are polite evasions. Few Christian novelists are willing to 'fess up that it's an imposition to ask a busy author to spend hours of time reading and evaluating a manuscript. That chore belongs to the writer's close friends, to the members of his or her critique group, or to the volunteers who read manuscripts at a writers' conference.

# Work to Grow Christian Publishing

There's one more responsibility I want you to consider: your duty to support the growth of Christian publishing. Writing Christian fiction is your chosen vocation. Even more important, Christian fiction is your ministry. Find ways to expand the reach of Christian fiction. Choose Christian novels as gifts for family and friends. Give away the best novels you've read—perhaps to members of your church, perhaps to your nonbelieving friends. A good novel deserves to be in a reader's hands, not sitting on your shelf.

## The Least You Need to Know

- You *do* have to help market your own book. Strike a comfortable balance when you plan your marketing campaign.

- Your readers do expect you to answer their letters—how you answer them is up to you.

- You need to strike a balance when you support Christian novelists who have just begun their journeys.

- The "fellowship of Christian novelists" is not a slogan—it's real, and it's wonderful!

- Find ways to expand the reach of Christian fiction by choosing Christian novels as gifts for family and friends.

# Appendix A

# Resources

I've had to be selective with the resources I presented in this appendix, because there are so many available. You'll find many more in bookstores and on the Internet.

## Books

Bell, James Scott. *Write Great Fiction: Plot & Structure: Techniques and Exercises for Crafting a Plot That Grips Readers from Start to Finish.* Cincinnati, OH: Writer's Digest Books, 2004.

Browne, Renni, and Dave King. *Self-Editing for Fiction Writers: How to Edit Yourself into Print.* New York: Collins, 2004.

*Chicago Manual of Style, The, 15th edition.* Chicago: University of Chicago Press, 2003.

Collins, Brandilynn. *Getting into Character: Seven Secrets a Novelist Can Learn from Actors.* New York: John Wiley & Sons, 2002.

Gardner, John. *The Art of Fiction: Notes on Craft for Young Writers. Reissue Edition.* New York: Vintage, 1991.

Herr, Ethel. *An Introduction to Christian Writing: An In-Depth Companion to the Complete Writing Experience. Second Edition.* Phoenix, AZ: Write Now Publications, 1999.

Hood, Ann. *Creating Character Emotions: Writing Compelling, Fresh Approaches That Express Your Characters' True Feelings.* Cincinnati, OH: Story Press Books, 1998.

Jenkins, Jerry B. *Writing for the Soul: Instruction and Advice from an Extraordinary Writing Life.* Cincinnati, OH: Writer's Digest Books, 2006.

Kenyo, Sherrilyn. *The Writer's Digest Character Naming Sourcebook.* Cincinnati, OH: Writer's Digest Books, 2005.

King, Stephen. *On Writing: A Memoir of the Craft.* New York: Pocket Books, 2002.

Kipfer, Barbara Ann. *The Writer's Digest Flip Dictionary.* Cincinnati, OH: Writer's Digest Books, 2000.

Lamott, Anne. *Bird by Bird: Some Instructions on Writing and Life.* New York: Anchor Books, 1995.

Morris, Gilbert. *How to Write and Sell a Christian Novel.* Phoenix, AZ: Write Now Publications, 1994.

Prose, Francine. *Reading Like a Writer: A Guide for People Who Love Books and for Those Who Want to Write Them.* New York: HarperCollins, 2006.

Stein, Sol. *Stein on Writing: A Master Editor of Some of the Most Successful Writers of Our Century Shares His Craft Techniques and Strategies.* New York: St. Martins Griffin, 2000.

Stokes, Dr. Penelope J. *Writing & Selling the Christian Novel.* Cincinnati, OH: Writer's Digest Books, 1998.

Stuart, Sally E. *Christian Writer's Market Guide.* Colorado Springs, CO: WaterBrook Press. (This annually published guide has become the "publishing bible" for Christian writers.)

Strunk, William, Jr., E.B. White, and Roger Angell. *The Elements of Style, Fourth Edition.* Needham, MA: Allyn & Bacon, 2000.

Tobias, Ronald B. *20 Master Plots: And How to Build Them.* Cincinnati, OH: Writer's Digest Books, 2003.

Wiesner, Karen. *First Draft in 30 Days: A Novel Writer's System for Building a Complete and Cohesive Manuscript.* Cincinnati, OH: Writer's Digest Books, 2005.

# Christian Publishers

B & H Publishing Group (formerly
Broadman & Holman)
127 9th Avenue N.
Nashville, TN 37234-0115
www.broadmanholman.com

Barbour Publishing, Inc.
P.O. Box 719
1810 Barbour Drive
Uhrichsville, OH 44683-0719
www.barbourbooks.com

Bethany House Publishers
11400 Hampshire Avenue S.
Bloomington, MN 55438
www.bethanyhouse.com

Cook Communications Ministries
4050 Lee Vance View
Colorado Springs, CO 80918
www.cookministries.com

Crossway Books and Bibles
1300 Crescent Street
Wheaton, IL 60187
www.crosswaybooks.com

Doubleday Religion
1745 Broadway
New York, NY 10019
www.randomhouse.com

Faith Words/Hachette Book Group
10 Cadillac Drive
Suite 220
Brentwood, TN 37027
www.hachettebookgroup.com

GuidepostsBooks
16 E. 34th Street
21st Floor
New York, NY 10016-4397
www.guidepostsbooks.com

HarperSanFrancisco
353 Sacramento Street
Suite 500
San Francisco, CA 94111-3653
www.harpercollins.com

Harvest House Publishers
990 Owen Loop N.
Eugene, OR 97402
www.harvesthousepublishers.com

Heartsong Presents
Barbour Publishing Inc.
P.O. Box 721
1810 Barbour Drive
Uhrichsville, OH 44683
www.heartsongpresents.com

Heartsong Presents/Spyglass Lane
Mysteries
Barbour Publishing Inc.
P.O. Box 721
1810 Barbour Drive
Uhrichsville, OH 44683
www.barbourbooks.com

Howard Books/Simon & Schuster
(formerly Howard Publishing)
3117 N. 7th Street
West Monroe, LA 71291
www.simonandschuster.com

Jireh Publishing Company
P.O. Box 1911
Suisun City, CA 94585-1911
www.jirehpublishing.com

Kregel Publications
P.O. Box 2607
Grand Rapids, MI 49501-2607
www.kregelpublications.com

Meredith Books/Jordan House
(formerly Meredith Books)
1716 Locust Street
Des Moines, IA 50309-3023
www.meredithbooks.com

Mountainview Publishing
1284 Overlook Drive
Sierra Vista, AZ 85635-5512
www.trebleheartbooks.com

Multnomah Publishers
Waterbrook Press
Suite 200
12265 Oracle Boulevard
Colorado Springs, CO 80921
www.randomhouse.com

Navpress
P.O. Box 35001
Colorado Springs, CO 80935
www.navpress.com

Revell (Imprint of Baker Publishing
Group)
P.O. Box 6287
Grand Rapids, MI 49516
www.bakerbooks.com

RiverOak Publishing
4050 Lee Vance View
Colorado Springs, CO 80918
www.cookministries.org

Steeple Hill/Harlequin (Single Title)
233 Broadway
Suite 1001
New York, NY 10279-0001
www.Steeplehill.com

Steeple Hill/Love Inspired
233 Broadway
Suite 1001
New York, NY 10279-0001
www.Steeplehill.com

Steeple Hill/Love Inspired Historical
233 Broadway
Suite 1001
New York, NY 10279-0001
www.Steeplehill.com

Steeple Hill/Love Inspired Suspense
233 Broadway
Suite 1001
New York, NY 10279-0001
www.Steeplehill.com

Strang Communications/Realms
600 Rinehart Road
Lake Mary, FL 32746
www.strangbookgroup.com

Thomas Nelson/Westbow
P.O. Box 14100
Nashville, TN 37215
www.WestBowPress.com

Treble Heart Books
1284 Overlook Drive
Sierra Vista, AZ 85635
www.trebleheartbooks.com

Tyndale House Publishers
351 Executive Drive
Carol Stream, IL 60188
www.tyndale.com

Waterbrook Press
12265 Oracle Boulevard
Suite 200
Colorado Springs, CO 80921
www.randomhouse.com/waterbrook

Zondervan
5300 Patterson S.E.
Grand Rapids, MI 49530-0002
www.zondervan.com

# Christian Self-Publishing Companies

ACW PRESS
American Christian Writers
P.O. Box 110390
Nashville, TN 37222
www.acwpress.com

Winepress Publishing
P.O. Box 428
1730 Railroad Street
Enumclaw, WA 98022
www.winepresspub.com

Xulon Press, Inc.,
2180 W. State Road 434
Longwood, FL 32779
www.xulonpress.com

# Websites

## Christian Manuscript Submission Services

Christian Manuscript Submission Services
www.christianmanuscriptsubmissions.com

The Writer's Edge
www.writersedgeservice.com

## Christian Writing Blogs

charisconnection.blogspot.com
*Charis Connection* is a must-read blog with thoughtful essays and Q&A from a talented group of popular Christian novelists.

www.faithinfiction.blogspot.com
*Faith in Fiction* is a frequently interesting Christian fiction blog led by a leading editor.

tpr.typepad.com/themastersartist
*The Master's Artist* is another must-read blog about Christian fiction with several well-known novelists as "guest bloggers."

noveljourney.blogspot.com
*Novel Journey* is a fascinating blog about different aspects of Christian fiction that includes interviews with leading novelists.

## Christian Writing

www.AdvancedFictionWriting.com
An e-zine on advanced writing published by Randy Ingermanson, a Christian novelist.

www.wherethemapends.com
A website devoted to speculative Christian fiction published by Jeff Gerke, a Christian novelist and editor.

## Writing and Editing Services

www.coachingthewriter.com
A website by a certified writing coach.

www.fictionfixitshop.com
A website that provides editing services for adult and young adult fiction.

## Christian Novelists

I've listed the personal websites of many leading Christian novelists as "resources," because they offer much more than "self-promotion." You'll find advice for first-time novelists, helpful tips, and useful information about Christian publishing. Don't think about these writers as your "competition"; rather, view them as your future colleagues—experienced writers who are happy to help first-time novelists join the fellowship of published Christian authors.

www.angelahuntbooks.com
Angela Hunt

www.anntatlock.com
Ann Tatlock

www.atholdickson.com
Athol Dickson

www.benrey.com
Ron and Janet Benrey

www.bjhoff.com
B. J. Hoff

www.brandilyncollins.com
Brandilyn Collins

www.carolcoxbooks.com
Carol Cox

www.carolumberger.com
Carol Umberger

www.carolyneaarsen.com
Carolyne Aarsen

www.coggins.ca
Dr. James R. Coggins

www.colleencoble.com
Colleen Coble

www.crestonmapes.com
Creston Mapes

www.daveneta.com
Dave and Neta Jackson

www.deannajuliedodson.com
Deanna Julie Dodson

www.deborahraney.com
Deborah Raney

www.denneybooks.com
Jim Denney

www.elizabethwhite.net
Elizabeth White

www.gailmartin.com
Gail Gaymer Martin

www.gayleroper.com
Gayle Roper

www.hannahalexander.com
Hannah Alexander

www.jamesscottbell.com
James Scott Bell

www.JeffersonScott.com
Jefferson Scott (Jeff Gerke)

www.johnrobinsonbooks.com
John Robinson

www.judithmccoymiller.com
Judith Miller

www.judykbaer.com
Judy Baer

www.karenkingsbury.com
Karen Kingsbury

www.kathleenmorgan.com
Kathleen Morgan

www.lindaford.org
Linda Ford

www.lissahallsjohnson.com
Lissa Halls Johnson

www.loisricher.com
Lois Richer

www.lorenamccourtney.com
Lorena McCourtney

www.marloschalesky.com
Marlo Schalesky

www.martaperry.com
Marta Perry

www.maureenlang.com
Maureen Lang

www.meredithefken.com
Meredith Efken

www.nancymoser.com
Nancy Moser

www.paulmccusker.com
Paul McCusker

www.rachelhauck.com
Rachel Hauck

www.renegutteridge.com
Rene Gutteridge

www.robertelmerbooks.com
Robert Elmer

www.robingunn.com
Robin Gunn

www.robinleehatcher.com
Robin Lee Hatcher

www.roxannehenke.com
Roxanne Henke

www.sandrabyrd.com
Sandra Byrd

www.sarahannesumpolec.com
Sarah Anne Sumpolec

www.sharondunnbooks.com
Sharon Dunn

www.sharonhinck.com
Sharon Hinck

www.stephaniewhitson.com
Stephanie Whitson

www.sunnijeffers.com
Sunni Jeffers

www.susanmeissner.com
Susan Meissner

www.tamaraleigh.com
Tamara Leigh

www.tameraalexander.com
Tamera Alexander

www.terriblackstock.com
Terri Blackstock

www.tlhines.com
T. L. Hines

www.tommorrisey.com
Tom Morrisey

www.tracidepree.com
Traci Depree

www.veronicaheley.com
Veronica Heley

www.writerhall.com
Linda Hall

## Organizations for Christian Novelists

American Christian Fiction Writers
www.americanchristianfictionwriters.com

Association of Christian Writers (United Kingdom)
www.christianwriters.org.uk

The Word Guild (Canada)
www.thewordguild.com

# Christian Writers' Conferences

Blue Ridge Christian Writers Conference
www.lifeway.com/christianwriters

Glorieta Christian Writers Conference
www.classervices.com/CS_Glorieta_Conf.html

Mount Hermon Christian Writers Conference
www.mounthermon.org/writers

Writing for the Soul
www.christianwritersguild.com/conferences

Write! Canada
www.thewordguild.com/writecanada/

# Technology for Christian Writers

Voice-to-text software:

Dragon NaturallySpeaking
Nuance Communications, Inc.
www.nuance.com/naturallyspeaking

Text-to-voice software:

TextAloud
NextUp Technologies, LLC
www.nextup.com

Text-to-voice:

Paraben Shareware
www.paraben.com/html/voice.html

# Online Backup Storage Services

iBackup Online Backup & Data Storage
www.ibackup.com

Mozy Online Backup
www.mozy.com

# My Chapter Checklist

I put this simple checklist together years ago. Besides highlighting common fiction problems, it reminds me to look for practical solutions and provide detailed suggestions. That way I provide constructive criticism to help other members improve their manuscripts—and I develop self-editing skills I can apply to my own work.

Make plenty of copies so you have a clean checklist for each chapter you evaluate. And don't merely check the boxes—use the space provided to jot down relevant thoughts and comments. Remember: the purpose of evaluating each chapter is to improve the author's writing skills.

❏ Did the opening grab my attention? If not, what changes will make it more compelling?

_____

_____

_____

❏ Does this chapter give the lead character a well-defined problem or conflict that moves the story forward? If not, what problem/conflict will boost dramatic energy?

_____

_____

_____

❑ Does the writing convey time and place quickly? If not, what additional hints do readers need?

_____

_____

_____

❑ Did the chapter start "in media res"—in the middle of things—to maximize dramatic impact, or did it start with details that slowed the action? If the latter, where should the chapter begin?

_____

_____

_____

❑ Did the chapter seem compelling? If not, what action, events, or complications will increase dramatic energy?

_____

_____

_____

❑ Does the chapter advance the main plot or subplot(s)? If not, what changes will give the chapter real purpose?

_____

_____

_____

❑ Did the chapter have a page-turning ending? If not, what changes will make the ending more compelling?

_____

_____

_____

❑ Were flashbacks necessary? Were they handled well? If not, how can the same information be delivered to readers without a flashback?

_____

_____

_____

❑ Did exposition seem natural? If not, what changes will improve exposition?

_____

_____

_____

❑ Was there enough sensory description to keep the "fictional dream" alive for me? If not, what additional descriptions will be useful?

_____

_____

_____

❑ Was dialogue consistent with each character's personality, ethnicity, education, age, and experience? If not, what changes will restore consistency?

_____

_____

_____

❑ Did the lead characters do anything out of character? If so, what changes will bring them back in character?

_____

_____

_____

❑ Did the dialogue convey emotions, intent, and characterization without the need for explanatory adverbs? If not, what dialogue changes will make adverbs unnecessary?

_____

_____

_____

❑ Are there instances of "telling" rather than "showing" sense reactions? If so, suggest ways to show rather than tell.

_____

_____

_____

❑ Is it clear which character speaks each dialogue block? If not, what changes will eliminate the confusion?

_____

_____

_____

❑ Are there instances of "head-hopping" or poorly signaled point-of-view shifts among characters? If so, what changes will eliminate POV problems?

_____

_____

_____

## Miscellaneous Problems

Once you've identified any major plot, voice, POV, and dialogue problems, you can turn your attention to minor consistency, continuity, and language issues. Listing them is usually sufficient; you don't have to go into lengthy explanations of the author's mistakes.

Inconsistencies with previous chapters

_____

_____

_____

Time and place mistakes and other "continuity errors"

_____

_____

_____

Essential facts/details that should be included

_____

_____

_____

Incorrect facts/details

_____

_____

_____

Clichés

_____

_____

_____

Inappropriate language

_____

_____

_____

# Index

## N

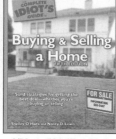

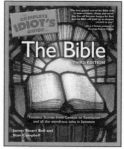
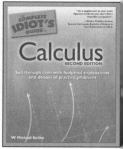